westermann

CAMDEN TOWN
Oberstufe

Arbeitsheft zu den Pflichtmaterialien

Erarbeitet von

Svenja Alpen-Kühne
Anne-Kathrin Böker
Florian Brauel
Ilka Kratz
Alexander Kuhrs Woltin
Jana Oldendörp

Abkürzungen:

AE	American English	*infml.*	informal
BE	British English	*pl.*	plural
e.g.	exempli gratia (Latin) = for example	*sb*	somebody
i.e.	id est (Latin) = that is	*sth*	something

Webcodes
Auf manchen Seiten findest du Webcodes, die dich zu zusätzlichen Materialien im Internet führen. Gib dazu einfach den Code auf www.westermann.de/webcode ins Suchfeld ein.

Filmauszüge
Je nach Abspielgerät und verwendeter Software kann es vorkommen, dass die Zeitangaben zu den Filmauszügen nicht exakt mit den im Kapitel angegebenen übereinstimmen.

Atonement
Die Verweise zu *Atonement* beziehen sich auf diese Ausgabe, die bei Westermann erhältlich ist: Ian McEwan, *Atonement*, ISBN: 978-3-425-73069-1. Kostenlose Annotationen finden sich auf www.westermann.de.

seven methods of killing kylie jenner
Die Verweise zu *seven methods of killing kylie jenner* beziehen sich auf diese Ausgabe, die bei Westermann erhältlich ist: Jasmine Lee-Jones, *seven methods of killing kylie jenner*, ISBN: 978-3-425-73070-7. Kostenlose Annotationen finden sich auf www.westermann.de.

Verweise auf *Skills pages* und *Workshops*
Die Verweise auf *Skills pages* und *Workshops* beziehen sich auf das Schulbuch *Camden Town Oberstufe Qualifikationsphase Niedersachsen*, ISBN: 978-3-425-73642-6.

---

westermann GRUPPE

© 2023 Westermann Bildungsmedienverlag GmbH, Georg-Westermann-Allee 66, 38104 Braunschweig
www.westermann.de

Das Werk und seine Teile sind urheberrechtlich geschützt. Jede Nutzung in anderen als den gesetzlich zugelassenen bzw. vertraglich zugestandenen Fällen bedarf der vorherigen schriftlichen Einwilligung des Verlages.
Nähere Informationen zur vertraglich gestatteten Anzahl von Kopien finden Sie auf www.schulbuchkopie.de.
Für Verweise (Links) auf Internet-Adressen gilt folgender Haftungshinweis: Trotz sorgfältiger inhaltlicher Kontrolle wird die Haftung für die Inhalte der externen Seiten ausgeschlossen. Für den Inhalt dieser externen Seiten sind ausschließlich deren Betreiber verantwortlich. Sollten Sie daher auf kostenpflichtige, illegale oder anstößige Inhalte treffen, so bedauern wir dies ausdrücklich und bitten Sie, uns umgehend per E-Mail davon in Kenntnis zu setzen, damit beim Nachdruck der Verweis gelöscht wird.

Druck A^1 / Jahr 2023
Alle Drucke der Serie A sind im Unterricht parallel verwendbar.

Redaktion: Isabel Klein, Schönau
Umschlaggestaltung: Gingco.Net Werbeagentur GmbH & Co. KG, Braunschweig
Layout: Visuelle Lebensfreude, Hannover; thom bahr GRAFIK, Mainz
Druck und Bindung: Westermann Druck GmbH, Georg-Westermann-Allee 66, 38104 Braunschweig

ISBN 978-3-425-**73684**-6

Contents

			Abiturvorgaben / Themen
Part 1	**Atonement**		
6	Novel	Pre-reading While reading Post-reading	Roman: Ian McEwan, *Atonement* (2001)
24	Topic	**Britishness**	Britishness
27		**Innocence and guilt**	Innocence and guilt
28		**Perception(s) of reality**	Perception(s) of reality
Part 2	**Short stories**		
29	Short stories	Pre-reading While reading Post-reading	Kurzgeschichte: Nafissa Thompson-Spires, *Heads of the Colored People: Four Fancy Sketches, Two Chalk Outlines, and No Apology* (2018)
38		Pre-reading While reading Post-reading	Kurzgeschichte: Camille Acker, *Mambo Sauce* (2018)
53	Post-reading	The short stories	Ethnic, cultural and linguistic diversity Ethnic identity Discrimination The American experience
54	Topic	**Ethnic identity and discrimination**	Ethnic, cultural and linguistic diversity Ethnic identity Discrimination The American experience
Part 3	**The Founder**		
57	Film	Pre-viewing While viewing Post-viewing	Film: John Lee Hancock (Regie), *The Founder* (2016)
65	Topic	**The American Dream**	The American Dream
66		**Ethics in the world of business**	Ethics in the world of business
Part 4	**Boy Erased**		
71	Topic	**Religion and sexual diversity** Terms and concepts regarding sexual diversity The Bible Belt Conversion therapy	Sexual diversity Tolerance and discrimination
76		**Discrimination** Stereotypes – The basis of discrimination Forms of discrimination Diversity and discrimination	Sexual diversity Tolerance and discrimination

Contents

			Abiturvorgaben / Themen
81	Film	Pre-viewing: A film poster Revisiting cinematography While viewing: Characters Practices of conversion therapy Portrayals of homosexuality Homosexuality as God's test? Time and symbolism Post-viewing	Film: Joel Edgerton (Regie), *Boy Erased* (2018)
94	Topic	**Coming of age**	Coming of age
95		**Sexual diversity – Tolerance and discrimination**	Sexual diversity Tolerance and discrimination

Part 5   seven methods of killing kylie jenner

100	Play	Pre-reading While reading Post-reading	Kurzdrama: Jasmine Lee-Jones, *seven methods of killing kylie jenner* (2019, Neubearbeitung 2021)
114	Topic	**The influence of social media on young people's identity**	The influence of social media on personal life and public opinion
116		**The role of ethnic identity on (social) media**	Ethnic identity The influence of social media on personal life and public opinion
118		**Images of black female identity**	Ethnic identity

Part 6   A Midsummer Night's Dream

121	Play	Pre-reading	Shakespeare: The world that made him Drama: Auszüge aus: William Shakespeare, *A Midsummer Night's Dream* (ca. 1595 / 1596)
124		While reading: Act I	
135		While reading: Act II	
145		While reading: Act III	
154		While reading: Act IV	
159		While reading: Act V	
165		Post-reading	
166	Film	Pre-viewing While viewing Post-viewing	Film: Michael Hoffman (Regie), *A Midsummer Night's Dream* (1999) Shakespeare: Modern adaptations
170	Topic	**Dream and reality**	Dream and reality
174		**Love and marriage**	Love and marriage
177		**Gender roles**	Gender roles

Introduction

Liebe Schülerin, lieber Schüler,
mit diesem Arbeitsheft kannst du dich ideal auf das Abitur vorbereiten. Du beschäftigst dich mit allen Texten und Filmen, die für das Abitur vorgeschrieben sind, und außerdem mit weiteren abiturrelevanten Themen.

Für das schriftliche Abitur 2025 müssen die folgenden Materialien unter den genannten inhaltlichen Gesichtspunkten behandelt werden:

Roman:
Ian McEwan, *Atonement* (2001)
→ verbindliche Unterrichtsaspekte:
- Britishness
- innocence and guilt
- perception(s) of reality

Kurzprosa:
Nafissa Thompson-Spires, *Heads of the Colored People: Four Fancy Sketches, Two Chalk Outlines, and No Apology* (2018)
Camille Acker, *Mambo Sauce* (2018)
→ verbindliche Unterrichtsaspekte:
- ethnic identity
- discrimination

Kurzdrama (Allgemein bildende Schulen):
Jasmine Lee-Jones, *seven methods of killing kylie jenner* (2019, Neubearbeitung 2021)
→ verbindliche Unterrichtsaspekte:
- ethnic identity
- the influence of social media on personal life and public opinion

Film (Berufliche Gymnasien):
John Lee Hancock (Regie), *The Founder* (2016)
→ verbindliche Unterrichtsaspekte:
- American Dream
- ethics in the world of business

Film:
Joel Edgerton (Regie), *Boy Erased* (2018)
→ verbindliche Unterrichtsaspekte:
- coming of age
- sexual diversity
- tolerance and discrimination

Drama:
Auszüge aus: William Shakespeare, *A Midsummer Night's Dream* (ca. 1595/1596)
Film:
Michael Hoffman (Regie), *A Midsummer Night's Dream* (1999)
→ verbindliche Unterrichtsaspekte:
- dream and reality
- love and marriage
- gender roles

Aufbau des Arbeitshefts

In **Part 1:** *Atonement*, **Part 2:** *Short stories*, **Part 3:** *The Founder*, **Part 5:** *seven methods of killing kylie jenner* und **Part 6:** *A Midsummer Night's Dream* erfolgen zunächst eine inhaltliche Sicherung und allgemeine Bearbeitung der jeweiligen Materialien. Auf speziell ausgewiesenen *Topic*-Seiten werden die verbindlichen Unterrichtsaspekte generell eingeführt, bevor sie im Kontext der jeweiligen Materialien noch einmal vertieft werden. Wo es sich anbietet, werden auch weitere Themen aus dem Lehrplan (Kerncurriculum) aufgegriffen.

In **Part 4:** *Boy Erased* werden zunächst auf *Topic*-Seiten für die Erarbeitung relevante thematische Aspekte behandelt, und dann wird in die Arbeit mit dem Film eingestiegen. Die thematischen Aspekte werden auf zusätzlichen *Topic*-Seiten wieder aufgegriffen und vertieft.

An vielen Stellen findest du Verweise auf *Skills pages* und *Workshops* im Schulbuch *Camden Town Oberstufe Qualifikationsphase* (ISBN: 978-3-425-73642-6). Die *Skills pages* geben dir Hilfestellungen zu wichtigen Aufgabenformaten. In den *Workshops* werden bestimmte Kompetenzen intensiv trainiert. Im Schulbuch werden außerdem weitere Aspekte der Themen dieses Arbeitsheftes behandelt.

| Novel | Atonement |

Pre-reading

1

You are going to read the novel *Atonement* by Ian McEwan (2001).

a) Read the following quotations. Choose the one that you like best. Explain your choice.

> "The beginning of atonement is the sense of its necessity."
> – Lord Byron

> "Forgiveness is not an occasional act, it is a constant attitude."
> – Martin Luther King Jr.

> "Always forgive, but never forget, else you will be a prisoner of your own hatred, and doomed to repeat your mistakes forever."
> – Wil Zeus, Sun Beyond the Clouds

> "The whole essence of the Christian religion is based on the atonement of Christ, his death and his resurrection."
> – Gordon B. Hinckley

> "I guess forgiveness, like happiness, isn't a final destination. You don't one day get there and get to stay."
> – Deb Caletti

b) What associations does the title *Atonement* bring to your mind?
What different definitions of the word "atonement" can you find?
Make a mind map and note down your first ideas about the plot of the novel.

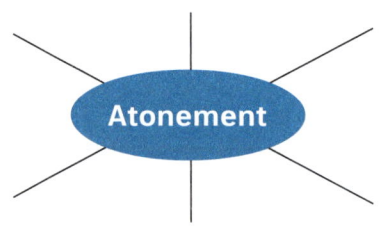

2

a) Use the internet to find out about the author's life.
b) Write a short biography of Ian McEwan for a website on modern English literature.
→ **S8:** How to improve your text

While reading

> **Info**
>
> Keeping a **reading journal** will help you follow and keep track of aspects of a novel such as the plot, the characters and the setting. Your notes will make it easier for you to understand the structure of the novel and the issues it deals with. Initial responses to the text or questions can be noted down, as well as the corresponding lines to help you find the relevant chapters and quotations more quickly. You should take notes in the simple present tense.

3
Now start reading *Atonement*. While reading the book, fill in your reading journal.
Take notes on what you consider to be most important in each section.

Atonement	
Author	
Year of publication	
Genre	
Part One	
Setting (time and place)	
Type of narrator	
Purpose of narrator	
Characters	
Main plot	
Main themes	

1 Novel — Atonement

	Part Two
Setting (time and place)	
Type of narrator	
Purpose of narrator	
Characters	
Main plot	
Main themes	
	Part Three
Setting (time and place)	
Type of narrator	
Purpose of narrator	

Atonement — Novel 1

Characters	
Main plot	
Main themes	
London, 1999	
Setting (time and place)	
Type of narrator	
Purpose of narrator	
Characters	
Main plot	
Main themes	

Novel — Atonement

PART ONE: CHAPTER ONE

4

a) Note down facts about the characters mentioned in the first chapter, their relationships and the setting (time and place).
b) Sum up what Briony's play *The Trials of Arabella* is about.
c) Explain why Briony is not enthusiastic about Lola wanting to be Arabella in her play.

5

Describe Briony as she appears in this chapter. Use some of the adjectives from the box. You can add more adjectives if needed.

> self-pitying | talented | jealous | naive | selfish | petulant | precocious | childlike | stubborn | bossy | shy | sensitive | talkative | curious | obsessed | stoical | inquisitive | meticulous | devoted | clever | manipulative | kind | …

6

Examine how the narrator describes Briony and Lola's relationship.

PART ONE: CHAPTERS TWO–THREE

7

Read the statements below. Decide whether the statements are true or false. Tick (✓) the correct box. Provide evidence for each statement. Find a suitable quotation from the novel to support your answer.

	Statement	True	False	Quotation
1	The vase is so important to the Tallis family because Jack Tallis's great-great-grandfather made it when visiting Belgium.			
2	Cecilia disrobes and goes swimming for the two missing pieces that have fallen into the fountain after the vase has broken.			
3	When Briony witnesses the scene at the fountain between Robbie and Cecilia, she assumes that Robbie saved her sister from drowning.			
4	Robbie and Cecilia used to be best friends back at university.			

8

Sum up what the reader finds out about Robbie Turner in these chapters.

9

State what Briony means by "The sequence was illogical […]" (p. 39).

10 Group work → Workshop: Analysing characters

a) CHOOSE

Analyse the relationship between Cecilia and Robbie.

OR

Analyse Cecilia's character and her relationship to Briony.

b) Present your results in class.

11

a) To Briony "a story was a form of telepathy" (p. 37). Explain the meaning of this statement.
b) Explain why the scene Briony witnesses at the fountain changes her whole perspective on writing.
c) Analyse the role of the narrator. Why do you think the narrator is going back and retelling the same episode through different eyes?
→ **Workshop:** Analysing narrative perspective

12 Pair work

Think about the significance of the following passage for Briony:
"[…] the simple truth that other people are as real as you. And only in a story could you enter these different minds and show how they had an equal value." (p. 40)
Discuss your ideas with a partner.

PART ONE: CHAPTERS FOUR–SEVEN

13

Match the sentence parts. Write the letters A–F in the boxes.

1 Cecilia attempts to comfort Briony
2 Paul begins flirting with Cecilia
3 Leon and Cecilia start an argument
4 In the nursery,
5 Emily considers her oldest daughter to be an "impossible prospect" (p. 64) as a wife
6 Briony meditates on being a fencing champion instead of becoming a writer

A Paul starts flirting with Lola and tells her and the twins about his chocolate factory.
B when thinking about Cecilia's time at Cambridge.
C while spending time at the temple.
D when Cecilia finds out that Leon has invited Robbie to join them at dinner.
E when she notices her crying in the front hall and destroying her playbill.
F when he enters the house with Leon.

14

Sum up what the reader finds out about Paul Marshall.

15

Examine how Paul Marshall is characterized by the narrator.

16

Describe the Tallis home (place, people, surroundings, atmosphere). Which words are used? What is their effect on the reader?

17 → Workshop: Writing an interior monologue

Briony has given up on her play and abandons the rehearsals without any explanation. Write an interior monologue in which she explains her reasons for cancelling the play.

18 → Workshop: Analysing characters

Analyse Emily's character as she is portrayed in Chapter Six.

Novel — Atonement

19 Group work

a) CHOOSE

Discuss possible reasons why Jack Tallis doesn't make an appearance in the story.

OR

Discuss whether Emily Tallis could be considered the head of the family.

b) Present your results in class.

PART ONE: CHAPTERS EIGHT–ELEVEN

20

Tick (✓) the correct box to complete each sentence.

1. Robbie writes Cecilia a letter in order to …
   - ❏ a) confess his love.
   - ❏ b) tell her his sexual desires.
   - ❏ c) apologize for breaking the vase.
   - ❏ d) tell her about his family background.

2. Robbie's father walked out on the family …
   - ❏ a) because he was called up for military service.
   - ❏ b) because he fell in love with another woman.
   - ❏ c) because he was sent to prison.
   - ❏ d) with no explanation.

3. Robbie asks Briony to pass the letter to Cecilia because …
   - ❏ a) he doesn't want to give it to Cecilia in front of others.
   - ❏ b) he is ashamed of his feelings for Cecilia.
   - ❏ c) he wants to spend some time alone with Briony.
   - ❏ d) he assumes Cecilia is still upset about the vase and doesn't want to talk to him.

4. When Cecilia asks Briony if she has read the letter, …
   - ❏ a) Briony admits she has opened the envelope.
   - ❏ b) Briony just ignores Cecilia's inquiry.
   - ❏ c) Briony says the note was passed to her without an envelope.
   - ❏ d) Briony blames Lola for having opened the envelope.

5. Lola starts crying because …
   - ❏ a) she feels threatened by Paul's attempt to flirt with her.
   - ❏ b) she is homesick.
   - ❏ c) Robbie accuses her of having opened Cecilia's letter.
   - ❏ d) her brothers blame her for being stuck at the Tallises' house.

6. When Briony enters the library and discovers Robbie und Cecilia in an intimate moment, …
   - ❏ a) she is jealous of her sister because she is in love with Robbie.
   - ❏ b) she believes Cecilia is being attacked and being held by Robbie against her will.
   - ❏ c) she is shocked because her sister is committing a sin.
   - ❏ d) she is embarrassed because she is disrupting an intimate moment.

21

Describe Cecilia and Robbie's relationship.

22

Explain what makes Briony and Lola's relationship change in these chapters.

23
Speculate why Cecilia is not offended by Robbie's letter.

24 Group work
a) **CHOOSE**

Lola calls Robbie "a maniac" (p. 119) when Briony tells her about the letter. What does this term imply? Discuss.

OR

Robbie decides to go out alone and search for the twins:
"This decision, as he was to acknowledge many times, transformed his life." (p. 144)
Speculate what this last sentence of Chapter Eleven could be foreshadowing.

b) Present your results in class.

PART ONE: CHAPTERS TWELVE–FOURTEEN

25
Organize the information about the Tallis home in a mind map. Try to be as detailed as possible. You can also use information from the previous chapters.

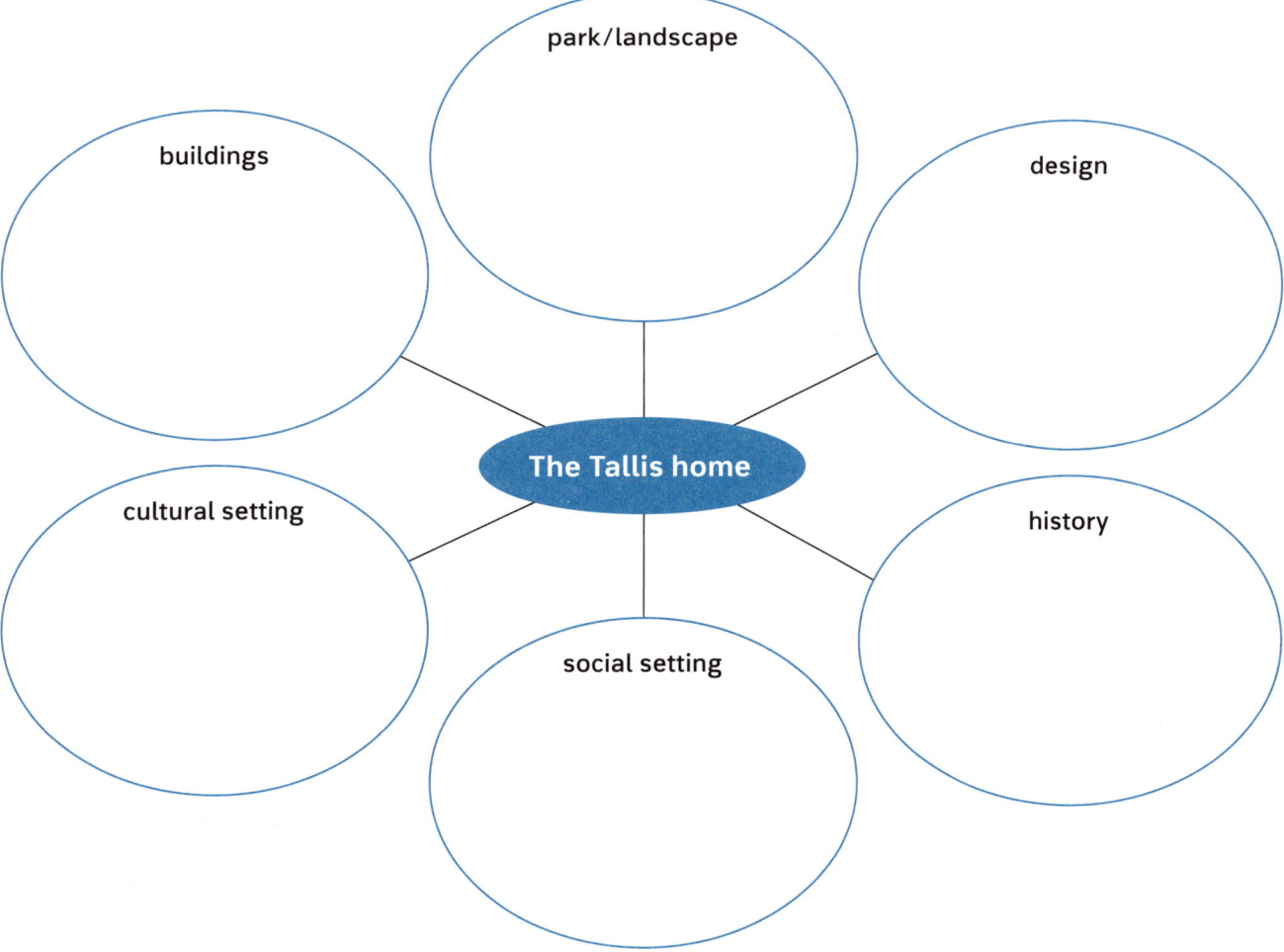

26
Sum up what the reader learns about Jack Tallis.

27
Analyse what Chapter Twelve reveals about the Tallis family and the family members' emotions being repressed.

Novel — Atonement

28 Answer the questions about Chapter Thirteen.

a) Why does Briony make her way towards the island?

b) What happens to Lola by the lake?

c) Why is Briony inferring that Robbie has harmed Lola?

29
a) Read the following information about prolepsis.
b) Examine how this technique is used in Chapters Twelve and Thirteen.

> **Info**
>
> **Prolepsis** refers to a rhetorical device by which possible objections to an argument are anticipated and answered in advance. The word derives from the Greek "prolambanein", which means "to anticipate".
> In literature or film, prolepsis refers to a scene that temporarily takes the story forward in time and represents future events. A modern English term would be "flashforward", revealing crucial aspects of the story that have not yet occurred, but will occur later in the story.

30 → **Workshop:** Analysing narrative perspective

Analyse Briony's perspective of the rape concerning the details included and omitted. Why do you think the author chose her point of view for the narration?

31
Briefly sum up the interrogation and testimony in Chapter Fourteen.

32
Speculate why Briony sticks to her testimony with such unwavering commitment.

| | Atonement | Novel |

33 → **S2:** Checklist: Creative writing

In Chapter Fourteen, a policeman interrogates Briony:
"'You saw him then.'
'I know it was him.'
'Let's forget what you know. You're saying you saw him.'" (p. 181)

a) Imagine Briony not being certain about the suspect and what has happened. How would this change the course of the conversation and the plot?
b) Write an alternative story based on plausible deductions (answering the questions: Who? What? When? Why?).

34 Group work

a) CHOOSE

"How guilt refined the methods of self-torture, threading the beads of detail into an eternal loop, a rosary to be fingered for a lifetime." (p. 173)
Explain this statement and its possible significance for the plot.

OR

"Forgiveness. The word had never meant a thing before, though Briony had heard it exulted at a thousand school and church occasions." (p. 185)
Analyse why this statement could mark a critical turning point in Briony's biography. How and why does "forgiveness" acquire a new meaning for her?

b) Present your results in class.

35

In class, discuss the importance of Briony being the only witness to the crime.

36 → **Workshop:** Analysing narrative perspective

Explain the role of the narrator in Part One. Speculate why the author chose this narrative style.

PART TWO

37

The Second World War is used as a setting in the second part of the novel.
a) Use the internet to find out about "Dunkirk 1940".
b) Use the information to fill in the fact file.

Dunkirk 1940	
Who?	
When?	
Where?	
Why?	
How?	

Novel — Atonement

38

Read the statements below. Decide whether the statements are true or false. Tick (✓) the correct box. Provide evidence for each statement.

	Statement	True	False	Evidence
1	Robbie Turner and Corporals Mace and Nettle take refuge in the barn of an old French woman.			
2	They have to stay in Dunkirk because they weren't able to catch a Naval ship back to England.			
3	Turner is haunted by nightmares because of his time in prison and his war experiences.			
4	While Robbie Turner was imprisoned, Cecilia remained supportive of his innocence.			
5	When Robbie and Cecilia meet again at a café in London, their relationship is still strong.			
6	Robbie forgives the Tallis family for putting him to prison and encourages Cecilia to reach out to her family.			
7	After an aerial assault, Turner denies his major's orders to sneak-attack the German machine gun location.			
8	Turner recalls a summer day in 1932 when Briony faked a drowning to test Robbie to see if he would save her because she is in love with him.			
9	Turner successfully rescues a boy and his mother as the bomber nears.			
10	Turner's wound leads to his strong delusion.			

39
Describe the change in setting (time and place) that takes place in Part Two of the novel.

40
"There were horrors enough, but it was the unexpected detail that threw him and afterwards would not let him go." (p. 191)
Contrast the narrative style at the beginning of Part Two to the one in Part One.

41
Examine how the narrator shows the horror of war and its consequences using implicit words and pictures. Find suitable examples from the text.

42 Group work
a) **CHOOSE**
"I keep thinking of her. To go into nursing, to cut herself off from her background, is a bigger step for her than it was for me." (p. 212)
Analyse the importance of family for both Robbie and Cecilia taking into account background knowledge from Part One.

OR

"He wanted a father, and for the same reason, he wanted to be a father. It was common enough, to see so much death and want a child." (p. 241)
Examine why seeing the horrors of war makes Robbie long for an intact world.
b) Present your results in class.

43 Pair work
Discuss why the narrator draws the reader's attention to the acts of kindness by Turner, Mace and Nettle. What might this reveal about their characters?

44 → S2: Checklist: Creative writing
Reread Cecilia's letter in which she tells Robbie that everyone has turned on him (p. 209). Write Robbie's reply to Cecilia's letter.

45
The narrator relates Robbie and Cecilia to some other famous romantic couples who have overcome all odds for their love (p. 204).
a) List the couples and find background information on them.
b) Discuss why the narrator brings up those couples. What does this tell the reader about Robbie and Cecilia's relationship?

46
Describe and analyse what the reader learns about Briony in Part Two of the novel.

47 Group work
Imagine you were turning Cecilia and Robbie's reunion at the café (pp. 204–207) into a short screenplay.
a) Answer the following questions to prepare the screenplay.
   – What would the stage look like?
   – How would the actors be dressed?
   – What would the actors say? Refer to Robbie and Cecilia's conversation in the text.
b) Act out the scene.

Novel: Atonement

PART THREE

48

Answer the following questions about Part Three.

a) What made Briony become a nurse?

b) Why has Briony detached herself from her family?

c) Why does Briony keep a journal?

d) How does Briony react when she gets to know that Paul and Lola are getting married?

e) How does Briony cope with taking care of wounded soldiers returning from the war?

f) Why does Briony visit the church where Paul and Lola are getting married?

_____
_____
_____
_____

g) What happens when Briony visits Cecilia's apartment?

_____
_____
_____
_____

49
Describe the shift in narrative style in Part Three compared to the previous parts.

50
Examine the fact that Betty drops Uncle Clem's vase on the steps (p. 279). What could this incident represent?

51 → Workshop: Analysing atmosphere
"The unease was not confined to the hospital. It seemed to rise with the turbulent brown river swollen by the April rains, and in the evenings lay across the blacked-out city like a mental dusk which the whole country could sense, a quiet and malign thickening, inseparable from the cool late spring, well concealed within its spreading beneficence. Something was coming to an end." (p. 269)
State what imagery is used to create a sense of unease in the reader about what is going to happen at the hospital.

52
Reread the letter on pp. 311–315.
Sum up what CC criticizes about Briony's story.

53
Write Briony's reply to CC's letter.
→ **S2:** Checklist: Creative writing
→ **S3:** Checklist: Formal letter

> **Info**
> The initials "CC" stand for Cyril Connolly (1903–1974), an influential English literary critic and writer. He founded and edited the important literary magazine _Horizon_.

54
Reread the end of Part Three and speculate how the story could go on.
"She knew what was required of her. Not simply a letter, but a new draft, an atonement, and she was ready to begin.

BT
London 1999" (p. 349)

55

Did World War II hinder Briony from atoning or rather enable her to do so? Discuss in class.

LONDON, 1999

56

Sum up what happens in the final section of the novel.

57

Reread the lines from *The Trials of Arabella* on pp. 367–368. Analyse why Briony's teenage play appears again at the end of the novel.

58

Briony has just been diagnosed with vascular dementia (pp. 353–355).
a) Use the internet to gather information on vascular dementia.
b) Assess the significance of the fact that Briony is suffering from vascular dementia. Does this affect her credibility as a writer/narrator/person trying to atone?
c) **Group work**
   Discuss whether Briony's disease could be seen as a kind of salvation or a punishment for her crime.

59 **Group work**

Reread the scene when Briony returns to her former home (pp. 363–365). Compare the description of the place in this chapter with the Tallis home in Part One.

60 **Group work**

"I've been thinking about my last novel, the one that should have been my first. The earliest version, January 1940, the latest, March 1999, and in between, half a dozen different drafts." (p. 369)

"It is only in this last version that my lovers end well, standing side by side on a South London pavement as I walk away." (p. 370)

Discuss what Briony's statement at the end of the novel implies for the story as a whole and the reliability of the narrator. You can also use information from the previous pages (especially pp. 356–360) and the box below.

Info

An **unreliable narrator** is usually a first-person narrator and character within the story whose narration and perception are not completely credible due to the character's affected mental condition or maturity. As a result, this narrator has a distorted view of events, gives illogical or contradicting information and speaks with a bias or even lies.

Accordingly, a **reliable narrator** is considered a credible storyteller being fully aware of the circumstances around him/her. His/Her perception of the world is trustworthy and coherent.

Reliable and unreliable narration has been widely debated within literary scholarship since some literary critics argue that there is no such thing as a reliable first-person narrator at all. According to them, every literary character is affected by his or her past experiences and perception in the telling of a story. However, generally most first-person narrators attempt to give the most accurate and therefore reliable version of the events told in the story. One reason for creating an unreliable narrator is to make the reader reconsider their point of view and create dramatic suspense by making the truth unclear.

61

"The problem these fifty-nine years has been this: how can a novelist achieve atonement when, with her absolute power of deciding outcomes, she is also God? There is no one, no entity or higher form that she can appeal to, or be reconciled with, or that can forgive her. There is nothing outside her." (p. 371)

Explain why Briony compares her novelist self to God.

Post-reading

62 Group work

Comment on the ending of the novel. Who does Briony seek atonement from?

63 Group work

Discuss the thematic focus of the novel. Is it a novel about …?

> identity | coming of age | perception | social class | redemption | innocence | guilt | war

Find arguments for and against the different options.

64 → **Workshop:** Analysing characters → **S8:** How to improve your text

Choose one of the following characters and write a characterization.
- Cecilia Tallis
- Emily Tallis
- Robbie Turner
- Paul Marshall

65 Group work

Discuss the importance of water in the novel. Find passages that relate to water and are crucial to the course of the story.

66 Group work

Discuss how the theme of war and its consequences is presented in the novel.

67 → **Workshop:** Analysing characters

Analyse the development of Briony throughout the novel.

68 Group work

Reread the final two paragraphs of the novel (pp. 371–372). Discuss whether Briony successfully atones for the events in 1935 by writing her novel.

69

a) Read the review on *Atonement* from *The Guardian*. Discuss whether (or not) you agree with the review.
b) Write your own review of the novel. → **S8:** How to improve your text

---

GEOFF DYER   Sat 22 Sep 2001

Who's afraid of influence?
In his latest book Atonement Ian McEwan brings the British novel into the 21st century, says Geoff Dyer

The twists and turns of Ian McEwan's fiction are built on a knack for sustained illusion. When he writes "a glass of beer" we do not just see it; we are willing to drink from it vicariously. The ballooning
5 accident (imaginatively derived from footage of an actual incident) that opens Enduring Love is a spectacular example, but the ability to make the invented seem real animates every page of his work.
10 The novels' psychological acuity[1] derives, always, from their fidelity to a precisely delineated[2] reality. Needless to say, the more disturbing or skewed that reality (in the early stories and novels, most obviously), the more finely McEwan attunes
15 his readers to it. Moral ambiguity and doubt are thereby enhanced – rather than resolved – by clarity of presentation. This is why the themes of the novels (with the exception of the enjoyably

Annotations
[1] **acuity** = *Schärfe*
[2] **delineated** = *skizziert*

Novel — Atonement

forgettable Amsterdam) linger and resonate beyond the impeccable³ neatness of their arrangement. McEwan is, in other words, a thoroughly traditional original.

Atonement does not feel, at first, like a book by McEwan. The opening is almost perversely ungripping. Instead of the expected sharpness of focus, the first 70 or so pages are a lengthy summary of shifting impressions. One longs for a cinematic clarity and concentration of dialogue and action, but such interludes dissolve before our – and the participants' – eyes. [...]

Various characters come and go but the novel, at this point, seems populated mainly by its literary influences. Chief among these is Virginia Woolf⁴. The technique is not stream of consciousness so much as "a slow drift of association", "the hovering stillness of nothing much seeming to happen". The book later contains a critique of its own early pages – or at least of the draft from which they derive – in the guise of a letter from Cyril Connolly, editor of Horizon, who advises that "such writing can become precious when there is no sense of forward movement". The requisite propulsion is provided by the unexpected intrusion, as it were, of two other novelists from the interwar years.

Cecilia, the eldest daughter of the family in whose house we are imaginatively lodged, was at Cambridge with Robbie, the son of the Tallises' cleaning lady, whose education was funded by Cecilia's father. They become aware, on this sultry day, of some kind of current – animosity? irreconcilable attraction? – passing between them. Robbie tries to articulate this in a letter, at the bottom of which he scribbles the naked truth: "In my dreams I kiss your cunt." He discards that draft and intends to send another, blander one but, in keeping with Freud's analysis of such slips, accidentally sends the shocking letter to Cecilia via her adolescent sister, Briony, who opens and reads it. [...]

Another crisis soon follows, this one imported from EM Forster's India. Cecilia's young cousin, Lola, is sexually assaulted in the grounds of the house. Lola does not know by whom, but Briony – an aspiring writer – compounds her earlier transgression⁵ by convincing her and everyone else (except Cecilia) that Robbie is the culprit. Unlike the incident in the Marabar caves, this one does not end in a retraction and Robbie, the proletarian interloper, is convicted.

In the second section of the novel, the pastel haze of the first part gives way to an acrid⁶, graphic account of Robbie's later experiences in the British rout at Dunkirk. McEwan is here playing more obviously to his strengths. The highly decorated novelist deploys his research in an effective if familiar pattern of narrative manoeuvres. Refracted through Robbie's exhausted, wounded view of history in the making, the retreat unfolds in a series of vividly realised details and encounters. In the atrocious context of battle, Briony's apparently motiveless crime is rendered almost insignificant. "But what was guilt these days? It was cheap. Everyone was guilty, and no one was."

In similar fashion, the partial democratisation of Britain that results from the social upheaval of war is prefigured by Cecilia's turning her back on her family and allying herself with Robbie, the working-class graduate (whose smouldering sense of grievance and displacement would be vehemently embodied on the postwar stage by Jimmy Porter).

Part three shifts back to London, where Briony is training as a nurse, struggling to cope with the influx of casualties from Dunkirk. McEwan's command of visceral shock is here anchored in a historical setting thoroughly authenticated by his archival imagination. The elliptical style of the opening part has no place in these pages, as the graphic horrors of injury, mutilation and death pile up before Briony's eyes. She loosens the bandage around a patient's head and his brain threatens to slop out into her hands. Does this devotion to the victims of war wash her hands of her earlier guilt? Does her atonement depend on Robbie's survival? Or can it be achieved through the eventual realisation of her literary ambitions – through a novel such as the one we are reading? Who can grant atonement to the novelist, whose God-like capacity to create and rework the world means that there is no higher authority to whom appeal can be made?

It is a tribute to the scope, ambition and complexity of Atonement that it is difficult to give an adequate sense of what is going on in the novel without preempting – and thereby diminishing – the reader's experience of it. Suffice to say, any initial hesitancy about style – any fear that, for once, McEwan may not be not in control of his material – all play their part in his larger purpose. [...]

Annotations
³ **impeccable** = *tadellos*
⁴ **Virginia Woolf** (1882–1941) was a British writer. She is considered one of the most important authors of modernist literature. She experimented with different forms of writing and was a pioneer in using stream of consciousness as a narrative device.
⁵ **transgression** = *Verstoß, Überschreitung*
⁶ **acrid** = *beißend, scharf*

Atonement | **Novel**

ATONEMENT – THE FILM: PRE-VIEWING

70

Atonement was turned into a romantic war drama film, released in 2007. It was directed by Joe Wright, starring James McAvoy, Keira Knightley, Romola Garai, Saoirse Ronan, Vanessa Redgrave and Benedict Cumberbatch.
Describe the film poster and identify the characters shown.

_____

_____

_____

_____

_____

WHILE VIEWING

71

Watch the film. Answer the following questions.

a) What is Briony like in the film?

_____

_____

_____

b) How is Cecilia shown in the film?

_____

_____

_____

c) What happens to the frame story?

_____

_____

_____

POST-VIEWING

72 Group work

a) Compare the ending of the novel to the final scenes of the film.
b) Discuss to what extent the film and the novel differ in terms of concepts of atonement.

73 Pair work

Novel or film? Discuss which of the two versions of *Atonement* you prefer. Justify your opinion.

Topic 1 | Atonement

Britishness

1 → **S15:** How to describe pictures

Describe the pictures below. Which aspects of British tradition and culture are depicted?

2

Read the findings from the research study "Citizenship and Belonging: What is Britishness?" by the Commission for Racial Equality (2005).

What is Britishness?

Most of the research participants shared a common representation of Britishness, ranging over eight dimensions:

- **Geography:** Britishness was associated with the British Isles, and with typical topographic features, such as the Scottish Highlands, lochs, Welsh valleys, and rolling hills.
- **National symbols:** Britishness was symbolised by the Union Jack and the royal family.
- **People:** Three different ways of thinking about the British people emerged: for some participants, the British included all British citizens (that is, those who hold UK passports), regardless of region or ethnicity; for others, the British were exclusively associated with white English people; and for others still, the British included people of very diverse ethnic origins.
- **Values and attitudes:** These included upholding human rights and freedoms, respect for the rule of law, fairness, tolerance and respect for others, reserve and pride (generally valued by white English participants and criticised by white Scottish and white Welsh participants, as well as those from ethnic minority backgrounds), a strong work ethic, community spirit, mutual help, stoicism and compassion, and drunkenness, hooliganism and yobbishness.
- **Cultural habits and behaviour:** These included queuing; watching and supporting football, cricket and rugby; and consuming food and drink such as 'fish and chips', 'English breakfast', 'Yorkshire pudding', 'cream teas', 'cucumber sandwiches', 'roast beef', 'Sunday lunch', 'curries' and 'beer'.
- **Citizenship:** For Scottish and Welsh participants, and for most participants from ethnic minority backgrounds, Britishness was very much associated with holding a UK passport. This was not salient among white English participants.
- **Language:** English was seen as a common language that unites the British people. The array of British accents (in terms of regional and class differences) was also seen as typically British.

- **Achievements:** Britishness was associated with political and historical achievements (the establishment of parliamentary democracy, empire and colonialism); technological and scientific achievements (the industrial revolution, medical discoveries); sporting achievements (the invention of many sports); and 'pop' cultural achievements.

Identification with Britishness

While the content of 'Britishness' was shared across most groups, there were important differences in the ways in which participants personally related to, and identified with, Britishness.

As UK passport holders, all the participants *knew* they were British citizens, but not everyone attached any *value significance* to being British. In Scotland and Wales, white and ethnic minority participants identified more strongly with each of those countries than with Britain. In England, white English participants perceived themselves as English first and as British second, while ethnic minority participants perceived themselves as British; none identified as English, which they saw as meaning exclusively white people. Thus, the participants who identified most strongly with Britishness were those from ethnic minority backgrounds resident in England. […]

 S8: How to improve your text

Write your own definition of the term "Britishness" using additional information from the internet.

MEDIATION

 → **Workshop:** Mediation → **S19:** How to improve your mediation skills → **S7:** Checklist: Writing a blog post

Imagine you are an exchange student at a school in Britain. Your class is doing a project on Britishness and patriotism. You are asked to contribute a German perspective on the matter and found an article from *Der Spiegel*. Read the article below and write a blog post for the school website.

Wie ein Schülerlied Großbritannien entzweit

„Untersteht euch, meinem Kind das Gehirn zu waschen!"
Der britische Bildungsminister wünscht sich, dass in allen Schulen am Freitag ein patriotisches Lied gesungen wird. In Schottland und anderen Landesteilen fühlen sich viele an Nordkorea oder die DDR erinnert.
Von Jörg Schindler, London   24.06.2021, 20.12 Uhr

„Wenn die Musik der Liebe Nahrung ist, spielt weiter", schrieb William Shakespeare – aber der hatte auch gut reden. Als der Barde vor mehr als 400 Jahren zur Feder griff, gab es noch kein Ver-
5 einigtes Königreich. Und erst recht keinen Brexit. Im heutigen Großbritannien würde womöglich gar Shakespeare lieber betroffen schweigen, bevor er einen Shitstorm riskiert.
Im heutigen Großbritannien ist öffentliches Gezänk
10 über ein Lied entbrannt, das Außenstehenden schwer vermittelbar ist. Also das Gezänk. Wobei: das Lied eigentlich auch.
Geschrieben haben es angeblich Schüler der St. John's Primary School im englischen Bradford. Es
15 handelt von einer großen Inselnation, die „viele Stürme und viele Kriege" überlebt, ihre Grenzen in der Welt „erweitert" hat und dabei „immer geeint, niemals entzweit" auftrat. Es endet mit der inbrünstig und gleich viermal hintereinander
20 vorgetragenen Zeile: „Strong Britain, Great Nation" – starkes Britannien, große Nation. […]
Das Problem mit dem Lied ist nun jedoch nicht, dass es eine gewisse patriotische Schlagseite der Heranwachsenden von Bradford offenbart. Das
25 Problem ist, dass es am morgigen Freitag möglichst in allen Schulen des Vereinigten Königreichs

gesungen werden soll. Idealerweise von in Rot, Weiß und Blau gewandeten Kindern – den Farben des Union Jack.
30 So wünscht es sich die kleine Initiative „One Britain One Nation", die nicht zufällig ebenfalls aus Bradford stammt und den letzten Freitag im Juni zum „One Britain One Nation Day" erklärt hat. So wünscht es sich auch der britische Bildungsminis-
35 ter Gavin Williamson, der im britischen Parlament wissen ließ, er halte es für „unglaublich wichtig", dass die Schulen des Landes dem Aufruf folgen. [...]
Seit Williamson dem Kinderlied ausgerechnet am
40 fünften Jahrestag des Brexit-Referendums quasi den Regierungsstempel aufgedrückt hat, kann von einem immer einigen, niemals entzweiten Königreich keine Rede mehr sein. In den sozialen Netzwerken machten sogleich Fotomontagen die
45 Runde, die Williamsons Chef als Kim Jong-Johnson zeigten. [...]
Vor allem aber kommen der Song und seine Begleitumstände in jenen drei Landesteilen des Vereinigten Königreichs, bei denen es sich nicht
50 um England handelt, weniger gut an. In Schottland, Wales und Nordirland betrachtet man den chauvinistischen Überschwang, mit dem Johnson und seine Brexitclique das Land seit geraumer Zeit überziehen, mit wachsendem Befremden. [...]
55 Dass die Regierenden in London neuerdings auf jedem Regierungsgebäude den Union Jack sehen wollen, dass sie für schlappe 200 Millionen Pfund das National-Flaggschiff „Britannia" nachbauen lassen, dass zuletzt jede Kritik am britischen Kolo-
60 nialreich und seinem profitablen Sklavenhandel regierungsamtlich niederkartätscht wurde, ist selbst manchem Brexitfreund nicht mehr ganz geheuer.
In bester Erinnerung ist vielen auch noch die boshafte Auseinandersetzung von Ministern Ihrer
65 Majestät mit der BBC, die im vergangenen Jahr den traditionellen Schlussakkord des Klassikfestivals „Proms" – „Rule Britannia" – in seiner bisherigen Form aus dem Programm streichen wollte. Über Wochen mussten sich BBC-Journalisten dafür als
70 vaterlandslose Gesellen beschimpfen lassen.
Nun also setzt sich der Streit auf Grundschulniveau fort. Mit einer gewissen Fassungslosigkeit wiesen Vertreter der britischen Teilnationen darauf hin, dass der patriotische Ohrwurm aus Bradford eher
75 das Zeug zum Spalten als zum Vereinen habe. So sei Nordirland mit dem Slogan „Strong Britain" schlicht vergessen worden. Nicht von ungefähr laute der offizielle Name des Landes: Vereinigtes Königreich von Großbritannien UND Nordirland. [...]
80 Die Schotten wiederum finden es typisch Englisch, dass der Song ausgerechnet am Freitag landesweit geträllert werden soll – just an jenem Tag, an dem schottische Schüler bereits in den Ferien sind oder geschickt werden sollen. Und in Wales wiesen
85 Lehrer und Eltern darauf hin, dass Erziehung eine originäre Zuständigkeit der Regionen sei, man aber von niemandem vorab informiert worden sei.
Die Stimmung dort brachte eine Mutter ganz gut auf den Punkt, die über soziale Medien wissen
90 ließ: „Untersteht euch, meinem Kind das Gehirn zu waschen! Vier Nationen – Cymru am byth". Das ist Walisisch für „Lang lebe Wales".
Im englischen Bradford saß derweil ein einigermaßen indignierter Kash Singh, jener Mann, der die
95 Initiative „One Britain One Nation" vor acht Jahren ersonnen hat. Die Reaktionen auf das gut gemeinte Lied seien „diabolisch", seufzte der Ex-Polizist. Man lebe doch gemeinsam in einem „brillanten Land", und es sei notwendig, den dort herrschen-
100 den „Geist der Einheit und des Zusammenhalts" gelegentlich zu feiern.
Die Frage muss allerdings erlaubt sein: Von welchem Geist redet der Mann?

BRITISHNESS IN *ATONEMENT*

5

Reread Chapter Twelve in Part One of the novel. Sum up and identify characteristics about the Tallis household that can be considered typically British.

6

Social context and social class are an important setting in the novel. Examine to what extent social context and class matters are related to Britishness in the novel.

7

Part Two deals intensively with central events of the Second World War from a British perspective. When Robbie and the other soldiers meet a major from the Buffs (a regiment of the British Army), he is depicted as follows:

"The major had a little toothbrush moustache overhanging small, tight lips that clipped his words briskly. 'We've got Jerry trapped in the woods over there. He must be an advance party. But he's well dug in with a couple of machine guns. We're going to get in there and flush him out.'
Turner felt the horror chill and weaken his legs. He showed the major his empty palms.
'What with, sir?'
'With cunning and a bit of teamwork.'
How was the fool to be resisted? Turner was too tired to think, though he knew he wasn't going." (p. 220)

Examine how the major resembles the stereotype of a British gentleman. Speculate why the author created this character as part of the novel.

8 Pair work

Is it important that the story is (for the most part) set in England? Discuss your ideas with a partner and justify your answer.

Innocence and guilt

1

Look at the cartoon and describe it. What does it tell you about innocence in relation to guilt?

2 Pair work

Explain the message of the cartoon and its reference to the novel.
→ **Workshop:** Analysing a cartoon
→ **S17:** How to work with cartoons

3

Look up definitions of the words "innocence" and "guilt". How do they differ in meaning and connotation?

"It's innocent or guilty. There are no do-overs."

INNOCENCE AND GUILT IN *ATONEMENT*

4

Speculate who else could be at fault for the crime committed in the summer of 1935.
Is Briony the only one who should feel guilty? Is Lola guilty for not saying anything? What role do their parents play?

5

Explain why Briony made a false statement (pp. 173–183). Can you understand why she acted as she did?

6 Pair work

Briony is only thirteen when she is interviewed by the police. Discuss the role of adults in Part One of the novel. Why do adults fully rely on the observation of a child?

Topic: Atonement

7 **Pair work**

Reread the end of Part Two (pp. 261–265). Examine the significance of innocence and guilt for Robbie. You can also use information from other chapters.

8

In class, discuss whether the outbreak of the Second World War in Part Two of the novel can be seen as a loss of innocence in broader scope.

Perception(s) of reality

1 → **S15:** How to describe pictures
Describe the picture.

2

Explain its message and what it tells us about the perception(s) of reality.

3

Comment on the following quote.

> "Perception is more important than reality. If someone perceives something to be true, it is more important than if it is in fact true."
> – *Ivanka Trump, The Trump Card*

What dangers might be in this opinion?

PERCEPTION(S) OF REALITY IN *ATONEMENT*

4 **Group work**

An essential theme of *Atonement* is the way an individual's perspective shapes the perception of reality.
- **a)** Go back to Part One, Chapters Two and Three. Sum up how the fountain scene is perceived differently by Cecilia and Briony.
- **b)** Examine the significance of the mirror in Chapter Nine.
- **c)** Analyse how Briony perceives crucial events (for example, the scene at the fountain, the scene in the library, the assault by the lake and Robbie's arrest in front of the house) in Part One.

5 **Pair work**

Analyse how your interpretations of the characters alter once you know that Briony is the author of the novel.
→ **Workshop:** Analysing characters   → **Workshop:** Analysing narrative perspective

6

Atonement is said to be a narrative within a narrative. Comment on this statement.

7

"I know there's always a certain kind of reader who will be compelled to ask, But what *really* happened?" (p. 371)
In class, discuss how you would answer the question of what really happened.

Heads of the Colored People: Four Fancy Sketches, Two Chalk Outlines, and No Apology – A short story (2018)

PRE-READING

1
Below is the title of the short story you are going to read. Read it step by step. Make predictions about what each part might reveal about the plot of the story.

"Heads of the Colored People":
_____

"Four Fancy Sketches":
_____

"Two Chalk Outlines":
_____

"and No Apology":
_____

2
Read the information about the main characters. Try to predict what their roles in the plot of the story might be.

Riley: A young black man with bleached-blond hair; he loves dressing himself up as characters from his favourite books, movies, manga and anime series.
_____
_____

Brother Man: A black man whose real name is Richard Simmons; he hands out pamphlets in the street and is ignored by Riley, which he can't handle.
_____

Kevan Peterson: Father of five-year-old Penny; he is on his way to a meeting to pitch a business idea concerning black art.
_____

Paris Larkin: Riley's girlfriend; she is a sketch artist who calls her sketchbooks "a collection of heads" because she never draws bodies.
_____
_____

Heads of the Colored People:
Four Fancy Sketches, Two Chalk Outlines, and No Apology

by Nafissa Thompson-Spires

1.

Riley wore blue contact lenses and bleached his hair — which he worked with gel and a blow-dryer and a flatiron[1] some mornings into Sonic the Hedgehog[2] spikes so stiff you could prick[3] your finger on them, and sometimes into a wispy[4] side-swooped bob with long bangs — and he was black. But this wasn't any kind of self-hatred thing. He'd read *The Bluest Eye*[5] and *Invisible Man*[6] in school and even picked up *Disgruntled*[7] at a book fair, and yes, they were good and there was some resonance in those books for him, but this story isn't about race or "the shame of being alive" or any of those things. He was not self-hating; he was even listening to Drake — though you could make it Fetty Wap[8] if his appreciation for trap music changes something for you, because all that's relevant here is that he wasn't against the music of "his people" or anything like that — as he walked down Figueroa[9] with his earbuds pushed in just far enough so as not to feel itchy.

Riley was wearing the wispy swooped version of his bangs[10] and listening to Drake or Fetty, and he was black with blue contacts and bleached-blond hair. And, yes, there are black people who have both of those things naturally, without the use of artificial accouterments[11], so we can move past the whole phenotypically this or biologically that discussion to the meat of things[12]. And if there is something meta in this narrator's consciousness and self-consciousness or this overindulgent[13] aside, it isn't meta for the sake of being meta; this narrator's consciousness is just letting you know about said consciousness up front, like a raised black fist, to get the close reading out the way and make space for Riley, who was the kind of black man for whom blue eyes and blond hair were not natural. He was the kind of black that warranted — or invited without solicitation — comparisons to drinks from Starbucks or lyrics from "Lady Marmalade"[14] or chocolate bars, with nuts.

You would think with his blue contacts and unnaturally blond hair set against dark chocolate mocha-choca-latte-yaya skin — and yes, there is some judgment in the use of "you" — that Riley would date white or Asian women exclusively, or perhaps that he liked men. But you'd be wrong on all counts[15], as Riley was straight, and he dated widely among black women, and he was neither in denial, nor on the down-low, nor, like John Mayer[16], equal opportunity and United Colors of Benetton in life but as separate as the fingers of the hand in sex, nor like Frederick Douglass[17] or many others working on black rights in public and going home to a white wife (and there is no judgment against Douglass here, just facts for the sake of descriptive clarity). Riley liked black women, both their blackness and womanness and the overlap between those constructs; nor was Riley queerphobic[18] or the type of man to utter "no homo" in uncomfortable situations, because Riley was comfortable enough, if "enough" expresses a sort of educated awareness. There is so much awareness in these two paragraphs that I have hardly made space for Riley, who in addition to black women liked cosplay[19] — dressing up as characters from his favorite books and movies — and *Dr. Who*[20] and *Rurouni Kenshin*[21] and the Comic-Love convention, and especially *Death Note*, his favorite manga and anime series. And though that day he was dressed as Tamaki Suoh[22] (per his girlfriend's request), in a skinny periwinkle[23] suit with a skinny black tie, his appearance gave him the flexibility to on other occasions dress as Kise Ryouta[24] or Naruto[25], or, if he was feeling especially bold, Super Saiyan[26].

So it was bothersome, then, to Riley/Tamaki as he walked

Annotations
[1] **flatiron** = a hot tool to straighten hair
[2] **Sonic the Hedgehog** = the main character of a video game series
[3] to **prick** = to stick into your skin and cause you pain
[4] **wispy** = fine, thin
[5] *The Bluest Eye* = title of a novel written by Toni Morrison
[6] *Invisible Man* = title of a novel written by Ralph Ellison
[7] *Disgruntled* = title of a novel written by Asali Solomon
[8] **Fetty Wap** = an American rapper
[9] **Figueroa** = a major north-south street in Los Angeles County, California
[10] **bangs** = a hairstyle with the hair being cut so that it hangs over your forehead
[11] **accouterments** = accessories
[12] **the meat of things** = (figurative) the most important part of a topic
[13] **overindulgent** = excessive, having more of something than is good for you
[14] **"Lady Marmalade"** = a song recorded in 1974 by the American R&B group Labelle
[15] **on all counts** = in every way
[16] **John Mayer** = an American singer, songwriter and guitarist
[17] **Frederick Douglass** was an African-American social reformer, statesman and writer in the 19th century. He became famous for his anti-slavery writings.
[18] **queerphobic** = fearing or hating queer people
[19] **cosplay** = short for: costume play
[20] *Doctor Who* = a famous British science-fiction TV series
[21] *Rurouni Kenshin* = a Japanese manga series
[22] **Tamaki Suoh** = a character from the manga and anime series *Ouran High School Host Club*
[23] **periwinkle** = lavender blue
[24] **Kise Ryouta** = a character from a Japanese sports manga series
[25] **Naruto** = a character (a young ninja) from a Japanese manga series
[26] **Super Saiyan** = a form of transformation in the Japanese manga and anime series *Dragon Ball*

toward the Los Angeles Convention Center, when Brother Man at the corner of Figueroa and Fifteenth — not to be confused with the Original Bruh Man, whose actual origins or current whereabouts are unknown, but Bruh Man's gradated type, this particular yet stock Bruh Man, Brother Man — accosted[27] Riley after he brushed away the pamphlet Brother Man was trying to hand him and put his hand on Riley's shoulder and ventured to violate Riley's personal space even further by using that large hand with cigarette-stained fingernails to turn Riley toward him. I am saying Brother Man stopped Riley on the street, singled him out in front of people dressed, respectively, as Princess Mononoke[28], Storm[29], Daleks[30], Cybermen[31], and Neil deGrasse Tyson[32] (both in blackface and in their own black faces), put his hands on him, and forced him to look into Brother Man's own face with the familiarity of a friend yet, contextually, with the violence of a stranger.

On any other day Riley might have acknowledged that he was wrong to walk past Brother Man's initial "Howyoudoin," which he pretended not to hear on account of the Fetty. On this day, however, Riley felt that since he was inhabiting the character of Tamaki, his decision to ignore Brother Man was just right, an exercise in method acting.

Riley was more than surprised — and did not need to borrow Tamaki's affectations to feel slighted — that Brother Man had touched him, and by that point, even though he might have been just the kind of buyer for what Brother Man was selling, his pride wouldn't let him concede[33].

...

It had long irked[34] Riley that his blackness or the degree of his loyalty to the cause should be suspect because he wore blue contacts and bleached his hair blond and because, on top of all that, his name was also Riley, and not, say, Tyreke. It irked him that he might be mistaken for a self-hating Uncle Tom because he enjoyed cosplay and anime and comic book conventions and because he happened to be feeling the character of a rich Japanese schoolboy a little too much at that very moment.

By the time Brother Man said, "Uppity[35], gay-looking nigga," Riley had bypassed logic and forgotten that he held none of the privileges of his costume.

There ensued then what Riley, in his costume, might have called fisticuffs[36], though in everyday life he would have simply said they got to scrappin[37], right on Figueroa Street.

The people who watched and filmed and circulated the scene from inside one of the lobbies of the convention center said it was just like Naruto v. Pain, only with two black guys, so you couldn't tell if either one was the hero.

2.

In truth Brother Man was burly[38] but not violent and rather liked to regard himself as an intellectual in a misleading package. If he could have made a wish before the end of that day, it would have been that he, too, had worn a costume to soften the effects of his image.

When he put his hand on Riley's shoulder, it was only because he disliked the sight of someone, especially one of his own, turning his back to him without hearing him out. It was also because he needed to promote *Brother's Spawn* and had thus far convinced a meager[39] four passersby to buy a $4 copy that day, and because Brother Man felt, unapologetically[40], that black people should stick together and that the blue-eyed, wig-wearing brother in the purple suit should have at least acknowledged him with a nod, if not a handshake or a howyoudoin.

Though in the aftermath, people would call his papers religious tracts, indoctrination[41] materials, and "some kind of gang documents," *Brother's Spawn* was Brother Man's self-published dystopian[42] comic series set at Pasadena City College[43], where he first learned of Octavia Butler[44] and her work. The comics were hand-drawn with the dimensions of a postcard, though he also hoped to sell broadsides featuring a poem he had written. Brother Man — aliases[45] Kyle Barker, Cole Brown, Overton Wakefield Jones, Tommy Strawn, and pen name

---

[27] **to accost** = to stop somebody and speak to them in a rude or threatening way
[28] **Princess Mononoke** = a main character of a 1997 Japanese animated epic historical fantasy film
[29] **Storm** = a fictional character from American comic books
[30] **Daleks** = a fictional extraterrestrial race of mutants in the British science-fiction TV series *Doctor Who*
[31] **Cybermen** = a fictional race of cyborgs in the British science-fiction TV series *Doctor Who*
[32] **Neil deGrasse Tyson** = an American astrophysicist, planetary scientist and author
[33] **to concede** = to admit (often unwillingly)
[34] **to irk** = to irritate or annoy
[35] **uppity** = (informal) haughty or snobbish
[36] **fisticuffs** = a not very impressive fight
[37] **scrappin'** = fighting (without the intention of causing serious pain)
[38] **burly** = having a broad body and strong muscles
[39] **meager** = very little, not enough
[40] **unapologetic** = without feeling sorry or expressing regret
[41] **indoctrination** = the process of teaching someone a particular belief so that they accept it uncritically and reject other beliefs
[42] **dystopian** = an imagined world or society in which life is characterized by fear and the loss of freedom and individuality
[43] **Pasadena City College** = a public community college in the city of Pasadena
[44] **Octavia E. Butler** (1947–2006) was an American science-fiction author.
[45] **alias** = another (false) name someone uses

Short stories — Heads of the Colored People

Brother Hotep — was selling the postcard comics illegally
145 (he preferred the term "without official city permits")
between a food truck and a juice cart that day. On other
days he sold them near the Century City Mall, in Ladera
Heights[46], in Little Ethiopia[47], and as far as Inglewood[48].
That day, he banked on the convention center's Comic-
150 Love traffic and the potential readers it might attract,
boasting to his girlfriend earlier in the morning that
he would probably sell out, "even without one of those
official tables in the convention center, watch."
And though he would say he was not usually the type to
155 call Riley a sellout[49] or an Uncle Tom[50], that day, Brother
Man (real name Richard Simmons, yes, Richard Simmons)
could not handle Riley's refusal to acknowledge him or
his art. He could find reasons to dismiss the hundred
or so people in costumes, some speaking English, some
160 other languages, who shook their hands no at the
laminated mock-ups he tried to show them, but he could
not abide a black refusal, especially one from a black guy
in a Japanese prep-schoolboy costume, the very kind of
audience Brother Man hoped to cultivate.
165 Thus, when he put his hand on Riley's shoulder, he
never meant to hit him, and if he could, Brother Man,
hereafter Richard, would have imagined that Riley didn't
plan to fight him either. And neither man ever would
have thought that amateur karate (pronounced in the
170 authentic Japanese accent) would be involved, their arms
flailing and legs kicking out in poorly choreographed
mortal combat.

3.

On his way to a meeting, Kevan stopped at the SweetArt
Bakeshop in Saint Louis to purchase a vegan brownie for
175 himself and a purple cupcake with tiny candy hearts for
his daughter Penny, who was with him for the weekend.
The whole shop was lined with canvases of varying sizes,
painted by the owners and sold from the bakery, which
served as a gallery and community meeting space. Tiny
180 vases holding local flowers adorned each table. Kevan
wore a black T-shirt that said in white letters, "Eff Your
Respectability Politics." He liked the irony of the word
"eff" instead of the F-word, but he still debated whether
it was better to change "your" to "yo." He wasn't sure
185 if anyone understood the stakes in these decisions or in
any of his other art, which he sold online, from his car,
and occasionally from a small suitcase in the barbershop
on Washington Avenue.
He had one hour left with Penny before her mother
190 would pick her up so Kevan could meet a potential
business partner and pitch an idea that he couldn't shake.
He chose a table in the middle of the nearly empty
shop, with yellow-and-green flowers in the vase. "She's
a superhero," Penny said, pointing to the largest canvas
195 on the wall adjacent to the bakery case, and inhaling
another glob of frosting. The frosting accumulated at the
corners of Penny's smile, but her tongue missed those
spots each time it swept her mouth.
"She's cute. Daddy can teach you to paint like this," Kevan
200 said, passing Penny a napkin across the table.
Kevan wasn't a vegan, but he supported black business
and black art, and regarded SweetArt as a place where
his own work might one day be represented. The T-shirt
sales provided him a stash[51] of petty cash, but Kevan
205 had sold only three paintings, and that grieved him. He
supported his daughter Penny with a court order and
a "real job" as a UPS deliveryman, but he "always took
care of my responsibilities," even before Penny's mother,
whom he alternately called a gold digger[52], that whore,
210 and my queen, demanded official monthly payments.
"My superhero name is gonna be" — Penny paused to
pull back the wrapper and expose the last quarter of the
cupcake, its frosting smooshed and all the candy hearts
gone — "my name's gonna be Purple. Purple Penny
215 Powers. I will make things purple like this," Penny said,
zapping something with her arm.
"Purple Penny Powers." Kevan pretended this was cuter
than it was. "Wow."
He was trying not to think about a joke he had seen
220 earlier in the day, trying not to remember the sight of two
dead bodies that had appeared casually in his news feed,
trying to rehearse instead his pitch for the realization of
something he had read in a book that he found in a used
bookstore.
225 *The Afric-American Picture Gallery* was a series of written
sketches by William Wilson, under the pen name Ethiop
and following the form of similar sketches — which Kevan
found with more research — by James McCune Smith in
The Heads of the Colored People and Jane Rustic (a.k.a.
230 Frances Ellen Watkins Harper, a black abolitionist[53] poet
and suffragist[54]). Kevan wanted to commission painters,
including mostly himself, to create a full exhibit of heads
of the colored people, now and then, to take the written,

Annotations

[46] **Ladera Heights** = an area in Los Angeles County, California
[47] **Little Ethiopia** = a neighborhood in Los Angeles, California
[48] **Inglewood** = a city in the Los Angeles metropolitan area
[49] **sellout** = somebody who is considered to have done something which used to be against their principles
[50] **Uncle Tom** is the main character of Harriet Beecher Stowe's novel *Uncle Tom's Cabin* (1852). Here the name refers to a person regarded as very subservient, thus betraying their ethnic and cultural community.
[51] **stash** = a secret store of something
[52] **gold digger** = here: a woman who strives to marry a wealthy man
[53] **abolitionist** = a person who is in favour of the end of slavery
[54] **suffragist** = a person who is in favour of women having the right to vote

literary work and render it visually. The idea intrigued him, the heads talking to him like the books in Equiano[55] — though he didn't know that reference yet.

In Kevan's collection, there would be, as in Ethiop's original, Phyllis Wheatley[56], Nat Turner[57], and a doctor, but he would update his favorite sketch, "Picture 26," of the "colored youth" who was "surrounded by abject wretchedness[58]" to reflect a sort of current abjection. To these he would add a superhero for Penny and a collage of the black men (and women, he would concede, with some coaxing[59] later from Paris Larkin) who had been killed by police and other brutalities.

"Now what's your name going to be?" Penny's voice seemed especially shrill at the moment.

"I don't know." Kevan was still thinking about the bodies and the grainy[60] video of the two men arguing and the way one of the men had held out his hand when the police officer entered the scene; it was clear that the man wasn't holding a gun or a knife, but something soft, like paper.

"Daddy, your name," Penny demanded.

"I don't know," Kevan repeated, and blurted out the first thing that came to his mind: "Bruh Man."

"Bruh Man?" Penny jutted[61] her head back. "What does he do?"

"He paints, and whatever he wishes, he can paint it and make it happen." Kevan made Penny lick a napkin so he could wipe the leftover icing from her face. "And he can make bad things unhappen, if he paints them right."

"That's gonna be my power, too," Penny said, pulling away from his grooming and hesitating in the way of five-year-olds, "but I'm just gonna think and make it happen or unhappen."

He wished briefly that things were so simple and then began to outline something on a napkin.

4.

Paris Larkin was meeting Riley at the convention center after two shifts at her part-time job for Dark Shadows Hollywood Cemetery Tours. Her official job description said, "Tour Narrator: Vocal talent. Must be able to memorize stories and stand for long periods of time on moving bus while engaging audiences." I ain't saying she a gravedigger, Riley liked to begin when he introduced her as his girlfriend, but really, she digs graves, like, loves them. It was one of the things that had attracted him to her when they first met, her dark cheeriness and her nonjudgmental approach to his lifestyle. And his soft-landing punch lines were one of the things Paris liked about him, and his interesting face, and the way he wasn't at all who she expected him to be.

When he took his contact lenses out at night and tied his hair down with a durag[62], Riley looked just as comfortable and kind as when he dressed up and hung out at his favorite comic café in Pasadena, drinking boba tea[63] and playing chess with kids from Caltech[64], where he studied engineering and was one of a handful of black students on campus.

If Paris could have a superpower, it would be to make herself visible, because even though she stood at the front of the bus with a microphone, pointing out alleged sightings of Marilyn Monroe to hungry tourists with camera phones and fake Gucci sunglasses, she wasn't the main attraction, and she preferred to narrate the tours with reverence[65] instead of theatrics, to fade into the background and let the spirits speak for themselves. With Riley she could be seen, since they got a decent amount of attention when they were together and especially when they dressed up. Certain cosplay purists (read: racists) did not always approve of Paris's or Riley's respective costume choices or the idea of black people dressed as nonblack characters. Paris had come to anticipate and almost enjoy the surge[66] of anxiety that came with entering these spaces, had felt her flight-or-fight instinct the closest thing to being fully alive. And the ghost tours, too, made her think that by comparison, she was at least more alive than the bodies that filled those holes.

That day was not her day off, so she took the Metro and two buses to meet Riley at the convention after work, after showering and changing into her long silver wig and meticulously[67] sewn necromancer[68] dress, her dark skin contrasting with the purple-and-white pinstripes of the dress, the gray armor on her arms and legs elevating

---

[55] **Olaudah Equiano** was a writer and abolitionist in the 18th century. As a child, he was enslaved in Africa and taken to the Caribbean. He purchased his freedom in 1766. Later he went to London, where he supported the abolitionist movement.
[56] **Phyllis Wheatley** was an African-American author in the 18th century. As a child, she was sold into slavery and taken to North America. She learned to read and write and became the first African-American author whose poetry was published.
[57] **Nat Turner** was an enslaved preacher who organized a four-day rebellion of enslaved and free African Americans in Southampton County, Virginia, in 1831.
[58] **wretchedness** = the feeling of being ill, very unhappy or unfortunate and suffering greatly
[59] to **coax** = to gently try to persuade someone to do something
[60] **grainy** = looking as if it is made up of lots of spots so that it is difficult to see something
[61] to **jut** = to move a part of your body in a determined way
[62] **durag** = a cloth tied around the hair
[63] **boba tea** = bubble tea
[64] **Caltech** = California Institute of Technology, a private research university in Pasadena, California
[65] **reverence** = a feeling of great respect for someone or something
[66] **surge** = a sudden powerful movement
[67] **meticulous** = very careful
[68] **necromancer** = someone who claims to be able to communicate with the dead

Short stories — Heads of the Colored People

her mood. She had debated dressing as Haruhi Fujioka[69], the counterpart to Riley's costume from *Ouran High School Host Club*, but her choice of Eucliwood Hellscythe[70] created a bigger impact, she thought. Though she kept her blue contacts down and focused on her sketchbook, her eyelids, adorned with heavy black-and-white shadow, warned other transit passengers to dare her, that day.

When Paris entertained visitors from out of town, or when she and Riley caught the spirit, she liked to ride the Metrolink from Highland Park to Glendale to visit Michael Jackson's mausoleum, which you couldn't exactly get close to, but which still sent a melancholy shiver through her and her guests. During most of her time on the bus or the Metrolink, Paris drew Riley and many other people — you could call her a sketch artist, though not in any official, paying capacity.

She called her sketchbooks a collection of heads, for she never drew bodies, and anyway, Paris was lighthearted and laughed frequently, showing the gap between her teeth, not nearly as morbid as her job and curated[71] heads make her sound. She called Riley Fuzzy Lumpkins[72], and he called her Bubbles[73]. She was listening to "Say My Name,"[74] attached as she was to all things nineties, even though she was nineteen and had been born after Tupac[75] and Biggie[76] were already dead. That morning, Paris had watched reruns of *Martin*[77] and laughed at a character's plea for a wish sandwich. In the nineties, she felt — and you should fill in for yourself a kind of longing here — something melancholy, plaid, flannel, but not overwrought[78].

It isn't true, at least not in Paris's case, that you can sense what the future holds. That day, she had jokingly, in an exercise of character acting, avoided pronouncing Riley's name near the word "death" or at the graveyard or while dressed as Eucliwood, lest she kill him. But no psychic, metaphysical force warned her to tell Riley not to go to Comic-Love or to avoid arguments without spoils or to immediately put his hands up when instructed to do so. Nothing told her, still humming "Say My Name" in her best humming voice, not to walk toward the large crowd of flashing lights, police cars, and costumed and uncostumed bystanders. Her stomach urged her to look away, once she got close enough to be sickened, but she couldn't then.

She didn't feel more alive from the surge of panic in her body or in comparison to Riley on the ground.

Years later, she would regret not drawing the offending officer that day. Since then, she has sketched his face over and over, penciling his name and image in her notebook as a sort of plea, saying it aloud, wishing that she, like Eucliwood, could pronounce the names of those she wanted to die and make it so.

When an artist named Kevan Peterson wrote to her about a project he wanted to finish — really, to finally begin — Paris was glad for her sketches of Riley.

5.

A well-read, self-aware, self-loving black man with blue contact lenses and blond hair and a periwinkle suit was shot down in Los Angeles after a reportedly violent altercation[79] with a well-read street promoter, who was also shot, after police officers answered a complaint. "Who was also shot" here signals the afterthought that was Brother Man, Richard, because he was not the one with the blond hair or blue contacts or in any way exceptional, except for his size and the things he had overcome (too many to name here), and his comic books. And you should fill in for yourself the details of that shooting as long as the constants (unarmed men, excessive force, another dead body, another dead body) are included in those details. Hum a few bars[80] of "Say My Name," but in third person plural if that does something for you.

A few more points I should not leave to the imagination: in the chalk drawing on Fifteenth, you can see Riley's leg kicking out like Spike Spiegel[81] and an additional rectangle above the outline of Richard's hand, where he might have held his comic books or a laminated mock-up.

The picture the Associated Press chose came from a Throwback Thursday photo that Riley had posted on social media, a picture of him in a costume from an undergrad party, at which he wore an oversize blue shirt and a bedazzled[82] blue bandana over cornrows. His mother, and girlfriend, Paris, explained repeatedly that he was not dressed as a thug[83], but as nineties Justin Timberlake.

Annotations

[69] **Haruhi Fujioka** = the main character of the manga and anime series *Ouran High School Host Club*
[70] **Eucliwood Hellscythe** = a main character of *Is This a Zombie?*, a Japanese light novel series
[71] **curated** = organized and presented professionally
[72] **Fuzzy Lumpkins** = a villain in *The Powerpuff Girls*, an American superhero animated TV series
[73] **Bubbles** = a main character of *The Powerpuff Girls*
[74] **"Say My Name"** = a song released in 1999 by the American girl group Destiny's Child
[75] **2Pac** = Tupac Amaru Shakur (1971–1996) was an American rapper and actor.
[76] **Biggie** = Christopher George Latore Wallace (1972–1997) was an American rapper and songwriter.
[77] ***Martin*** = an American TV sitcom (1992–1997)
[78] **overwrought** = extremely excited or upset and worried
[79] **altercation** = a noisy argument or fight
[80] **bar** = one of the small equal parts into which a piece of music is divided
[81] **Spike Spiegel** = the main character of the 1998 anime series *Cowboy Bebop*
[82] **bedazzled** = sparkly
[83] **thug** = a violent person or criminal

Brother Man's picture was an old mug shot, accompanied by a story that emphasized a criminal charge from five years ago — for child support nonpayment and tax evasion — and his penchant[84] for false names.

Both men's families would say the pictures didn't say anything, that that's not how anyone who knew them would remember them.

The Neil deGrasse Tysons disagreed over the number of gunshots they heard; the one in blackface said ten, while the one with a brown face called black said thirteen. The autopsies would not conclude, but there might have been marijuana in Riley's or Richard's systems, at some point.

6.

I think a cop shooting is too melodramatic when the story was interesting on its own, and my preoccupation with race is perhaps overdone, but it was O'Connor, I think, who said — and I say "I think" here more as a device, to affect a sort of nonchalance, when in fact I know she said — everything that rises must converge or something like that ("or something like that" serving as another affected clause). But that makes the ending sound intentional or overdetermined, when it wasn't, though I believe — I know — it was Donika Kelly[85] who said "the way a body makes a road," or in this case an outline, impression.

How to end such a story, especially one that is this angry, like a big black fist? The voice is off-putting. All the important action happens offscreen; we don't even see the shooting or the actual bodies or the video. Like that one guy in fiction workshop said, meta is so eighties. The *mise en abyme*[86] is cool but overdone. This is a story of fragments, sketches. Dear author: Thank you for sharing this, but we regret.

I concede that it might have been so much more readable as a gentle network narrative, with the cupcakes and the superheroes and the blue eyes and the nineties image-patterning. But I couldn't draw the bodies while the heads talked over me, and the mosaic formed in blood, and what is a sketch but a chalk outline done in pencil or words? And what is a black network narrative but the story of one degree of separation, of sketching the same pain over and over, wading through so much flesh trying to draw new conclusions, knowing that wishing would not make them so?

...

[84] **penchant** = a special liking for something
[85] **Donika Kelly** = an Assistant Professor of English at the University of Iowa, specializing in poetry writing and gender studies in contemporary American literature
[86] ***mise en abyme*** = a formal technique of creating an image that contains a smaller copy of itself

WHILE READING

3

Read the short story. Match the sentence parts. Write the letters A–E in the boxes.

1. Riley and Paris often hang around the town
2. On his way to the Convention Center, where he is meeting Paris, Riley ignores Brother Man's greeting
3. Not being pleased about Riley's lack of interest, Brother Man
4. The confrontation between Riley and Brother Man leads to a fight
5. Both Brother Man and Riley are shot although

A violates Riley's personal space by turning Riley toward him.
B wearing costumes as characters from manga and anime series.
C ending with police intervention.
D being unarmed.
E brushing away the pamphlet Brother Man was trying to hand him.

4

a) Divide the story up into different parts and sum up what happens in each part in no more than four sentences.

b) **Group work**
Compare the structure you came up with and your summaries with your group.

Short stories — Heads of the Colored People

5 Group work

a) Read the short story again. Work in a group of four. Each of you chooses one of the following characters. Note down what you have learned about them and provide references from the text.

b) Present your results to your group members and add the missing information.

Character	Personal information	Outer appearance	Beliefs and values	Relationship to other people	Text reference
Riley					
Brother Man					
Kevan					
Paris					

6 → Workshop: Analysing narrative perspective

Analyse the narrative perspective of the short story. How does it challenge the reader's perceptions of the story and its characters?

7

a) Several important African-American personalities are mentioned in the short story. Do some research on:
- Frederick Douglass (l. 46)
- Uncle Tom (ll. 103 and 155)
- William Wilson and *The Afric-American Picture Gallery* (ll. 225–226)
- James McCune Smith and *The Heads of the Colored People* (ll. 228–229)
- Jane Rustic a.k.a. Frances Ellen Watkins Harper (ll. 229–230)

b) Present your findings in class. Speculate on why the narrator mentions these people and their work.

POST-READING

8 Think-Pair-Share
a) **Think:** Make a list of three themes you consider central to your understanding of the short story.
b) **Pair:** Explain your choices to your partner and agree on two major themes.
c) **Share:** Discuss your results in class. Give reasons for your choices by presenting examples from the short story.

9 → Workshop: Analysing characters
Compare Riley and Brother Man: What similarities are there between them? How are they different? What separates them?

10 Pair work
Discuss which "apology" the title of the short story refers to.

11
Go back to your assumptions from task 1 and 2 (p. 29).
a) How was the story different from your predictions?
b) Which character stood out the most to you and why?

12
The narrator portrays Brother Man as follows:
"In truth Brother Man was burly but not violent and rather liked to regard himself as an intellectual in a misleading package. If he could have made a wish before the end of that day, it would have been that he, too, had worn a costume to soften the effects of his image." (ll. 118–122)
Explain what this reveals about Brother Man.

13
Comment on the ending of the short story.

14
Analyse the significance of the title of the short story.

15
Read three comments on Nafissa Thompson-Spires's story from an online forum of a reading group.

Anonymous *March 26, 2021 at 4:43 PM*
I was very interested in how the author was able to weave these narratives together but the moment that stood out to me the most was the reality they were able to combine with the creativity in order to send a message. Specifically when it came to Riley and Brother Man, though both did not fit the typical definition of a black man brought on by society as well as our people they were still gunned down like a typical black
5 man. The message I received from this being that black society, as well as general society, needs to cultivate this type of creativity from our black men. So that others can view this creativity as a natural pathway from the harmful rhetoric of not being a typical black man. Not to say that being a typical black man is bad but that younger generations know that they do not have to be made to feel weird for expressing themselves in different ways.

Danielle Hawthorne *March 26, 2021 at 6:19 PM*
Nafissa Thompson-Spires is a unique story teller. Usually in novels, American Americans don't have this much variety. The characters were all unique and different aside from the fact that they are African American. I think this is a very important read because it emphasizes that people in one race are not all the same.

2 Short stories | Mambo Sauce

> It is kind of breaking that stereotype people have about race. For example a black man with blue eyes was introduced in this section of the book. The author stated that they were his real eyes but people may stereotype and think they are fake just because this is uncommon. At the end of the day same race or not, we are individuals and can express ourselves as such. I enjoyed this section of the book.
>
> **Phoenix Johnson** March 25, 2021 at 7:05 PM
> Thompson-Spires has a special writing style in this particular sequencing by showing how 4 people are different in personality and in life, but could still fall to a same fate. Each character has a personality or style that doesn't fit the stereotypes that come with their race. Though in society every one of those four could die because of their skin. At the end of the day the author shows how these four different lives can come together and be connected in a way because of discrimination to their race.

a) Pair work
Discuss whether (or not) you agree with each post. Give reasons for your answers.

b) Write your own short comment on the short story.

c) Present your comment in class.

16
Find an alternative ending to the story. Include information the narrator deliberately left out.

17 Group work
Write a film script based on the short story. Answer the following questions to prepare the film script.
- What would the setting look like?
- What would the actors look like? Which actors would you employ for the film? Why?
- Which sentences from the short story would you keep to be acted out? What would you change? Why?
- Would you alter the ending of the story? Why (not)?

Mambo Sauce – A short story (2018)

PRE-READING

1 → **S15:** How to describe pictures
Describe the photo below. Use the picture to speculate on the content of the short story and the topics it might be dealing with. The phrases in the box on the right may help you.

Language support
The story might revolve around …
I expect a story about …
It's most likely a story about …
I would imagine that the story's main theme is …
I think the story/characters …

2

Initially, read only the first paragraphs of the story (ll. 1–30).

a) **Think:** Characterize the couple's relationship on the basis of this extract. Choose adjectives from the box to describe the couple and their relationship. Add at least two more adjectives.

> loving | balanced | serious | strong | reciprocal | meaningful | harmonious | special | stable | romantic | complex | difficult | …

b) **Pair:** Share your results with a partner. Decide on three adjectives that you think describe their relationship best.

c) **Share:** In class, discuss reasons why the narrator introduces the couple in this specific way.

Mambo Sauce

by Camille Acker

He had good bones, the archways[1] of his arms when he hugged her, the strong lines of his frame. Constance met him at a bar in Brooklyn. Brian wasn't who she had been looking for, in a place she didn't frequent. A black woman in a mostly white bar talking to a white guy over white music she didn't know. She marveled[2] at his views nonetheless, the intellectual skyline dotted with feminism, prison reform, and progressive economic policy. The negotiations that night took so long she began to wonder if she were making a mistake. He wanted to go out Friday night. She thought Friday was too large a commitment to make. She argued for Sunday brunch. He countered with Saturday night. She held firm: Sunday brunch. Final offer. They shook on it, and when she tried to pull away he held on to her hand and she remembered the good bones, the sturdiness[3] missing from the lean-to[4] men she had dated before.

He became hers. She owned him outright, paid in full. He said so in the midst of a weekend sleepover.

"I should post a sign," he told her, his finger tracing the lines of a rectangle on the left side of his chest. "Property of Constance."

"Is this what you expected?" she said.

"You're what I've been looking for."

"Exactly?" she asked. She had seen pictures of his ex-girlfriends. He had dated black women before, he told her that first night. Dated black women before, sure, but he had never had a black girlfriend — that word so precious it had been like a child asking for a toy when he first used it to introduce her to a friend.

"Yes. Exactly."

Ownership had been her lifelong dream, not that he didn't require some improvements, the rickety[5] way he told jokes and the creak of a man who at thirty-five strummed a guitar and told stories about the band he had always wanted to start. He got a new job in DC as a charter-school[6] lobbyist and asked if she would come with him. It had only been six months, but Constance surveyed their landscape, even the rockiness of their interracial terrain, took in the height of their possibilities, and said yes. She could always unload him if she decided to move on, but for now, she was invested.

And in DC, Constance could be different. She wouldn't be the part-time teacher and full-time dreamer she had been in New York. She could pursue art, call herself an artist. Brian insisted on it, that she take the time she needed to sculpt and find her voice. Once, Brian had gotten out of bed in the middle of the night, naked and hair tousled, to touch each of the pieces Constance had sculpted. "And what's this one?" he said. "And this?" he asked. He came back to bed and she told him, his face close enough that she could whisper and even then, she felt that if she hadn't spoken the words he would have heard them anyway. She told him about her first sculptures and what impossible work it was until what was once only in her mind formed itself in the world. "You form it," he'd said. He listened and then asked questions, his eyes closing when he did, searching for the right phrase. And one time with his eyes closed, she had mouthed *love* when it was much too early to think such a word, much less press lips, even soundless ones, into forming it. Now, they said that word to each other all the time. Him, first. Him, most often.

Annotations

[1] **archway** = a passage or an entrance with a curved roof
[2] **to marvel** = to show great surprise, wonder or admiration
[3] **sturdiness** = physical strength
[4] **lean-to** = a small building which is attached to one side of a larger building
[5] **rickety** = shabby, of low quality or in bad condition
[6] **charter school** = a school in the US which is paid for with public money and operated by private organizations

The broker[7] took them all over DC, but the neighborhoods where they really wanted to live — Adams Morgan, Dupont Circle, Shaw — were all out of their price range. Brian had gone to Georgetown but told Constance from the beginning that wasn't the neighborhood for them. They finally found an apartment in Far Northeast, the broker assuring them that the neighborhood was up-and-coming.

"I haven't seen many white people," Constance told Brian after their first visit to the place.

Brian said only, "This place gets so much light." He fingered the old window casements in the apartment and smiled.

The second time she brought it up, over Ethiopian food in Shaw, she asked, "And you'll be comfortable there?"

"My king bed won't fit, but that thing's old anyway and your queen is enough space for us." Brian tore off more injera[8]; he scooped up some of the doro wat[9] with the spongy bread. He swallowed the mouthful and after he sucked on each food-stained finger, he smiled.

The third time, she finally said it outright because she had to be sure. "We're the only interracial couple in the neighborhood," she said.

He laughed. "Connie, how many couples have you seen? The neighborhood is changing. I'm sure we won't be the only ones." Constance was unconvinced. Brian moved toward her, stroking her close-cropped hair. "And so what if we were?"

They moved in the next week. Her parents sent a gift card to help them decorate their new home and promises of coming to visit from California. Her mother had been surprised by Constance's worry about dating a white guy. Her mother was more surprised to discover she hadn't dated one before.

"I always kind of thought that was you," she had told Constance. She yelled to Constance's father just then, a *what* that was impatient and harsh. "I'll have to call you later," her mother said before hanging up and before Constance could ask what her mother had seen in her. She liked living in New York because she could find mixed crowds and parties where she didn't have to skillfully work her body to the ground like other black women could. As a girl in San Francisco, she hadn't learned to do that. Rock and pop had been the soundtrack to her teenage years, when she was just as likely to sing into the hairbrush of her Chinese American best friend as the hair pick of her black one.

Brian's mother — his father dead since he was a teenager — sent love and a hundred-dollar bill in a card from Virginia. She wrote inside, *You'll get the real money when I can call Connie my daughter-in-law.* Brian laughed. "How long should I tell her that will take?" he asked Constance. She was hanging their curtains.

"Is that at the right height?" she asked, but before he could answer, the rod[10] fell to the floor, heavy with its own weight.

★★★

The first day of Brian's job, Constance began sculpting not long after he left, eager to have something to show him when he got home. Four hours in and she had progressed little. She wandered a circuitous[11] path through their apartment. Brian had a beat-up[12] car that he'd kept in New York, mostly for major grocery store runs, that she could use. She didn't want to drive. In Brooklyn, she walked all the time. One block became ten and she could peer into the open windows of brownstones or eavesdrop[13] on the closest sidewalk conversation.

She got out of their apartment and onto their block, the silence of this city foreign to her. She turned onto a major street and was the only one walking. People waited at a bus stop, the Metro wasn't close. Brian biked the distance and he must have gotten stares on his route. The blocks of the neighborhood had few businesses: a check-cashing place, a Chinese carryout, a furniture-rental store. Then, across the street, Constance saw a pink-and-white striped awning[14] with script that read *Winging It!*

Inside the chicken joint, the air felt heavy with grease. The paint saturated with it. The floor waxed with it. This was where the neighborhood was at lunchtime on a Monday: crowding together to put in orders for fried chicken and fries. The cost of two wings and fries was laughable, only two dollars and twenty-five cents. The price was once lower, the *$2.25* written on paper that had been taped over the last price. One of the women behind the counter was at least in her forties or fifties, another might have been as young as twenty, and a third woman looked to be in her sixties. Age was always hard to tell with black folk.

People clumped together with no sense of a line, but the women, especially the oldest one, knew who was next, as if an invisible number popped up above their head when the bell above the door announced their arrival. The women would point and ask, "What you want, honey?"

Annotations

[7] **broker** = a person whose job is to buy and sell things for other people
[8] **injera** = a type of flat, thin bread, usually made from fermented teff flour and eaten in Ethiopia and Eritrea
[9] **doro wat** = a spicy Ethiopian chicken stew
[10] **rod** = a long, thin bar made of wood or metal
[11] **circuitous** = long and complicated, not straight or direct
[12] **beat-up** = in bad condition, damaged
[13] **to eavesdrop** = to listen secretly to what someone is saying
[14] **awning** = a cloth or plastic cover attached to a building to provide shelter from the rain or sun

A short and stout[15] light-skinned man tended most of the fryers, setting them down into the bubbling grease. The women lifted them up and drained them. They tonged the freshly fried chicken into checkerboard-patterned[16] baskets and then held one large salt and one large pepper shaker above the food. Some of the customers, mostly men, simply nodded for the seasonings. Others said "Everything," and then the women would reach for a bottle of hot sauce too. Constance stood back, she didn't want to come off as a newcomer. She had hit the tail end of the rush it seemed, and once most of the customers cleared, it was her, one burly man up to his elbows in his meal, an older gentleman sitting on one of the few stools in the small place, and the staff.

"Honey?" one of the women asked. She pointed the same finger at Constance she had at everyone else.

"Three chicken wings and fries." The woman nodded and the fry cook dropped a new basket in.

"Best wings in DC," the older gentleman said to her. He moved the brim of his hat up to wipe sweat from his forehead.

"Smells like it," Constance said back.

"Never been here before?" he asked. He had a cane[17] and he leaned into it to get nearer to her. Constance shook her head. She glanced at the women to make sure that wasn't a problem.

"What you doing over here, honey?" the oldest woman asked. Her voice was sly and soft. She wiped the counter down, but kept her eyes on Constance.

"I just moved here," she said. She had thought *we*, but the sentence came out with an *I*.

"From where? Over in Northwest?" one of the other women, the youngest and chubbiest, asked. She had curls under her hairnet.

"No, from out of the city," she said. The burly[18] man eating his chicken turned with a ketchup-laden fry in his hand.

"Baltimore or something?" the young chubby one kept up with her questions.

"New York," Constance said, and then, "Brooklyn, actually." It felt like it would give her more credibility[19].

"Where Brooklyn at?" the young girl rapped, mimicking the famous hip hop line. She laughed and hit the fry cook in the back. He only grunted.

"That girl got too much energy for her own good," the oldest one said to Constance. Constance smiled at the ease between them.

"Well, it's so nice to see some young, single sisters in the neighborhood," the older gentleman said. He winked at her. The women dissolved into laughter[20]. Their shoulders shook with amusement and their heads shook in disbelief.

"Let me find out Mr. Bruce is in here trying to get himself a young girl," the third woman, who had kept quiet until then, said. She was tall and slight, all angles in her white uniform. Under her hairnet, she had a bun of what looked like fake hair on top of her head. "He got a chance?" the woman asked Constance, trying to get her in on the joke. She was eager to join the sorority[21].

"He might be too much man for me," Constance said. She had wanted a good line that was also a little bawdy[22], and the women loved it. They responded in choruses of elongated[23] "Girl" and then "You ain't never lied."

Mr. Bruce did his part by sitting up taller on his stool and tapping his cane on the scuffed linoleum. The oldest one slowed her laughing enough to raise the fry basket and put Constance's food in a container.

"Everything," Constance said. The woman smiled and nodded her approval, she sprinkled hot sauce on generously.

"You want mambo too?" she asked. Constance didn't know what that was and couldn't be sure if she'd said *mambo* or *mumbo*.

"She from New York, she don't know about mambo sauce," the young one said. She grabbed a couple of small plastic containers full of red sauce from a nearby counter. "Try it." She opened one and offered it to Constance, who dipped a finger in and put it in her mouth. It was sweet and spicy, like duck sauce and hot sauce combined. She wasn't sure she liked it, but the woman offered it again. Constance took another finger full, and liked it better that time. She nodded and grabbed two more containers and put them into a paper bag with her food. Constance reached into her pocket for some cash. She would bet they didn't take cards.

"Go on," the oldest one said. "Welcome to the neighborhood." She pushed the bag toward her.

"No, it's so cheap already. I can't let you do that."

"She said go on," the tall one said.

"Maybe we'll get Mr. Bruce to pay for it. He can't let his new girlfriend starve," the youngest said. They rocked with laughter again. Constance joined in and took her food.

"See you tomorrow," someone said just as she pushed her way through the door.

---

[15] **stout** = fat or thick and strong
[16] **checkerboard-patterned** = a pattern of squares in alternating colours
[17] **cane** = a long, thin stick used by people to help them walk
[18] **burly** = large and strong
[19] **credibility** = the fact that somebody can be believed or trusted
[20] to **dissolve into laughter** = to suddenly start laughing
[21] **sorority** = sisterhood, a strong feeling of friendship and support among women
[22] **bawdy** = containing humorous references to sex
[23] **elongated** = very long and thin

She thought of ideas to sculpt almost as soon as she got back to the house. She reached for her chisel[24] with chicken grease still on her fingers. After half of the second wing and the huge helping of fries, she couldn't eat anymore. Brian gnawed on the last piece of chicken when he came home that night and told her about his day.

"A lot to be done," he said, biting into some fried skin on the wing tip. "But everyone seems up for it."

Constance told him about walking around the neighborhood, but didn't relay her conversation in Winging It! She said only that the people were nice and that when the wings were hot and just out of the fryer, they were even better.

"What's this?" Brian asked, holding up one of the mambo-sauce containers.

"It's this special DC sauce," Constance said. "Try it."

Brian did, but he made a face after. "I don't get it. It's weird."

"I liked it," she said.

"Well you," he said, putting the small containers back into the fridge, "can have all of it."

Their first weekend in DC, Brian's old college friends had a welcome dinner for them. Constance found a colorful dress and wore large gold hoop earrings with it. Brian said she looked beautiful, but when they got to the friend's townhouse in Georgetown, Constance felt like she'd come to the wrong party. Everyone else was very casual, cargo shorts or jeans and flip-flops. One of the four women had a dress on, but she was unadorned[25]. The pale pink of the dress was pretty but barely registered between her complexion and light blond hair. They all lived in DC, had ever since they graduated from Georgetown together. A couple were lawyers who went from undergrad to Georgetown Law[26]. There was a teacher, Alissa, who grabbed Constance's hands when Brian said she taught in New York. Someone else worked in government like Brian, and others had corporate jobs that Constance lost track of during the introductions. They all knew a lot about politics and world events, and made witty[27] and obscure pop culture references some of her Brooklyn girlfriends wouldn't have caught. But the room didn't roll with laughter and Constance noticed early on that there was no music. She was used to get-togethers that ended in old-school Michael Jackson and hip hop that started with, "Six minutes, six minutes, six minutes, Doug E. Fresh, you're on." The home began to empty out, many of the friends saying their good-nights, until it was just Constance and Brian, and Alissa and her husband, Mark.

"You teach, is that right, Connie?" Mark asked. She would have preferred he call her Constance.

"No, she's a sculptor," Brian said. He turned to Constance and she nodded in approval. "Sculptress?"

"I'm a sculptor," she said, smiling at Alissa instead of Mark.

"Does that get lonely? Just you in the apartment, right?" Alissa asked.

"Oh, she gets out sometimes," Brian said. "Connie brought home this chicken, like the best chicken I've ever had. But then she tries to get me to try this stuff called, wait what is it?" Brian said. He had his hand around a bottle of beer, the other on Constance's knee.

"Mambo sauce," she said, wishing he hadn't brought it up.

"Oh yeah, we call it ghetto sauce," Alissa said. She laughed and the men joined. Constance strained a smile.

"They all talk about it like it's foie gras or something. You don't remember it from college, Bri?" Mark asked. Brian shook his head.

"And where are you guys again?" Alissa asked. "U Street and that area?"

"No. Far Northeast," Brian said.

"God, no idea where that is at all," Alissa said. She turned to Mark for his recognition, but he had none to offer her.

"We're so Northwest-bound."

"Well, your part of Capitol Hill[28] is Northeast. And H Street[29] is," Mark offered, parsing[30] the sections of the city. "And I hear Southwest has really been transforming," Alissa said. Mark nodded.

"We like it over there," Brian said. He squeezed Constance's hand and she limply squeezed his back.

"And it's safe?" Alissa asked. Constance wondered if she had ever even been to the other side of the city.

"Of course," Constance said.

"Any other restaurants besides the fried-chicken place?" Mark asked.

"Lots," Brian said. "The two Chinese carryouts." His friends collapsed in laughter. It was a joke Constance had made to Brian after their first week in the apartment, the place filled with too many boxes to think about cooking and their options limited to chicken wings or shrimp

---

Annotations

[24] **chisel** = a tool for cutting and shaping wood and stone
[25] **unadorned** = with little or no decoration
[26] **Georgetown Law** = the law school of Georgetown University in Washington, D.C.
[27] **witty** = clever and amusing
[28] **Capitol Hill** = a large neighborhood in Washington, D.C.
[29] **H Street** = the main commercial strip of the Near Northeast neighborhood in Washington, D.C.
[30] to **parse** = to examine something carefully

fried rice. The comparisons to their former hip Brooklyn neighborhoods had run roughshod[31] over Far Northeast.

"And I'm sure the liquor store has a fine collection of 40s[32] to choose from," Alissa said.

"Not every neighborhood needs to be Georgetown," Constance said. "Places like this are so," she searched for the right intellectually damning word, "stagnant. I wouldn't choose a place to live just so I could get an ego boost when I told people." Alissa reddened, her face now a better contrast to her pale pink dress.

"I thought that was the only reason people ever moved to New York," Mark said. He took a sip of his beer, but watched Constance over the bottle's rim.

"Well, that's not why I moved there," Constance said. Brian's fingers tapped out a fevered rhythm on her knee.

"People do lots of things for the reaction they get, right?" Mark looked at Constance and Brian's interlocked hands.

"Like that trick we played on Sigma Chi[33]?" Brian said, moving his hand off Constance's knee to offer Mark a high five. Mark pointed a finger at Brian and began laughing.

"Oh man, and your face when we almost got caught." They began to talk over each other to tell the story and Alissa stiffly asked Constance if she wanted anything else.

★★★

Constance endured another half an hour until finally Brian seemed ready to leave. They said their goodbyes, but Constance held her face away from Mark when he tried to give her a kiss on the cheek. Alissa told Constance she hoped they would see her again soon, but when she said it she looked as if something sharp and sour were contained in her cheeks.

"They're good people," Brian said, when they were in the car and on their way back home.

"I'm sure they are," Constance said.

"Then what was with the Georgetown takedown?" he asked. He pulled up to a red light and turned to face her.

"What about their takedown? And why did you tell them about mambo sauce?" she asked.

"What? They already knew about mambo sauce," he said. The light turned and Brian accelerated, the car jolting forward.

"No, why did you tell them about any of it? The chicken place, my joke about the Chinese carryouts?" she asked. He was driving too fast.

"Why did I make conversation? When clearly you weren't going to?"

"Is this the way we came?" she asked. She peered out at water, but she hadn't remembered any on the way there.

"They're not New Yorkers, okay? But they're still good people," he said. He made a U-turn[34] right before an oncoming car and the horn of the vehicle blared.

"Why do you keep saying they're good people? Like that makes up for being ignorant. *Ghetto sauce*?" she said, yelling this time.

"She didn't mean anything by it. Everyone says *ghetto*."

"I've never heard you say *ghetto*, Brian."

"Well, I've never heard you be a bitch to my friends," he said. He pulled the car over onto a small side street. "I need to goddamn map us back to Northeast."

"I wasn't a bitch. Don't you call me a bitch. You shared something you shouldn't have," she said. "And your friends said things they shouldn't have. Neither of those make me a bitch."

Brian tapped the screen of his phone, his face set aglow with its light and his anger.

"It doesn't even know the address." He typed on his phone, then struck[35] the screen, then banged it on the steering wheel. "We can't even get to the fucking neighborhood, but you want to defend it rather than, for just one night, being nice to my friends?"

"It isn't just one night," Constance said. She turned to look out the window, the lawn of a house before her, a tricycle abandoned until morning. Silence set in.

"No, it isn't. It's a lot of fucking nights," he said. He breathed out. He touched the side of her face, his fingertips on her cheek. "Of us."

Constance hadn't been talking about them. She had been talking about the anger at his friends' ignorance, the lopsidedness[36] of feeling defensive and never knowing when someone was coming to knock her sideways. She had said something about their dismissal of Far Northeast, but had smiled at ghetto sauce. She hadn't bothered to defend loving Brian, to question the look Mark had given. It wasn't just one night of excising the parts of her that didn't create the right picture, a paper doll with cutouts in the right places so that when she was strung up, over archways and doorframes, everyone would be ever so complimentary. It wasn't just one night. Brian was right. It was a lot of fucking nights.

★★★

---

[31] **roughshod** = completely ignoring
[32] **forty** = a 40-ounce bottle of malt liquor
[33] **Sigma Chi** = one of the largest and oldest all-male college fraternities in the US

[34] **U-turn** = a turn in a half circle to go back in the direction from which you have come
[35] **to strike, struck, struck** = to hit forcefully or violently
[36] **lopsidedness** = the quality of being not equally balanced

2 Short stories — Mambo Sauce

Constance's second visit to Winging It! was a whole week after the first. She came a little later that day to avoid the rush, and when she walked inside the oldest waitress pointed a finger at her and asked, "Where you been?"

Constance put her hands together as if pleading for forgiveness. "I know. Shame on me."

"See what happen when you give people free food?" It was the first time she heard the fry cook's voice.

"Earl's right," the woman said. Constance, when she had replayed her first visit, named all the ladies in her head after her girlfriends in Brooklyn. The oldest, bossy one was Gina. The young, sweet one was Joy, and the tall and quiet one was Tracy. She hadn't bothered to name the cook, so she subbed in Earl.

"You give someone the best fried chicken they ever laid lips to," Gina said, "and what you get? No visit, no call, no nothing."

Joy shook her head at Constance.

"How about I pay for this meal and the last one to make up for it?" Constance asked.

"Oh, now we need your charity?" Tracy said. They each tried to hold their belligerence[37], but Gina broke first, laughing off her indignation.

"Come on, what you want?"

Constance walked closer to the counter and relaxed. She ordered fish and asked for everything including the mambo sauce. She'd put some on her eggs one morning, dunked a piece of toast in it the next. They joked with Mr. Bruce again, and Constance found out that the burly, silent customer from last time who was there again was Gina's husband.

"He don't like to talk, and I don't like him to," she said. "It's a match, honey."

Constance laughed with the girls, slapping the counter when someone made an extra-funny joke. Mr. Bruce said he liked Constance eating lots of food. He liked a woman with some thickness. The women joked that he'd have to wait a long time to get that with her.

"Twig, is what she is," Tracy said.

"Look who's talking," Constance shot back. Gina and Joy about died. They slapped each other's backs when they weren't howling into each other's shoulders.

"She think she can come in here talking to anybody any way," Tracy said, but she grinned through the condemnation[38]. "Come on, let's see." Tracy came out from behind the counter and put an arm around Constance. "Call it."

"I don't know, think young Miss might win. She got a little more curve on hers," Joy said.

"What about this though?" Tracy turned around, and the women mm-hmmed.

"Now on that back there," Gina said, motioning for Constance to turn around. "Yup, you got her."

"Give me another order," Constance said. Everyone began to laugh, even Gina's husband.

"What do you do, Twig?" Tracy asked.

"I make art. I'm an artist," Constance said, the words dribbling out of her mouth.

"Like what?" Gina asked.

"You take pictures or something?" Joy asked. She posed with a hand on an errant hip and cast her eyes toward the tile floor. She jumped out of the pose just as quick presenting the palms of her hands to the room in a ta-da.

"No pictures," Constance said, laughing at Joy's enthusiasm.

"I don't know if I can sit long enough for a painting, but I could try." Joy hopped back to her pose and froze.

"I sculpt," Constance finally said.

"Like these statues we got all over this city? You might need to move somewhere else, where there's less competition," Gina said.

"You should do a statue for this place," Mr. Bruce said.

"Shoot, she might as well make you a statue, Mr. Bruce. Don't know the last time you weren't sitting on that stool," Tracy said.

"Ain't that the truth. I open up and seem like he's already sitting there. Sleeping upright in here," Gina said. She and Tracy celebrated their tag-team[39] comedy.

"I could do a statue of Mr. Bruce maybe," Constance said, hoping for Gina and Tracy's approval.

"No cane though, better to capture me when I was in my prime."

"Who says you aren't still?" Constance said. Joy began whooping in approval.

"We could see your work somewhere?" Gina asked.

"Probably in New York, one of those museums up there," Joy said.

"No, nowhere like that. Everything is just in the apartment right now," Constance said. At least this time she hadn't used "my apartment." "*The* apartment" betrayed no one.

"What you waiting for?" Tracy asked.

"Well, somebody's gotta want to see it," Constance said.

"You believe in you?" Gina asked. Constance nodded, afraid of chastisement[40] if she shrugged her shoulders or told her maybe. "You got somebody else who believe in you?" Gina asked. Constance nodded, picturing Brian

---

Annotations

[37] **belligerence** = the state of being hostile or aggressive, the wish to fight or argue
[38] **condemnation** = the act of saying that something is very bad
[39] **tag-team** = people who take turns to do something
[40] **chastisement** = severe criticism

that night in New York, Brian insisting that all she needed was the time to become a great artist. "Then you got everything. You bring one of those in here. We'll make space on the counter or something. Move Mr. Bruce over for a few days."

"That's too sweet of you," Constance said, waving away Gina's offer. She didn't know if they would like her work, if it might strike them as too foreign, as too little, as too much.

"You need something. We can give it to you. No museum in New York, but we can start calling that counter, the Winging It! Gallery. Might as well do it now before we can't anymore."

"What do you mean?" Constance asked. Joy and Tracy's heads were hung a bit and Mr. Bruce lowered the rim of his hat.

"We closing at the end of the month," Gina said.

Winging It! opened in 1968, Gina told her. She and her silent-type husband had watched DC burn after Martin Luther King's assassination. They didn't live in Shaw, where the most damage was done, but they had both grown up around H Street, which had burned almost entirely that day in April. They wanted to do something and they thought what the city needed was new black businesses, people who could show they believed in the city. They borrowed and begged from whomever they could to open and even bought the building.

"Nobody was thinking about this building, about this neighborhood. Scandal how cheap it was and now, they telling us we can get all kinds of money for it. We said no for a long time, but they get personal. They come in saying, 'Ma'am, you must want to do something else. You must not want to stand in here frying chicken for people. Who would want that?' Like my whole life don't mean a thing."

Developers were looking for areas for new condos[41]. This section was filled with single-family homes, not as easy to rent out to young professionals who wanted shiny new amenities[42] without the hassle[43] of a house. The privilege of ownership.

"You can't close," Constance told her. "What will the neighborhood do?"

"Change come for all of us, honey," Gina said and sent her on her way with three free chicken wings.

But that night, welcoming change wasn't what Constance wanted to do. She ranted to Brian instead.

"More than forty years," she told him, shaking a spatula at him as vegetables sizzled in a skillet. "They started because of the riots. This is how neighborhoods are destroyed."

Brian cracked open a beer and took a seat at the kitchen table. "Well, we should go and support them as much as we can before they close."

Constance nodded, but she didn't want him coming into Winging It! with her. She didn't want them to know that she was with a white guy and that the way she talked when she was with them wasn't the way she talked when she was with him.

"Someone decides that newer is better," she said. "People have no sense of their history. And this developer she's selling to, he's done this all over the city. Put developments in historically black neighborhoods, moved out small businesses." She got two plates down from the cabinet and began to dish up a plate for him. "I'm going to email some people. Maybe the *Washington Post*, the *City Paper*, local stations, tell them the story and see if I can get something to happen." She set his plate in front of him.

"You talked to them about this?" Brian said. He began eating, furrowing his brow as he did. "They want you to stop it?"

"You haven't even been in there," Constance said. She opened a beer for herself and took a long sip. She turned away from him.

"You're right. Maybe I should go in soon."

"Don't go just because I said to go," she said, pressing reprimand[44] into her voice so insistently that he would feel it.

"What? Who said that? And you didn't say I should go, you've never said that."

"The point is, it's a real shame," she said. Constance began to make a plate for herself.

"What's a shame is people burning their own neighborhoods. It's like, why do that?" he said.

"Rage," she said. One of her aunts had witnessed the Watts riots in '65. She had told Constance that all that love had to go somewhere. Constance had asked, "Love?"

"I guess you thought that was hate?" her aunt had said.

"Of course. But in the end, rioting accomplishes nothing." He laid his hands out on the table, open in supplication[45].

"I don't know if protest is always meant to be productive," she said. "Sometimes you just have to get something out of your system."

"Only to destroy yourself?"

---

[41] **condo** = condominium, an apartment building in which each apartment is owned by the person who lives in it
[42] **amenity** = something, such as a shopping centre or sports facilities, that is intended to make life more pleasant or comfortable for people
[43] **hassle** = a situation that causes difficulty or trouble
[44] **reprimand** = strong disapproval or criticism
[45] **supplication** = the act of asking a god or someone who is in a position of authority for something in a humble way

Short stories — Mambo Sauce

Television coverage was more than Constance expected, but the call to the *City Paper* had yielded interest. The reporter there had mentioned a reporter he knew at a local station. That reporter called Constance and said they could do a live remote the next day. Constance put on a bright orange dress, something vivid for the cameras, and got there just before noon.

"Anne won't come out," the reporter said to Constance after a brief hello and handshake. Constance turned to Winging It! and back to the reporter, doused in perfume and the irritation of someone with something better to do.

"Anne?"

"The owner." The reporter began to reek of her indignation. "She says she's running her business and doesn't have time for some news story."

"Well, it is the lunch rush." Inside Winging It!, the crowd was dense, hungry patrons[46] layered over one another. Constance couldn't find Gina/Anne in all of that thickness. "Maybe after, you could talk to her," Constance offered.

"It's a live remote. I told you. You're gonna have to talk." Constance craned again to see if she could spot Gina. She saw Tracy yelling over her shoulder, probably at Earl for an order. Constance couldn't catch her eye and going inside to talk to one of them felt pointless, casting her voice on too turbulent a sea. "Okay," she said.

Constance dabbed a tissue at her nose and cheekbones, hoping to clear any shine that the camera might catch. The cameraman counted them down to go live. The reporter struck a smile, her teeth shining brightly, and thanked the anchor miles away in the studio. Constance tried to construct sentences in her head to make sure she wouldn't fumble any words, but the reporter's intro was too short and the microphone was in her face too soon.

"And how long have you been coming to Winging It!?" the reporter asked.

"Forever it feels like," Constance said. Two times seemed an infinitesimal[47] number to tell her. "Gina and the girls have made it feel like home." Constance had used her private name, but there was no recovery on live television. "And what makes the food so good?"

"Well, it's the best fried chicken in the city," Constance parroted Mr. Bruce's pronouncement since she hadn't had fried chicken from anywhere else. "And of course, you have to get it with the mambo sauce."

"And what makes this place important?"

"It's a cornerstone of the community and when we allow developers to come in and take away these cornerstones, the whole structure collapses. This developer has done this all over DC and here's a place where we can take a stand against it. They think they know better than the people of this community what is best for them. We think they're wrong."

The reporter moved the mic away. "The developer has suggested a mixed-use complex, some condos as well as retail. But inside right now, lots of hungry Washingtonians are getting their fill of this institution before it closes. Anna Bruce and her husband, George, started this restaurant in the wake of the riots of 1968, and now this city will be losing a place to all sit down at the table of brotherhood as Dr. King would have said, with some of the best fried chicken in the city in hand." The cameraman swung toward the door of Winging It! just as Brian exited, a greasy white paper bag in his hands, Gina behind him.

"Back to you."

★★★

3. Climax

Gina had beckoned[48] Constance into Winging It! with just one wave of her hand and one set, stern line of her mouth. Constance asked Brian to wait outside, she wouldn't be long, she said. Brian followed her back inside anyway, as if the words she'd spoken had been no more than her own discarded thought. She tried to stand just a bit apart from Brian. Not that she was denying him or that they were together; she wouldn't do that. She just wanted to handle her own business with Gina, explain that it was like Gina had told her about bringing in a sculpture: they had needed something and Constance had been able to give it.

"Who asked you to do that?" Gina asked. Her hands rushed the air, propelled by anger toward Constance and the sidewalk that the news crew had abandoned only minutes ago. Constance opened her mouth to reply, but stopped. "You know my name?" Gina said. "Or hers?" She pointed at Tracy. "So, how you know what I want?"

"I just thought if you could stay here," Constance's voice began to rise, "it would be better," she said.

"For you?" Gina said. "So you can come in here and chat with women who work for a living?"

"I told you, I sculpt," Constance said quietly.

"And live with your white boyfriend," Gina said. Constance looked around Winging It!, but Mr. Bruce wouldn't meet her eyes and neither would any of the other women. "That's your man, sister?" Gina asked. She pointed her finger at Constance, her ordering finger, the one that gave you permission to ask for what you were willing to pay for, the one that allowed her to give you

---

Annotations

[46] **patron** = (formal) customer
[47] **infinitesimal** = extremely small
[48] to **beckon** = to signal somebody to come nearer

what you were looking for or tell you that they were all out of that.

"It's been six months," she said. Constance shrank inside, her courage fleeting enough to escape her in one short sneeze.

Gina lowered her finger and shook her head. "You think just because you black, you not changing this neighborhood?" she said. Constance's hand went to her hair, feeling for her blackness. Gina raised her finger again, this time for Brian. "He asked questions. Wanted me to tell him what was the best choice, how he should order, whether people really got salt, pepper, and hot sauce or if that would make it too salty. You came in here like you knew. You never asked anything. You thought you knew better. You thought you *were* better. Just because you live on this side of town don't mean you don't think like they do on the other side of town. Go save a business in Georgetown, honey," she said, punctuating the most important words with her finger. That finger ruled the whole place.

"I was helping."

"You were interfering. I knew who I was selling this place to. Maybe that developer puts a good grocery store in here or a drugstore that doesn't keep its soap under lock and key. I love this place, put my whole life into even the corners of it, but even I know there are better things in this world than two-dollar fried chicken wings." She pointed one red nail to the plateglass window and the gray of the neighborhood beyond it. "But you too busy knowing it all to ever figure out what someone else knows. You so sure of things, how come you didn't know to tell us you didn't move down here alone?" Gina thumbed in Brian's direction. "Now, I gotta hope this developer don't say to me, 'Never mind,' don't say, 'Maybe she's too much trouble to sell to and maybe those Chinese down the street might be easier to deal with.' Now, I gotta make sure that the life I decided I wanted isn't gonna get wrecked by some girl who don't even know what the hell my name is."

Gina slammed a fist onto the counter. She turned and walked through the doors to the back. Constance and the whole room watched her go. Then the others turned to Constance. She headed straight for the door, Brian stood still behind her. His face was filled with the fire that had just been on Gina's. Before she could reach the door, she caught her foot on Mr. Bruce's cane. He didn't give her any of his teasing, none of his innuendo. She was quiet too, begging in silence to just get out of the door. Outside, shame and the smell of grease clung to her.

★★★

[49] **rustle** = a soft, dry sound
[50] **neglected** = not receiving proper attention

Brian eventually came outside and began to walk to their house, in front of Constance. Her feet didn't bother to catch up, unsure of how deep the water was around her and with no insurance to take care of the damage after. In their apartment, Brian was hushed. The rustle[49] of the bag from Winging It! when he set it down with no gentleness, with no ease, was the loudest of anything.

"Why didn't they know about me?" he asked.

Constance didn't know what answer would be both true and painless. She could find none.

"She made it sound like I was hiding something," she said. "You never said, 'My boyfriend thinks' or 'My boyfriend says'?"

"I didn't talk to them like that."

"It's only been six months, right?"

"I was helping. I was doing my best."

"People are always lying when they say that."

"You don't understand anything," she said, but tried to bury the words in an exhale.

"Say that again," he said. Constance could not and she still could not look at him.

"No, I understand everything," he said. He walked away from her.

Before long, the apartment began to darken. Constance went into the kitchen, wanting a beer or perhaps nothing at all. The chicken, still in its white bag, sat on the table, cold and neglected[50]. It seemed a shame for it to be wasted, but Constance thought it best to get it out of the house. She would have scrubbed her memory of this afternoon if she could have, at least she could scrub the kitchen of it. She pushed the bag into the trash, ripping it as she did. Mambo sauce tumbled out and when she pushed more, the small plastic containers opened. Dark sauce spilled on its journey to the bottom of the bin. Maybe she had never even liked the taste of mambo sauce. The vinegar too sharp and the sweetness too thick. She hadn't been tasting the sauce as much as she had been tasting newness. That was what those developers wanted.

Gentrification[51] was always good at first: fresher produce at the grocery store, a cleaner subway station. Then, a new shop replaced the family-owned one that had been there for decades. The crumbling row house — an eyesore[52] for its boarded-up windows, but beautiful when the first snow collected in the jagged remnants[53] of its roof — is gone one day to make way for high-rise condos. This is what Brian didn't understand: once gentrification started it could not be stopped. And Constance was afraid love would do the same to her.

[51] **gentrification** = the process by which a part of a city changes from being a poor area to a more expensive place where wealthier people move in
[52] **eyesore** = a very ugly or unpleasant sight
[53] **remnant** = a small part of something that is left from a larger original piece or amount

2 Short stories — Mambo Sauce

WHILE READING

3 Read the short story. Then answer the following questions.

a) How did Constance and Brian start dating?

b) How does each of them benefit from moving to DC?

c) What is special about the neighborhood they moved to?

d) How do their parents react to their relocation?

e) What kind of place is Winging It! and who does Constance meet there?

f) What is Constance's reaction to trying mambo sauce? What is Brian's?

g) Why is the atmosphere tense at the welcome dinner Brian's old college friends prepared for them?

h) What is the reason for the dispute Brian and Constance have on their way home?

i) Why is Winging It! closing at the end of the month?

_____

_____

j) What does Constance do to prevent Winging It! from closing and what is the owner's reaction to it?

_____

_____

k) How does Brian react to the incident at Wining It! on their way home and in their apartment?

_____

_____

l) What does the narrator say about "gentrification" at the end of the story?

_____

_____

4

Read the statements below. Decide whether the statements are true or false. Tick (✓) the correct box. Provide evidence from the text for each statement.

	Statement	True	False	Evidence
1	Brian has never had a black girlfriend before.			
2	Brian ignores Constance's comment on the mostly black neighborhood.			
3	Constance tells Brian about her first visit to Winging It! and the amusing conversation she had there.			
4	Constance feels overdressed at the welcome dinner.			
5	Constance thinks Brian's friends acted ignorantly towards her.			
6	In 1968 Gina didn't open her business in Shaw because she was scared of riots after Martin Luther King's assassination.			
7	Constance doesn't care if anyone at Winging It! knows that she has a white boyfriend.			
8	The media coverage is different from what Constance has expected.			

Short stories — Mambo Sauce

5 Pair work

a) Use the internet to find out more about what is meant by the term "gentrification".
b) Exchange your findings with a partner. Talk about:
  - the definition of "gentrification"
  - causes of "gentrification"
  - effects of "gentrification"
  - different approaches to "gentrification": demographic-ecological, socio-cultural, political-economic, social movements, community networks
  - gentrifier types
c) Explain why "gentrification" is an important issue in "Mambo Sauce".
d) Create a mind map to illustrate your findings.

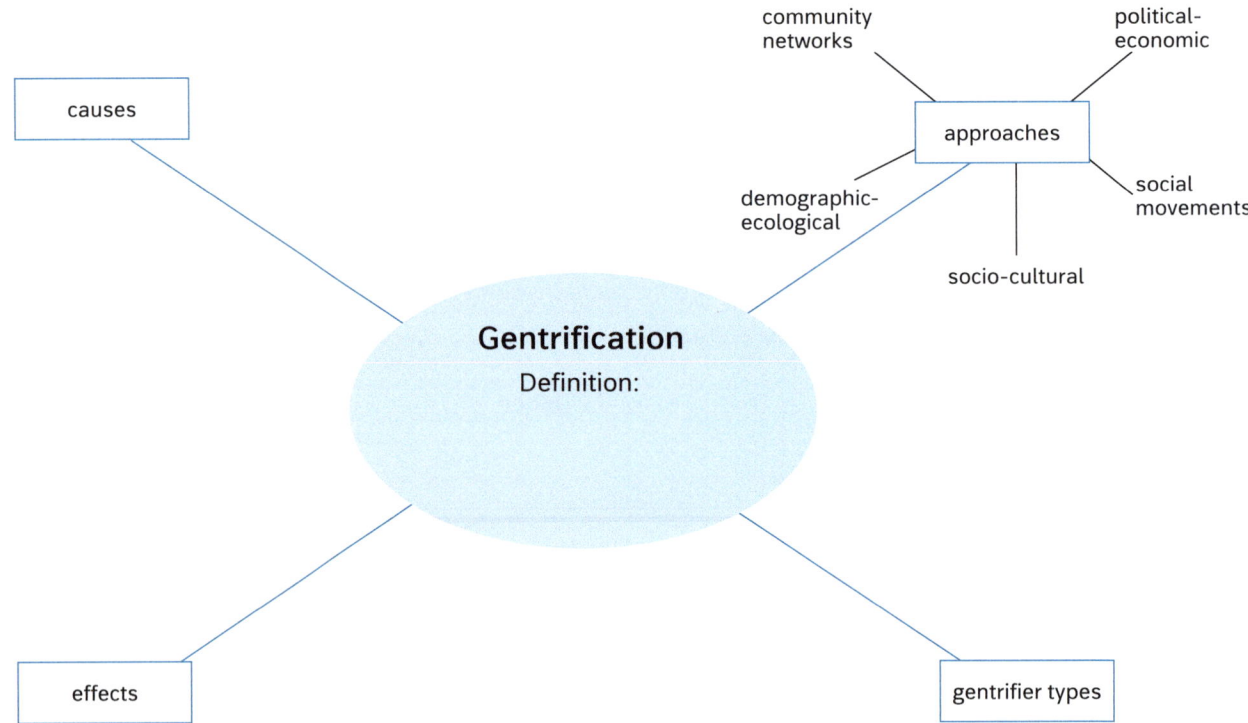

6

Evaluate the final sentence of the short story:
"This is what Brian didn't understand: once gentrification started it could not be stopped. And Constance was afraid love would do the same to her." (ll. 813–815)
What is meant by this? Do you agree with it?

Mambo Sauce | **Short stories**

POST-READING

7

Read the following quotes and fill in the grid. Note down the name of the character the quote refers to. In the last column, note down what the quote reveals about the character.

	Quote	Character	What it reveals
1	"Brian wasn't who she had been looking for, in a place she didn't frequent." (ll. 3–4)		
2	"Connie, how many couples have you seen? The neighborhood is changing. I'm sure we won't be the only ones." (ll. 87–89)		
3	"Not every neighborhood needs to be Georgetown," […]. (l. 346)		
4	"I wasn't a bitch. Don't you call me a bitch. You shared something you shouldn't have," […]. (ll. 402–403)		
5	"They wanted to do something and they thought what the city needed was new black businesses, people who could show they believed in the city." (ll. 551–554)		
6	"It's been six months," […]. (l. 721)		
7	"You think just because you black, you not changing this neighborhood?" […]. (ll. 724–726)		
8	"No, I understand everything," […]. (l. 789)		

8

The structure of a short story can often be divided into five parts. Identify the different parts in "Mambo Sauce" and explain their function. → **S11:** How to work with drama

> rising action | exposition | resolution (denouement) | falling action | climax

Part	Lines	Function
1		
2		
3		
4		
5		

Short stories — Mambo Sauce

9
Analyse to what extent the conflict is resolved at the end of the story.

10
a) Explain why the author might have called her short story "Mambo Sauce".
b) Analyse the narrative perspective in "Mambo Sauce" and explain its purpose for the overall message of the story. → **Workshop:** Analysing narrative perspective
c) **Group work** Discuss other titles that you think would fit the story.

11
a) Read the definition of "ethnic identity" from the APA (American Psychological Association) Dictionary of Psychology.
b) Describe the aspects of Constance's ethnic identity depicted in the short story.

> **Info**
>
> **Ethnic identity**
>
> An individual's sense of being a person who is defined, in part, by membership in a specific ethnic group. This sense is usually considered to be a complex construct involving shared social, cultural, linguistic, religious, and often racial factors but identical with none of them.

12
a) Explain what the narrator means by the following statement:
"Constance nodded, but she didn't want him coming into Winging It! with her. She didn't want them to know that she was with a white guy and that the way she talked when she was with them wasn't the way she talked when she was with him." (ll. 582–586)
b) Discuss possible consequences of the "them" and "us" mentality as shown in the extract above.
c) Analyse what issues of interracial relationships the couple is faced with in the short story. How could these challenges be met?

13
In class, discuss what the message of the short story "Mambo Sauce" is.

14
a) **CHOOSE**

Imagine Constance wants to explain her situation and her feelings to Brian. Write Constance's letter to Brian. → **S2:** Checklist: Creative writing

OR

Imagine Brian wants to explain to Constance how he feels about the incident at Winging it!. Write Brian's letter to Constance. → **S2:** Checklist: Creative writing

OR

Group work Discuss the following statement in your group:

> "I believe in recognizing every human being as a human being – neither white, black, brown, or red; and when you are dealing with humanity as a family there's no question of integration or intermarriage. It's just one human being marrying another human being or one human being living around and with another human being."
> – Malcolm X, The Autobiography of Malcolm X

b) Present your results in class.

Post-reading: The short stories

1 Group work
a) **CHOOSE** Get into groups of four to five students. Decide on a key scene of "Heads of the Colored People: Four Fancy Sketches, Two Chalk Outlines, and No Apology" **OR** "Mambo Sauce".
b) Create a freeze-frame. Your classmates can guess which scene you have chosen and explain why it is crucial for the overall message of the story.

2
Look at the following quotes taken from the two short stories that you have read. Choose the one you like best. Explain the context of the quote and analyse its relevance for the short story.

> "We could see your work somewhere?" Gina asked.
> "Probably in New York, one of those museums up there," Joy said.
> "No, nowhere like that. Everything is just in the apartment right now," Constance said. At least this time she hadn't used "my apartment." "*The* apartment" betrayed no one.
> – "Mambo Sauce" (ll. 517–522)

> When he put his hand on Riley's shoulder, it was only because he disliked the sight of someone, especially one of his own, turning his back to him without hearing him out.
> – "Heads of the Colored People: Four Fancy Sketches, Two Chalk Outlines, and No Apology" (ll. 123–126)

> It had long irked Riley that his blackness or the degree of his loyalty to the cause should be suspect because he wore blue contacts and bleached his hair blond and because, on top of all that, his name was also Riley, and not, say, Tyreke.
> – "Heads of the Colored People: Four Fancy Sketches, Two Chalk Outlines, and No Apology" (ll. 98–102)

> "And what makes this place important?"
> "It's a cornerstone of the community and when we allow developers to come in and take away these cornerstones, the whole structure collapses. […]"
> – "Mambo Sauce" (ll. 668–671)

> I think a cop shooting is too melodramatic when the story was interesting on its own, and my preoccupation with race is perhaps overdone, […].
> – "Heads of the Colored People: Four Fancy Sketches, Two Chalk Outlines, and No Apology" (ll. 412–414)

> "Mambo sauce," she said, wishing he hadn't brought it up.
> "Oh yeah, we call it ghetto sauce," Alissa said. She laughed and the men joined. Constance strained a smile.
> – "Mambo Sauce" (ll. 313–316)

3 Group work
Discuss what the quotes tell us about inequality in US society.

Topic: Ethnic identity and discrimination

Ethnic identity and discrimination

1
a) Look at the cartoon and describe it.
b) Analyse the people shown in the cartoon.
c) Explain the message of the cartoon.
→ **Workshop:** Analysing a cartoon
→ **S17:** How to work with cartoons

Language support

The cartoon shows …
On the left/right, you can see …
The figure represents/symbolizes …
The main issue addressed by the cartoon is …
The message of the cartoon is …

2
a) Do some research on the following terms:
- ethnic identity
- discrimination
- stereotype
- prejudice
- racism

b) Write your own definitions of these terms. How do they differ? → **S8:** How to improve your text
c) Find suitable examples from the short stories for each term and discuss them in class.

3 Pair work
a) **Think:** Each student deals with one of the two short stories.
Collect important aspects of
- ethnic identity
- discrimination
- racism

for each story. Use text references.
b) **Pair:** Compare your results with your partner showing differences and similarities.
c) Choose the short story you would recommend to someone interested in learning something about what it means to be African-American in the United States. Give reasons for your choice.
d) **Share** your results in class.

Ethnic identity and discrimination | Topic 2

4 Pair work
Research some background information on police violence and the Black Lives Matter movement and present your findings in class.

5 Group work
Do some research on one of the following topics:
- the American Civil Rights Movement
- Martin Luther King Jr.
- the March on Washington
- Rosa Parks and the Montgomery Bus Boycott

Prepare a short presentation.

VIEWING: WHAT IT MEANS TO BE BLACK AND GERMAN

6
You are going to watch a video by DW News (Deutsche Welle) about Black Germans and their identity and achievements.
First read the questions below. Then watch the video and answer the questions. **Webcode** DSW-73684-01

a) What is the difference between the terms "Afro-German" and "Black German"?

_____

_____

b) What is "ISD" and how did it start?

_____

_____

c) Who was Audre Lorde?

_____

_____

d) What is the issue of "Black in Tech Berlin"?

_____

_____

e) How are Black studies, African history or colonial history taught in Germany?

_____

_____

Topic: Ethnic identity and discrimination

f) Why are there so few Black German academics?

g) Who was "Milli" and why can she be considered as a gap in art history?

h) Which examples of Black Germans and their important works are given in the video?

i) What is "Each One Teach One"?

7 Group work

a) Watch the scene with Nana Titi Amoako (2:45–3:20) again. What does she say about white people? Explain what is meant by this statement.

b) Compare this statement with the depiction of Riley in "Heads of the Colored People: Four Fancy Sketches, Two Chalk Outlines, and No Apology".

8

Compare the reality of Black Germans as depicted in the video with the reality of African Americans as portrayed in the short stories. Discuss your results in class.

The Founder | Film | 3

The Founder

PRE-VIEWING

1

You are going to watch the film *The Founder*, which was directed by John Lee Hancock (2016).

a) Look at the film poster and the film still below.

b) What do you think? What will the film be about? What kind of person may the protagonist Ray Kroc be? Make a mind map and note down your first ideas about the film.

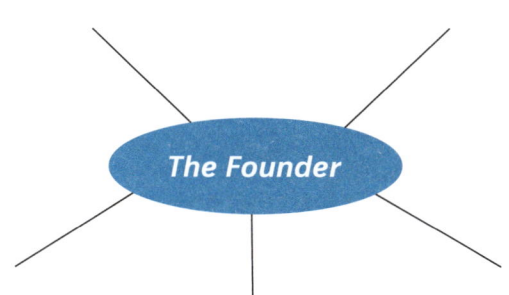

3 Film — The Founder

WHILE VIEWING

2

Look at the plot diagram and read the information below.
While you are watching the film, take notes and complete the plot diagram with the most important information.

> **Info**
>
> **A plot diagram – key terms explained:**
>
> **Exposition:** the introduction of the setting, the situation and the main characters
> **Rising action:** an important moment for the protagonist; the events focus on a conflict or a problem
> **Conflict:** a dramatic struggle between two forces; for example, character vs. character, character vs. society, or an inner conflict
> **Climax:** the point of highest tension; the turning point, which can change the protagonist's fate
> **Falling action:** the tension decreases and the main problem starts to resolve, leading to the ultimate resolution
> **Resolution:** the point when the conflict is finally (re)solved or determined unsolvable

The Founder – Plot diagram:

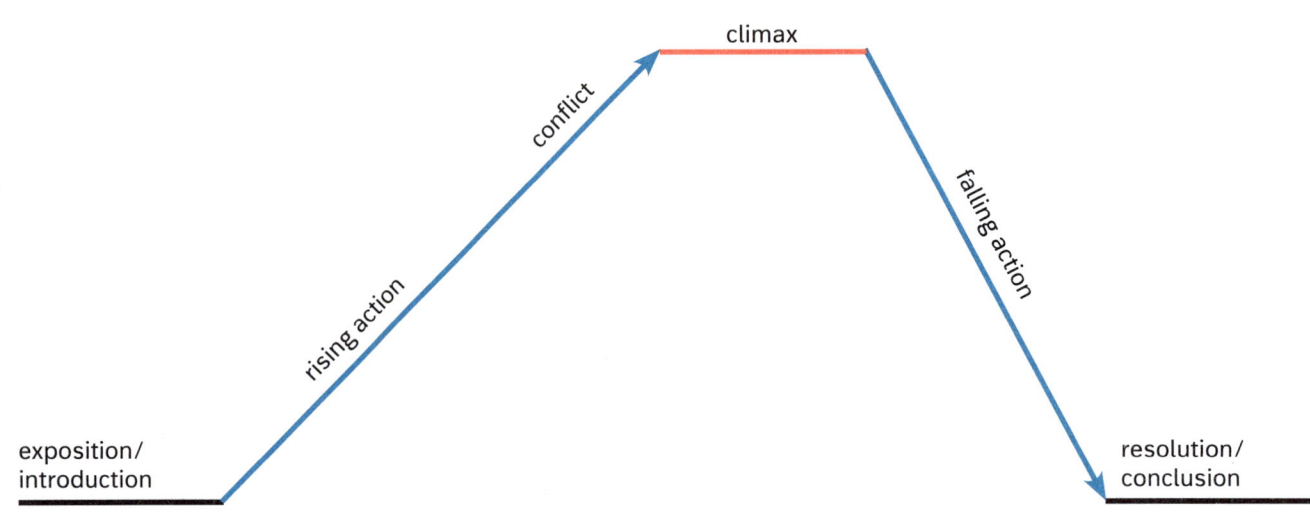

3

a) Sum up what the McDonald brothers tell Ray Kroc about their concept and the history of their business. (You can watch the following scenes again: 0:13:00 – 0:24:08)

b) Write a blog post on the McDonald brothers' idea. You can include your own experiences as a customer going to a restaurant.

→ **S7:** Checklist: Writing a blog post

The Founder | Film

4
Explain how Ray Kroc manages to make Dick and Mac McDonald's concept so successful.
You can create a chart to illustrate your findings.

5 Pair work
From the very first day, a pillar of McDonald's success has been quality management (QM). In the film Ray Kroc is shocked when he realizes that some of his franchisees and people who work in his restaurants do not stick to his quality standards.
What forms of quality management do you think are most important for McDonald's? Explain why.
The key words on the right can help you.

safety | supplies | food | products | cleanliness | financial | …

6
a) Examine what skills and qualities Ray thinks people who want to work for McDonald's should have.

responsible | curious | fair | conscientious | stress-resistant | well-organized | highly motivated | reliable | resilient | sociable | cooperative | diligent | modest | independent | flexible | calm | determined | practical | creative | open-minded | …

_____
_____
_____
_____

b) Write a job ad that Ray could have written. → **S8:** How to improve your text

7 → **S16:** Checklist: Analysis of a film scene   → **Workshop:** Analysing a feature film
Watch the scene "Welcome to Minneapolis" (0:57:08 – 0:58:07) again.

> Ray Kroc and Fred Turner have just landed in Minneapolis and a taxi has taken them to the opening of a new McDonald's franchise. The music starts, there is a close-up of Ray's shoe stepping out of the car, a tilting shot follows and the camera moves upwards – and Ray gets out of the car.

a) Describe your first impression of the scene.

_____
_____
_____
_____

3 | Film | The Founder

b) Describe the two film stills and the cinematic effects used.

c) Analyse how Ray is presented in the scene and how the film-makers have accomplished this.

8 → **S16:** Checklist: Analysis of a film scene → **Workshop:** Analysing a feature film

a) Watch the scene in which Ray buys Dick and Mac out. Complete the viewing log below (you don't need to fill in every single box). You can look up cinematic devices on pp. 87–88 in your book.

time	setting/characters	what is going on/ what they are talking about	cinematic devices	function/effect
1:34:25 – 1:34:28	a dark conference room; Dick and Mac and their lawyer, Ray and his lawyer	the business partners and their lawyers are sitting at a table; Ray's lawyer explains that he agrees to the brothers' conditions of sale but with one exception	tracking shot from right to left, starting from behind the stairs; full shot of the conference table; the lighting is quite dark, shady	voyeuristic, it seems as if the viewer witnesses the scene from some distance
1:34:29 – 1:34:33		the 1% royalty for the brothers won't be written into the contract		
1:34:34 – 1:34:36		Mac is shocked and turns his head to his brother and back to Ray		
1:34:37 – 1:34:41			close-up of Ray	
1:34:41 – 1:34:44			close-up of Mac	
1:34:45 – 1:34:48			close-up of Ray	
1:34:49 – 1:34:57		Ray promises that the brothers will get their full royalties	quick shots showing close-ups of Dick, Mac and Ray	

3 Film — The Founder

time	setting/characters	what is going on/ what they are talking about	cinematic devices	function/effect
1:34:58 – 1:34:59			over the shoulder shot showing Dick, Mac and their lawyer	
1:35:00 – 1:35:02		Ray stands up and gives them his word	full shot of the conference table from below the stairs	
1:35:03 – 1:35:21			quick shots showing close-ups of Ray, Mac, including Ray's outstretched hand, and Dick; medium shot: Ray standing, the others sitting at the table	
1:35:22 – 1:35:25	Ray and his lawyer			
1:35:26 – 1:35:34			close-up of Mac	
1:35:34 – 1:35:49	Dick and Mac		medium shot, filmed through a glass pane; close-up of the cheques	

b) Analyse the scene focusing on the characters' emotions, the audience's possible reaction and how those are created through acting and cinematic devices.

9 → **S1:** Checklist: Summary
Write a plot summary of the film *The Founder*. You can use your plot diagram from p. 58.

The Founder | **Film**

POST-VIEWING

10 Pair work

a) At the beginning of the film, Ray is listening to the motivational record "The Power of the Positive" by Dr. Clarence Floyd Nelson (0:04:15 – 0:06:25). Read the extract from the film script below. Assess to what extent the scene foreshadows Ray's character traits and the way he acts to reach his goals.

> "Persistence. Nothing in the world can take the place of persistence.
> Talent won't. Nothing is more common than unsuccessful men with talent.
> Genius won't. Unrewarded genius is practically a cliché.
> Education won't. The world is full of educated fools.
> Persistence and determination alone are all powerful.
> Show that you don't have to be defeated by anything. That you can have peace of mind, improved health and a never ceasing flow of energy. If you attempt each and every day to achieve these things, the results will make themselves obvious to you. While it may sound like a magical notion, it is in you to create your own future. The greatest discovery of my generation is that human beings can alter their lives by altering their attitudes of mind.
> Or as Ralph Waldo Emerson declared, "A man is what he thinks about all day long.""

b) Compare this scene with the end of the film, when Ray is practising his speech in front of the mirror (1:39:25 – 1:40:20).

c) Comment on whether you agree or disagree with this attitude that persistence and determination are more important than talent or education in the world of work.

11 → **Workshop:** Analysing characters → **S8:** How to improve your text
Write a coherent text to characterize Ray.

12
Analyse the development of Ray's relationship with his wife Ethel.

13 → **Workshop:** Analysing characters → **S8:** How to improve your text
Choose one of the following characters and write a characterization.
- Fred Turner
- Ethel Kroc
- Dick McDonald
- Harry Sonneborn
- Joan Kroc (previously Smith)
- Mac McDonald

14
a) **Pair work** Choose two of the following quotes by Ray Kroc and explain in what contexts in the film they are said.

> "McDonald's can be the new American church. Feeding bodies and feeding souls and it ain't just open on Sundays, boys. It's open seven days a week." (0:34:04 – 0:34:18)

> "Contracts are like hearts, they're made to be broken." (1:25:53 – 1:25:57)

> "Business is war. It's dog eat dog, rat eat rat. If my competitor were drowning, I'd walk over and I'd put a hose right in his mouth." (1:29:24 – 1:29:33)

> "Now, I know what you're thinking. How the heck does a 52-year-old, over the hill, milkshake machine salesman, build a fast food empire with 1600 restaurants, in 50 states, five foreign countries, with an annual revenue of in the neighborhood of 700 million dollars? One word, persistence." (1:39:25 – 1:39:52)

b) **Group work** Comment on the quotes: which ones do you agree or disagree with? Give reasons for your answers.

Film — The Founder

15 Group work
Discuss whether Ray Kroc can be considered an exceptional founder.
Comment on the film title, too.

16
Film directors and screenwriters often adapt real facts for a more dramatic effect, which is called 'artistic licence'. What is fiction and what is reality? What may be exaggerated, what was left out, what did not really happen? Check some facts and research how accurate the film is if you compare it with the historic events.

Ray Kroc, Chairman of the Board of the McDonald's Corporation

Fiction?	Reality?

17
a) Write a film review on *The Founder*.

Info

Tips on how to write a film review:
- Come up with a catchy heading for your review.
- Name essential information about the film (title, release date, genre, director, screenwriter, producer).
- Give a short plot summary, but do not give away too much of the story (such as a twist or the end) as you might spoil the film for a possible audience.
- Describe your personal impression of the film.
- Comment on the actors. (Were they convincing? Were they a good choice for the roles?)
- Describe how the cinematic devices contribute to the effect of the film (e.g. camera, editing, lighting, sound, special effects, …).
- Finally, say whether you would recommend the film (and, if so, to whom/what kind of audience). Give the film a rating (1–10 stars) and explain your decision.

---

b) Use the internet to find out how other viewers have rated the film. Think about whether you would like to upload your film review, too.

The American Dream

1
Read the information below.

> ### The American Dream
> The American Dream is a concept that generations of people in the United States have believed in and strived for. The term was coined by James Truslow Adams in his book *The Epic of America* (1931):
> "The American Dream is that dream of a land in which life should be better and richer and fuller for everyone, with opportunity for each according to ability or achievement."
> The American Dream is rooted in the Declaration of Independence (July 4, 1776), a document signed by the Thirteen Colonies seeking independence from British rule:
> "We hold these truths to be self-evident, that all men are created equal, that they are endowed by their Creator with certain unalienable Rights, that among these are Life, Liberty and the pursuit of Happiness."
> – Preamble to the Declaration of Independence
> For many people, the American Dream means that everybody has the freedom to do what they want and everybody who works hard can be successful and rise "from rags to riches".

2 Group work

There is a variety of individual interpretations of the American Dream, for example:

- getting rich, making it
- climbing up the social ladder
- leading a happy life
- living peacefully
- having a happy family and home
- being independent
- knowing that everything is possible
- doing what you love
- being able to do good in the world
- being self-employed
- owning your own company
- practising your religion freely
- being able to say your opinion
- being treated equally, no matter who you are or where you are from
- …

What do you think about the American Dream and the different interpretations? Can the American Dream come true for everybody? Discuss in your group.

hire and fire

3 Pair work

What is the American Dream for the following characters from the film *The Founder*? What is similar and what is different? Note down some ideas and fill in the Venn diagram below.

The American Dream for characters in *The Founder*

Ray Kroc

Ray's wife Joan

Dick and Mac McDonald

Topic: The Founder

4 Pair work

You are going to watch the CNBC video "Why McDonald's Failed In Iceland".

a) Pre-viewing: As the title of the documentary suggests, McDonald's tried to establish their business in Iceland. Despite being successful in more than 100 countries around the world, they failed in Iceland. Name possible reasons. Share your ideas with a partner.

b) Now watch the video. **Webcode DSW-73684-02**

While you are watching, list the reasons for McDonald's failure in Iceland. Compare your assumptions from a) with the actual reasons. Which aspects were you right about and which aspects were you wrong about?

c) Post-viewing: Imagine McDonald's wants to return to Iceland and make another attempt to establish their franchise there. Fill in the grid below. Then write a short text giving some advice to the McDonald's management.

McDonald's in Iceland?	
Things they can count on	Hurdles to overcome

Ethics in the world of business

1

Research online how McDonald's presents itself as a company. Find out more about their beliefs and values, priorities and activities. Present your findings in class.

2 → **Workshop:** Analysing a cartoon   → **S17:** How to work with cartoons

Look at the cartoon and describe it. Explain the message of the cartoon.

"Hangin' around McDonald's again, aren't you?"

The Founder | **Topic**

3 → **S15:** How to describe pictures

McDonald's has been criticised for different reasons. Look at the photos below and describe the different forms of protest against McDonald's.

4

Use the internet to find out more about the different reasons why McDonald's has been criticised. Present your findings in class.

5 Pair work

Examine how both positive and negative aspects of McDonald's are presented in the film *The Founder*.

6 Group work

Discuss whether or not you would like to work for McDonald's. Give reasons for your answers.

7 → **S3:** Checklist: Formal letter

Choose an international company that you find interesting. Use the internet to find out more about the company, their beliefs and values, and possible careers. Write a letter of application to the company.

MEDIATION

8 → **Workshop:** Mediation → **S19:** How to improve your mediation skills → **S5:** Checklist: Writing a speech

You are taking part in an international youth conference on environmental protection and sustainability. Read the article from the online magazine *BASIC thinking*. Use the information to prepare a speech for the conference. Explain how McDonald's has been working on changing its image in Germany and how the company can still improve.

Wie nachhaltig ist McDonald's Deutschland wirklich?

30. Mrz 2021
geschrieben von Marinela Potor

Im Klimacheck von *BASIC thinking* stellen wir die Nachhaltigkeitsstrategien von Konzernen auf den Prüfstand. Wie nachhaltig und grün sind die neuen Konzepte wirklich? Diesmal: McDonald's Deutschland.

Es war ein großes Zeichen, als McDonald's im Februar 2021 eine dreijährige Partnerschaft mit Beyond Meat ankündigte. Das Unternehmen für vegane Produkte soll für McDonald's weltweit den pflanzlichen McPlant-Burger liefern.

Solche Kooperationen sind fürs Klima weitreichender als man denkt. Sie signalisieren schließlich Produzenten und Lieferanten weltweit, dass der Trend weg vom Fleisch und hin zu pflanzenbasierter Ernährung geht.

Und auch McDonald's positioniert sich damit als Unternehmen, das verstärkt auf Klimaschutz achten will. Doch wie sieht das über den veganen Burger hinaus aus? Wir schauen uns die aktuelle Nachhaltigkeitsstrategie der Fast-Food-Kette in Deutschland an. […]

Regionale Priorität

Tatsächlich hat sich McDonald's Deutschland hier sehr bewusst für eine möglichst regionale Versorgung entschieden. Bis auf Tomaten, Zwiebeln, Kaffee sowie Shrimps und Fisch, die aus Europa oder aus weltweiten Quellen stammen, kommt die Mehrheit der Produkte aus Deutschland.

Das reduziert natürlich Lieferwege. Als Qualitätssiegel setzt McDonald's auf Nachhaltigkeitszertifikate.

Bio-Siegel und Co.

Dazu gehört das Bio-Siegel bei Obst und Gemüse. Das ist natürlich nicht das strikteste aller Nachhaltigkeitssiegel, aber immerhin.

Fischprodukte stammen zu 100 Prozent per MSC-Label und ASC-Label aus nachhaltiger Fischerei und der Kaffee kommt von Farmen, die zur Rainforest-Alliance gehören.

Tierhaltung

Bei den Hühnern achtet das Unternehmen darauf, dass die Tiere mit gentechnisch unveränderten vegetarischen Futtermitteln gefüttert werden und der Einsatz von Antibiotika gemindert wird. Heißt aber auch: Die Hähnchenprodukte sind nicht durchweg frei von Antibiotika.

Zur Tierhaltung der Hühner sagte McDonald's gegenüber *BASIC thinking*, dass alle Hühnerprodukte zu 100 Prozent von Tieren aus Freilandhaltung kämen.

Für Rindfleisch gibt es seit 2019 das Programm „Best Beef". Damit fördert das Unternehmen Rindbauern, die in ihren Nachhaltigkeitsansätzen über das gesetzlich erforderliche Minimum hinausgehen.

Das Schweinefleisch kommt sowohl von männlichen (nicht-kastrierten) und weiblichen Tieren und stammt aus dem Qualitätsprogramm QS. Dazu gehören sowohl artgerechte Fütterung als auch Transport.

Wie bereits erwähnt ist auch die neue Partnerschaft mit Beyond Meat und dem Ausrollen von veganen Burgern ein weiterer Aspekt für mehr Klimaschutz. Ebenfalls positiv: Den Januar 2021 erklärte McDonald's zum „Veganuary."

Verpackung

Als Fast-Food-Kette sind Verpackungen für McDonald's natürlich ein großes Thema. Hier hat das Unternehmen aber bereits einen grünen Ansatz.

Dessertverpackungen (Strohhalme, Eisbecher, Löffel) sind schon komplett plastikfrei. Für Einwegbecher (aus Papier) gibt es ein Recyclingprogramm, um daraus bedruckbare Papierbögen zu machen.

Die Happy-Meal-Verpackungen sind noch nicht komplett plastikfrei. Doch man bemüht sich, zunehmend mehr Papier und weniger Plastik zu nutzen. Das Spielzeug ist aber weiterhin aus Plastik. […]

Einweg-Papier ist auch Verschwendung

Klar ist: Diese Strategie stammt vor der neuen Vorgabe der Bundesregierung, die Einweg-Plastik verbietet. Tatsächlich hat McDonald's sein Plastikproblem aber schon so gut wie gelöst. Nur: Auch

Einweg-Papier ist im Grunde Ressourcenvergeudung.
Bis 2025 soll es aber nur noch Verpackungen aus erneuerbarem, recyceltem oder zertifiziertem Material geben. [...]

Energie

Im Bereich „Energie" konzentriert sich die Nachhaltigkeitsstrategie des Konzerns in Deutschland vor allem auf zwei Säulen: Mobilität und Strom.

Ökostrom und E-Autos

So nutzen die Betriebe in Deutschland zu 100 Prozent Strom aus Wasserkraft. [...]

Beim eigenen Fuhrpark setzt sich der Konzern Grenzwerte und bemüht sich zumindest die E-Flotte auszubauen. [...]

So bietet das Unternehmen seinen Mitarbeitern auch ein günstiges Fahrradleasing an (auch mit E-Bikes). Auch bei den Lieferungen setzt McDonald's in Deutschland offenbar auf zwei Räder. [...]

Fazit zur Nachhaltigkeitsstrategie von McDonald's in Deutschland

Verglichen mit den Anfängen von McDonald's hat die Fast-Food-Kette einen großen Wandel vollzogen. Klar: Schnelles Essen ist immer noch das Konzept und allein das mögen viele aus Klimasicht kritisieren.

Dennoch bemüht sich die Restaurantkette eindeutig um einen niedrigeren CO_2-Fußabdruck. In vielen Bereichen, wie etwa beim Recycling, Ökostrom oder der regionalen Produkt- und Lieferkette ist schon ein großes Bewusstsein für den Klimaschutz zu erkennen, auch wenn sicherlich noch Luft nach oben besteht.

Lobenswert ist auch der Transparenz-Ansatz des Unternehmens. Wer will, findet online oder per App eine detaillierte Auflistung aller Zutaten in den einzelnen Produkten. [...]

Wasserstrategie fehlt

Auffällig ist aber, dass McDonald's bestimmte Bereiche in seiner Nachhaltigkeitsstrategie gar nicht erst erwähnt.

Dazu gehören zum Beispiel:
- die Zubereitung der Gerichte
- Zusatzstoffe in Gerichten
- Wasserkonsum

Wie viel Wasser verbraucht McDonald's Deutschland beispielsweise in der gesamten Produktkette? Gibt es Ansätze, um Wasser zu sparen oder auch wenn möglich zu recyceln?

Auf Nachfrage von *BASIC thinking* sagt das Unternehmen, dass verantwortungsbewusstes Wassermanagement durchaus Teil der Nachhaltigkeitsstrategie sei.

„In Deutschland folgen wir diesem Grundsatz. So wurden unsere Restaurants unter anderem mit entsprechenden Reinigungsanlagen ausgestattet, um eine Abwasserbelastung möglichst zu minimieren", sagt das Unternehmen gegenüber *BASIC thinking*.

Was ist mit Plastikflaschen?

Und: Was ist eigentlich mit den Wasser- und Getränkeprodukten in den Restaurants? Diese werden nach wie vor in Plastik verpackt. Auch hier könnte sich die Kette künftig nachhaltigere Alternativen überlegen, die es ja durchaus gibt.

Dazu sagt McDonald's Deutschland Folgendes: „Apfelschorle und Wasser werden derzeit in Einwegpfandgebinden angeboten, da diese aus Verpackungs- und Recyclingprozessgesichtspunkten so bestmöglich in einen optimierten und geschlossenen Kreislauf zurückgeführt werden können."

Angesichts eines sehr guten Mehrwegsystems von Glasflaschen in Deutschland, ist dies aber nicht zu 100 Prozent nachvollziehbar.

Soziale Verantwortung von Fast Food

Die Zutaten der Gerichte wie Transfette, Zucker oder auch Stärken mögen etwa im Vergleich zu Fleisch keinen extremen Klimaeffekt haben. Doch sie schaden den Konsumentinnen und Konsumenten.

Menschen, die sehr viel Fast Food konsumieren, leiden öfter an Depressionen, ihre Haut altert schneller und Fast Food begünstigt auch Krankheiten wie Diabetes Typ 2 und Demenz.

Fairerweise muss man dazu sagen, dass dies meist daran liegt, dass Menschen, die viel Fast Food essen auch wenig Sport treiben und anderweitig ungesund unterwegs sind. Auch wird mal ein Burger hier oder dort keine Langzeitschäden hervorrufen.

Dennoch gäbe es in diesen Bereichen durchaus noch Verbesserungspotenzial für McDonald's. Darin steckt aber auch eine wirtschaftliche Herausforderung. Denn als günstige Fast-Food-Kette hat McDonald's natürlich auch einen strikten Price-Point.

Topic: The Founder

> Wer will schon so viel für einen Burger bei „Mickie D's" zahlen wie in einem Gourmet-Restaurant?
>
> **McDonald's muss mit der Zeit gehen**
> Gleichzeitig sieht natürlich auch der Konzern, dass sich das Bewusstsein der Kundinnen und Kunden wandelt, hin zu mehr Nachhaltigkeit und einem gesünderen Lifestyle. Fettige Pommes sind da einfach nicht mehr zeitgemäß.
>
> Es wird daher spannend zu sehen, wie McDonald's künftig mit den Verbraucherinnen und Verbrauchern mitgehen wird und gleichzeitig wirtschaftlich bleiben kann.

Notes for your speech:

Religion and sexual diversity

1 → **S15:** How to describe pictures

a) Look at the two photos below and describe them.
b) **Pair work** Talk to your neighbour:
- Explain in what way the two pictures deal with the same topic.
- Compare the pictures.
- Assess why the two pictures are contradictory.

GETTING STARTED – SEXUAL DIVERSITY

2 Think – Pair – Share
What do you know about queer people?

3
What do you think? Read five statements from *DoSomething.org* on queer youth life in America. Match the given percentages to the statements below.

90% | 42% | 80% | 92% | 60%

1. _____ of people who are LGBT report living in an unwelcoming environment.

2. _____ of gay and lesbian youth report severe social isolation.

3. _____ of LGBT students report feeling unsafe at school because of their sexual orientation. [...]

4. _____ of teens who are LGBT come out to their close friends.

5. In 2013, _____ of adults who are LGBT said they believe society had become more accepting of them than in the past 10 years. [...]

Topic: Boy Erased

LOVE IS LOVE – TERMS AND CONCEPTS REGARDING SEXUAL DIVERSITY

4

Love is love and it comes in many forms and facets. For a long time, there was talk of LGBTQ+. This acronym has now been extended as follows: LGBTQQIP2SAA. It stands for lesbian, gay, bisexual, transgender, queer, questioning, intersex, pansexual, two-spirit (2S), androgynous and asexual. Moreover, people define themselves as cisgender or non-binary. Match each term with its suitable description.

	Term		Description
1	lesbian	A	… describes the lack of a sexual attraction or desire for other people.
2	gay	B	… describes people who naturally (without any medical interventions) develop primary and/or secondary sex characteristics that do not fit neatly into society's definitions of male or female.
3	bisexual	C	… describes a woman who is emotionally, romantically, or sexually attracted to other women.
4	transgender	D	… describes a person who is not limited in sexual choice with regard to biological sex, gender, or gender identity.
5	queer	E	… describes a person who is emotionally, romantically, or sexually attracted to members of the same gender.
6	questioning	F	… describes a third gender in a ceremonial or social role found in some Native American cultures, often involving birth-assigned men or women taking on the identities and roles of the opposite sex; a sacred and historical identity, which can include but is by no means limited to LGBTQ identities.
7	intersex	G	… describes a person who is emotionally, romantically, or sexually attracted to more than one sex, gender or gender identity though not necessarily simultaneously, in the same way or to the same degree.
8	pansexual	H	… describes people who are in the process of exploring their sexual orientation or gender identity.
9	two-spirit (2S)	I	… refers to people identifying and/or presenting as neither distinguishably masculine nor feminine.
10	androgynous	J	… is seen as an umbrella term for people whose gender identity and/or expression is different from cultural expectations based on the sex they were assigned at birth. However, it does not imply any specific sexual orientation. These people may identify as straight, gay, lesbian, bisexual, etc.
11	asexual	K	… is used as an umbrella term for people who are not straight or cisgender. People often use it to express fluid identities and orientations.
12	cisgender	L	… describes a person whose gender identity corresponds with the sex assigned to them at birth.
13	non-binary	M	… describes a person who does not identify exclusively as a man or a woman. They may identify as being both a man and a woman, somewhere in between, or as falling completely outside these categories.

1	2	3	4	5	6	7	8	9	10	11	12	13

THE BIBLE BELT

5 Look at the map and read the information below.

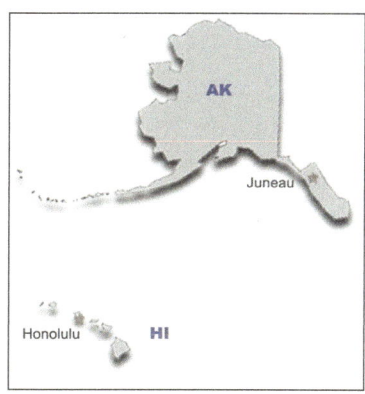
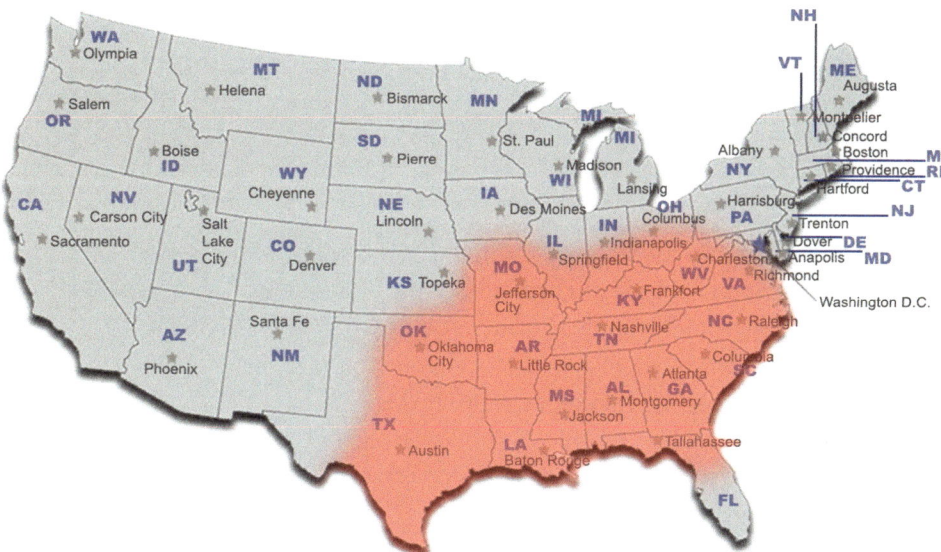

USA

Info

The Bible Belt

The "Bible Belt" includes several southern states in the United States and runs like a kind of belt from Texas to the southeast. The southern states are typically the stronghold of the Bible Belt due to the colonial foundations of state religions in the area. It is a region of highly conservative, religiously determined people whose beliefs in part stem from the Christian Bible.

One of the Bible Belt states is Arkansas. It got the official nickname "The Natural State" in 1995. Before that, it was called "Land of Opportunity" for about 40 years.

6 → **Workshop:** Analysing a cartoon → **S17:** How to work with cartoons
a) Look at the cartoon and describe it.
b) Examine the message of the cartoon.
c) **Think – Pair – Share** Think about what gay life might look like in Arkansas and state your speculations.

4 Topic — Boy Erased

> **Language support**
>
> - When I first saw the cartoon, I thought / felt / was reminded of …
> - My initial thought when seeing the cartoon was …
> - The cartoon illustrates / shows / depicts / deals with / points out …
> - It shows / deals with / refers to / comments on …
> - In the cartoon there is/are … / there seems to be … / one can see …
> - In the foreground/background …
> - In the middle/centre …
> - At the top/bottom …
> - On the right/left …
> - In the top left-hand corner … / In the bottom right-hand corner …
> - The cartoon implies … / is supposed to … / stands for … / represents … / is a caricature of …
> - It can be assumed that … because it brings its message across by …
> - The cartoonist tries to / aims to / intends to / is making fun of / criticizes / draws attention to …
> - The cartoonist skillfully/effectively shows …
> - In my opinion, …
> - I believe/think that the cartoon is convincing / too abstract / well composed / authentic / simplistic / confusing / … because …

7

a) Look at the symbols of different religions and spiritual/faith communities below. Do you know all of them? Which ones are unknown to you?

b) **Group work** Do some research on the following question:
Do the religions/faith communities officially accept/tolerate other sexual orientations or gender identities next to being heterosexual and cisgender? If not, what is their standpoint?
Present your results in a poster.

8

While the picture above represents Christianity as one religion, it can have different forms and facets just like all the other religions and faith communities, too. Baptism is one of those forms. Do some research on the Southern Baptist Convention, which is the largest religious group in Arkansas, USA.

a) Outline the religious community in general.
b) State information regarding their viewpoint on homosexuality and diverse gender orientations.

CONVERSION THERAPY

9
Read the information below.

Info

Conversion therapy

Conversion therapy (sometimes also known as Sexual Orientation and Gender Identity Change Efforts) refers to a wide range of different interventions that aim to change or suppress a person's sexual orientation, sexual expression or gender identity. Diverse practices and measures are used with the aim to change people from homosexual or bisexual to heterosexual and from trans or gender diverse to cisgender.

Next to private or public mental health care centres, religious or faith-based organizations have designed programmes of conversion therapy that see forms of sexuality other than being heterosexual and cisgender as a sin and so must be changed. The conversion practices are often represented as part of spiritual healing, mental health and religious freedom.

Believing that LGBTQ people are inferior and weak, the practices of conversion therapy are degrading and discriminatory. They often result in long-lasting psychological and physical damage. Although conversion practices are often represented in the media as outdated and homophobic, some countries and regions still allow conversion therapy on a legal basis.

---

10 → **Workshop:** Analysing a cartoon → **S17:** How to work with cartoons
a) Look at the cartoon and describe it.
b) Explain what the customer in the cartoon might have misunderstood.
c) Analyse in what way the cartoonist criticizes conversion therapy with his/her mode of presentation.

11
You are going to listen to John Smid, a former gay conversion therapist who is talking about conversion therapy in an interview with *60 Minutes Australia*. Watch the video and answer the following questions.
Webcode DSW-73684-03

a) What does the Bible say about homosexuality?

_____

_____

b) Why do people interpret the Bible with an anti-gay bias according to John Smid?

_____

_____

c) Which practices are common in gay conversion therapy?

_____

_____

| Topic | Boy Erased |

4

d) According to John Smid, these practices did not work. Which consequences did the people instead suffer from after gay conversion therapy?

_____

_____

e) How does John Smid feel now about himself having been a conversion therapist?

_____

_____

12
Do some more research on conversion therapy and give answers to the following questions.
a) Which other practices and therapy measures are known of?
b) In which countries and/or regions is conversion therapy still legal?
c) Which countries officially banned conversion therapy and why?

13
Use the information from the info box (p. 75), the interview **Webcode** DSW-73684-03 and your own research to create an infographic about conversion therapy that includes all the important information.

――― Info ―――

Infographics

An infographic is a concise visualization of a subject's most important facts on one single page using headings, bullet points and/or images and tables. Effective infographics split the information into different sections. The following guidelines will help you.
- ✓ 1. Organize your research well.
- ✓ 2. Make a simple outline.
- ✓ 3. Think of informative header information.
- ✓ 4. Design or choose an infographic template.
- ✓ 5. State your facts concisely.
- ✓ 6. Publish and present your fact file.

Tip: You may use free software tools to create your infographic.

Discrimination

Pre-viewing: Do not erase who you are
Every day people of different ethnic or social groups experience discrimination in various forms and facets. Being discriminated against because of who you are is also a major theme in the film *Boy Erased* (2018). In order to understand the underlying mechanisms, familiarize yourself with stereotypes and related concepts as well as with the different forms of discrimination.

STEREOTYPES – THE BASIS OF DISCRIMINATION

Read the information below.

> Info
>
> - A **stereotype** is a judgement (in the sense of an opinion) that can be adopted about specific types of individuals or certain ways of doing things. These thoughts or beliefs may or may not reflect reality accurately. It can be differentiated into:
>   - an **autostereotype**, which is a judgement (in the sense of an opinion) that one group forms about itself. The autostereotype is often more differentiated than the heterostereotype. The positive attributes are dominating.
>   - a **heterostereotype**, which is used by a group to define others. The heterostereotype tends to be a black-or-white pattern: it can be a stronger generalization or simplification.
> - A **prejudice** is an unfair and unreasonable opinion or feeling of dislike of a person or group, especially when it is formed without enough thought or knowledge.
> - A **cliché** is a popular or common idea or phrase that has lost originality and ingenuity by long overuse.

2

a) Using your knowledge from the info box above, decide whether the following statements are a stereotype (autostereotype or heterostereotype), a prejudice or a cliché. Draw lines.

autostereotype	Some foreigners believe that "all Germans are Nazis or fascists."
heterostereotype	A queer woman states: "Homosexuals are good lovers."
prejudice	A German friend of mine states: "All Latinos dance well."
cliché	"All gay men are hairdressers."

b) **Pair work** Talk to your neighbour:
- Have you ever been confronted with stereotypes and/or prejudices?
- If so, how did you feel? What did you do?
- If not, can you imagine how people might feel when being valued solely on the basis of stereotypes and prejudices?

FORMS OF DISCRIMINATION

3

Read the article "Discrimination" by Amnesty International. In order to raise awareness for discriminatory practices in everyday life, prepare an infographic (cf. the info box on p. 76) in which you define discrimination, describe possible forms of discrimination, and state the consequences of discrimination.

Discrimination

OVERVIEW

Discrimination strikes at the very heart of being human. It is harming someone's rights simply because of who they are or what they believe. Discrimination is harmful and perpetuates[1] inequality.

We all have the right to be treated equally, regardless of our race, ethnicity, nationality, class, [...] religion, belief, sex, gender, language, sexual orientation, gender identity, sex characteristics, age, health or other status. Yet all too often we hear heartbreaking stories of people who suffer cruelty simply for belonging to a "different" group from those in positions of privilege or power.

Discrimination occurs when a person is unable to enjoy his or her human rights or other legal rights on an equal basis with others because of an unjustified distinction made in policy, law or treatment. [...]

Discrimination can take various forms:

Direct discrimination is when an explicit distinction is made between groups of people that results in individuals from some groups being less able than others to exercise their rights. For example, a law that requires women, and not men, to provide proof of a certain level of education as a prerequisite for voting would constitute direct discrimination on the grounds of sex.

Indirect discrimination is when a law, policy, or practice is presented in neutral terms (that is, no explicit distinctions are made) but it disproportionately disadvantages a specific group or groups. For example, a law that requires everyone to provide proof of a certain level of education as a prerequisite for voting has an indirectly discriminatory effect on any group that is less likely to have achieved that level of education (such as disadvantaged ethnic groups or women).

Intersectional discrimination is when several forms of discrimination combine to leave a particular group or groups at an even greater disadvantage. For example, discrimination against women frequently means that they are paid less than men for the same work. Discrimination against an ethnic minority often results in members of that group being paid less than others for the same work. Where women from a minority group are paid less than other women and less than men from the same minority group, they are suffering from intersectional discrimination on the grounds of their sex, gender and ethnicity. [...]

WHAT DRIVES DISCRIMINATION?

At the heart of all forms of discrimination is prejudice based on concepts of identity, and the need to identify with a certain group. This can lead to division, hatred and even the dehumanization of other people because they have a different identity.

In many parts of the world, the politics of blame and fear is on the rise. Intolerance, hatred and discrimination is causing an ever-widening rift in societies. [...]

SOME KEY FORMS OF DISCRIMINATION

Racial and ethnic discrimination

Racism affects virtually every country in the world. It systematically denies people their full human rights just because of their colour, race, ethnicity, descent[2] [...] or national origin. Racism unchecked can fuel large-scale atrocities[3] such as the 1994 genocide in Rwanda and more recently, apartheid and ethnic cleansing of the Rohingya people in Myanmar. [...]

Discrimination against non-nationals, sometimes known as xenophobia

[...] discrimination against non-nationals is frequently based on racism or notions of superiority [...].

Since 2008, South Africa has experienced several outbreaks of violence against refugees, asylum seekers and migrants from other African countries, including killings, and looting or burning of shops and businesses. In some instances, the violence has been inflamed by the hate-filled rhetoric of politicians who have wrongly labelled foreign nationals "criminals" and accused them of burdening the health system.

Annotations
[1] to **perpetuate** = to make something such as a bad situation, belief, etc. continue for a long time
[2] **descent** = a person's family origins
[3] **atrocity** = a cruel and violent act, especially in a war

Discrimination has also been a feature of the response of authorities to refugees and asylum seekers in other parts of the world. Many people in countries receiving refugees and asylum-seekers view the situation as a crisis with leaders and politicians exploiting these fears by promising, and in some cases enacting, abusive and unlawful policies.

For example, Hungary passed a package of punitive laws in 2018, which target groups that the government has identified as supporting refugees and migrants. The authorities have also subjected refugees and asylum seekers to violent push-backs and ill-treatment and imposed arbitrary detention on those attempting to enter Hungarian territory. [...]

Discrimination against lesbian, gay, bisexual, transgender and intersex (LGBTI) people
Everywhere in the world, people face discrimination because of who they love, who they are attracted to and who they are. Lesbian, gay, bisexual, transgender and intersex (LGBTI) people risk being unfairly treated in all areas of their lives, whether it's in education, employment, housing or access to health care, and they may face harassment and violence.

Some countries punish people for their sexual orientation or their gender identity with jail or even death. For example, in October 2019, Uganda's Ethics and Integrity Minister announced that the government was planning to introduce the death penalty for consensual same-sex sexual acts. [...]

It is extremely difficult, and in most cases, impossible for LGBTI people to live their lives freely and seek justice for abuses when the laws are not on their side. Even when they are, there is strong stigma and stereotyping of LGBTI identities that prevents them from living their lives as equal members of society or accessing rights and freedoms that are available to others. That's why LGBTI activists campaign relentlessly for their rights: whether it's to be free from discrimination to love who they want, have their gender legally recognized or to just be protected from the risk of assault and harassment. [...]

Gender discrimination
In many countries, in all regions of the world, laws, policies, customs and beliefs exist that deny women and girls their rights.

By law, women cannot dress as they like (Saudi Arabia, Iran) or work at night (Madagascar) or take out a loan without their husband's signature (Equatorial Guinea). In many countries, discriminatory laws place limits on a woman's right to divorce, own property, exercise control over her own body and enjoy protection from harassment.

In the ongoing battle for justice, hundreds of thousands of women and girls take to the streets to claim their human rights and demand gender equality. In the USA, Europe and Japan, women protested against misogyny[4] and abuse as part of the #MeToo marches. In Argentina, Ireland and Poland, women demonstrated to demand a stop to oppressive abortion laws. In Saudi Arabia, they called for an end to the driving ban, and in Iran, they demanded an end to forced *hijab* (veiling[5]).

All over the world, women and girls have been at the forefront of demands for change.

Yet despite the stratospheric rise of women's activism, the stark reality remains that many governments around the world openly support policies, laws and customs that subjugate[6] and suppress women. [...]

Discrimination based on disability
As many as 1 in 10 people around the world lives with a disability. Yet in many societies, people with disabilities must grapple with stigma, being ostracized[7] and treated as objects of pity or fear.

Developing countries are home to about 80 per cent of people with disabilities. The overwhelming majority of people with disabilities – 82 per cent – live below the poverty line. Women with disabilities are two to three times more likely to encounter physical and sexual abuse than women without disabilities.

In Kazakhstan, current laws mean that thousands of people with psychosocial and intellectual disabilities have been declared "incapable" by law and put in the care of a guardian. Under this system they cannot exercise their rights and are not able to challenge the decision in court. [...]

Annotations
[4] **misogyny** = a feeling of hate or dislike towards women, or a feeling that women are not as good as men
[5] **veil** = a piece of thin soft cloth worn by women to cover their head or face
[6] to **subjugate** = to take complete control of somebody
[7] **ostracized** = excluded

Topic: Boy Erased

DIVERSITY AND DISCRIMINATION

4 **CHALLENGE**

Look at the graphic "Diversity Wheel" below.

a) Describe which categories are used to describe a personality.
b) Examine which of these categories are naturally given and which are socially constructed. Give reasons.
c) Discuss whether it is legitimate to put people in categories that are not natural but socially constructed and to discriminate against them on that basis.

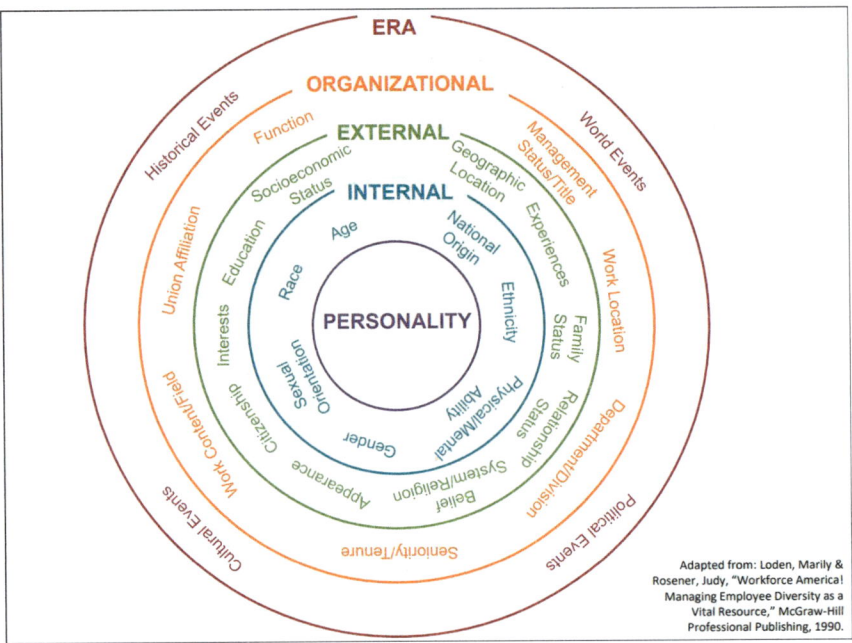

Adapted from: Loden, Marily & Rosener, Judy, "Workforce America! Managing Employee Diversity as a Vital Resource," McGraw-Hill Professional Publishing, 1990.

Boy Erased

You are going to watch the film *Boy Erased*, which was directed by Joel Edgerton (2018).
Film posters, DVD covers and trailers provide a selected visual preview attempting to catch and arouse the potential target groups' interest to advertise and promote the film.

PRE-VIEWING: A FILM POSTER

1
Look at the film poster below. Using it as a starting point, first describe the poster and then speculate about the content and the genre of the film. Give reasons for your answers.

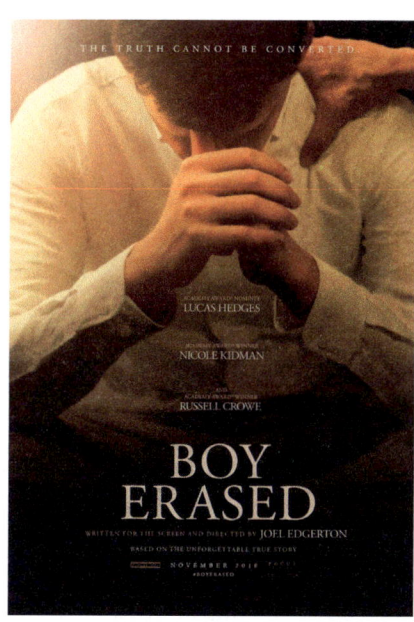

_____

_____

_____

_____

_____

_____

_____

_____

_____

Language support

Description / Layout of a poster

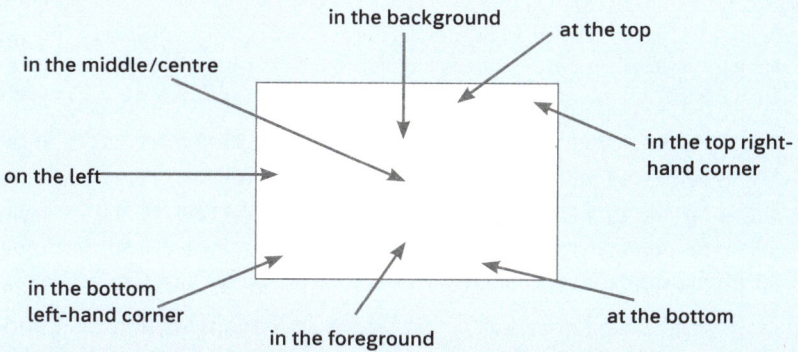

- On the film poster / In the picture I can see … / There is / are / seems to be … / One can see …
- The poster shows/illustrates/depicts …
- The field size is a close-up/medium shot/long shot …
- The layout emphasizes … / The layout is rather detailed/simple with …
- The focus of attention … / What strikes the eye is the key/main image / the image of … taking up the most space …
- There is a contrast between … / A contrast is clearly recognizable/visible.

4 | Film | Boy Erased

Language support

Talking about content und genre

- When looking at the film poster, I think/feel/am reminded of … / Initially the image makes me think / gives the impression of …
- The choice of colours supports the idea of / suggests / contributes to …
- The film's mood and tone are reflected/illustrated by … / It can be assumed that … because … / … is a symbol of …
- The film poster appeals to audiences that enjoy films containing dramatic tension / showing male views of the world / about protecting law and order, right and wrong / focusing on one protagonist, powerful and ready to take on the enemy …
- The film poster depicts/shows/portrays/represents/illustrates/conveys … which is why I believe/think …

✓ Use the simple present tense to talk about the poster.
✓ Use the present progressive if you refer to actions in the image. (This is not applicable to verbs of perception or verbs with static meaning, e.g. *be, believe, hate, like, love, mean, notice, see, think, wish, …*)
✓ Use specific descriptive expressions (e.g. *on the left, at the bottom, …*).
✓ Use suitable adjectives and adverbs.
✓ Employ linking words/connectives.

Info

Some examples of genres

action	crime	documentary	drama
• speed action • physical stunts and chases • rescues, battles, fights, escapes, destructive crises • often standard heroes and villains (good guy – bad guy)	• high speed with some mystery • action of a criminal mastermind versus the rise and fall of sinister criminals	• non-fictional • reporting on an issue of interest	• serious and plot-driven • rounded, real-life characters, settings, situations, and stories • characterized by an intense character development and interaction • vigorous human emotions

fantasy	horror	romance	suspense/mystery
• imaginative and fantasy themes • fairy-tale adventures or plots from Dark Ages • magic, supernatural elements	• large amount of violence in the plot • trying to awaken audience's worst fears and nightmares about the arrival of an evil force or event • often mythical creatures, such as ghosts, vampires, and zombies	• alternating tone from happy to tragic • love between two protagonists, e.g. love at first sight, forbidden love, love triangles and love requiring great sacrifices	• a person of authority, usually a detective, trying to solve a mysterious crime • clues, investigation, and logical reasoning • constant suspense created through visual cues or unusual plot twists

Boy Erased | Film | 4

PRE-VIEWING: REVISITING CINEMATOGRAPHY

In order to analyse and talk about *Boy Erased* properly you need some film specific terms and phrases. When dealing with films, camera operations and music or sound play a vital role in guiding and influencing the viewer as intended by the film-makers.

2 → **Workshop:** Analysing a feature film
Look at the most common cinematic devices that are used in films. Match the functions on the right to the given operations on the left.

I FIELD SIZE
Camera operations

A long shot
B full shot
C medium shot
D close-up shot
E extreme close-up shot

Functions

1 points out sth specific about sb/sth
2 provides a complete picture of sb/sth
3 points out a particular detail about sb/sth
4 presents the setting of the scene
5 provides a closer look at sb/sth

II CAMERA MOVEMENT
Camera operations

A static shot
B zooming in/out
C panning/tilting shot
D tracking shot

Functions

1 horizontal/vertical movement from a static position to shift focus towards or away from sb/sth
2 creates the impression of following sb/sth
3 no movement; creates a feeling of hesitation/calmness/slowness
4 puts focus on something or takes focus away

III CAMERA ANGLE AND POSITION
Camera operations

A overhead shot
B high-angle shot/bird's eye
C eye-level shot
D low-angle shot
E over-the-shoulder shot
F reverse-angle shot
G point-of-view shot
H establishing shot

Functions

1 creates an overall impression of the scene
2 creates a neutral impression
3 makes sb/sth seem unimportant
4 represents a character's perspective
5 creates the impression of being involved in a conversation
6 usually in connection with over-the-shoulder to show the other character's reaction/side
7 sets the scene that's to come
8 makes sb/sth look important

83

4 Film — Boy Erased

IV EDITING/MONTAGE

Techniques

A fast cuts ☐
B slow cuts ☐
C fade-in/fade-out ☐
D cross-cut ☐
E slow motion ☐
F fast motion ☐
G voice-over ☐
H flashback/flash-forward ☐
I floating, superimposed text ☐

Functions

1 opens/closes an action or a scene slowly
2 create focus on sth specific or create calm atmosphere
3 intensifying an action/moment
4 depict action vividly
5 focuses on contrast and thus creates suspense
6 provides a comment on the action
7 changing chronological order and therefore connecting/disconnecting action/moments
8 focus on text and its meaning, gives additional information without adding voices or stressing the meaning of voices
9 intensifies speed, creating the impression of change

Language support

Talking about cinematography

General phrases:
- The establishing shot of the film shows/portrays … / … is shown in a medium shot/(extreme) close-up / …
- … brings the viewer closer to … / creates a distance between …
- The focus is on … in detail.
- The movement of … is followed in a … shot.
- The shots follow each other quickly/slowly.
- The viewer sees the character in … / There is a close-up of the character …
- The scene is shot from X's point of view. / … is seen from the perspective of …
- The director uses a long shot of the setting. / … uses high-angle/low-angle/eye-level shots of …
- The camera pans from left to right / tilts up/down.

Effects of cinematography:
- … describes characters indirectly / shows a character's emotions / draws attention to sth / describes the setting / evokes a certain atmosphere …
- … is presented in a low-angle shot/high-angle shot, which illustrates inferiority/vulnerability/superiority/power …
- The point-of-view shots make the audience experience the (emotional) perspective of …
- The close-up is used to focus attention on … / reveals the character's feelings / makes the situation more intimate.
- … is shown in a close-up so the viewer can see the reaction in his/her face when …
- The over-the-shoulder shots include the viewers in the action.
- … uses a fade-in / fade-out to …
- The hand-held camera underlines … / gives the scene an unsteady quality / aims for authenticity …
- The light used in the scene is harsh/soft/bright/intense / …
- The … is used to focus on … / draw attention to … / This … emphasizes/stresses/indicates …
- … is used to build (up) suspense / tension / to create a certain effect / to convey a feeling of / to create a mood to set the scene …
- … affects/touches the viewers …
- … suggests/signifies that / provides a strong contrast to / serves as an insight into … / bridges two scenes …

Boy Erased — Film

Info

Music/Sound

1. **diegetic sounds**: sounds from 'the world inside the film', e.g. conversation, a window closing, footsteps
2. **non-diegetic sounds**: sounds from 'the world outside the film', e.g. film music, sounds creating suspense
3. **voice-over** (off-camera commentary): non-diegetic information by a narrator

→ to build up suspense
→ to develop a certain mood / to create a certain atmosphere
→ to describe a character
→ to foreshadow an event

Language support

Talking about cinematography

Music/Sound:
- The music is upbeat/gloomy/aggressive/slow/fast-paced …
- The rhythmic/background music contributes to the atmosphere of …
- The effect of this scene is enhanced by the music. / … contributes to the mood/atmosphere of the scene.
- The music provides an extra feeling of tension / adds to the atmosphere.
- The scene is accompanied by soft/alarming/melancholic music.
- The lyrics suggest …

WHILE VIEWING

Characters

3 Group work

Now you are going to watch the entire film. Form groups that focus on preassigned characters and take notes while watching the film.

- Jared
- Nancy Eamons (mother)
- Marshall Eamons (father)
- Victor Sykes (camp leader)
- Brandon Ellis
- Cameron
- Sarah
- Gary

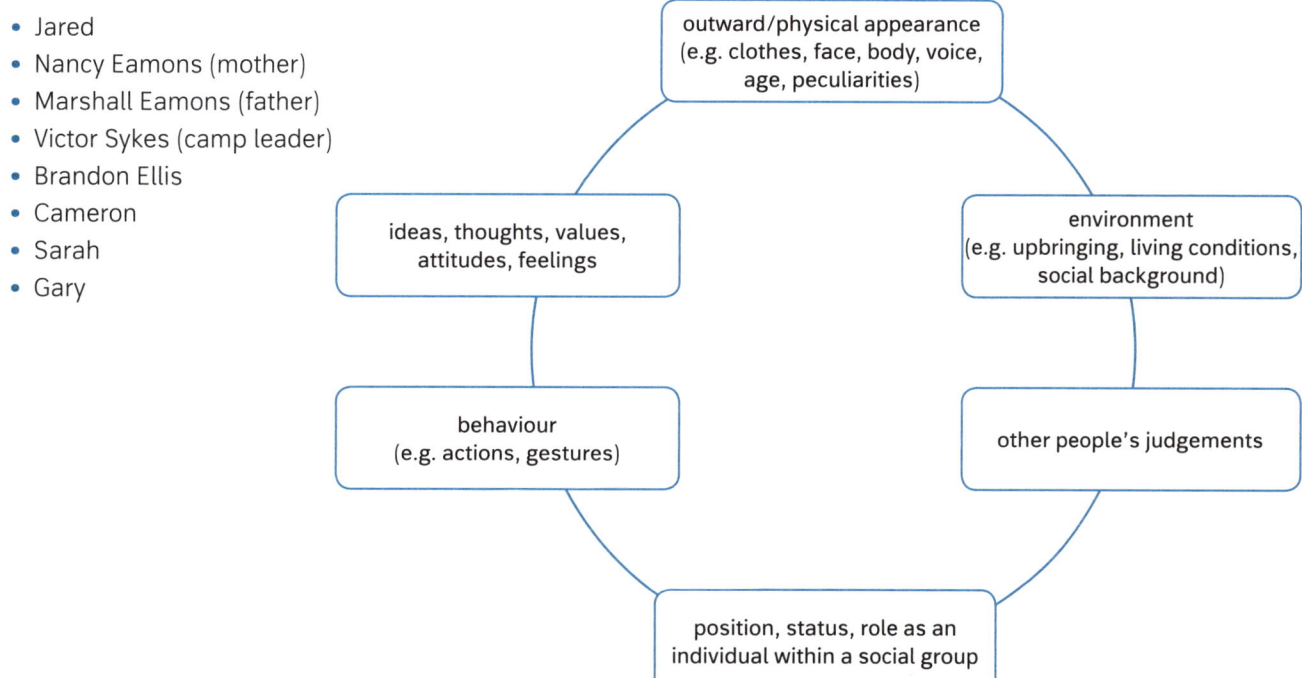

Compare your findings with classmates who have been dealing with the same character.
Design a (digital) poster and be prepared to present it to the class (→ gallery walk).

4 Film — Boy Erased

Language support

Talking about characters

General phrases:
- The main/principle character in the story is …
- Another central character is …
- … is characterized/described/portrayed/depicted/presented as … / … proves to be …
- As far as his/her character is concerned, it can be said that he/she is …
- Concerning his/her character, it can be said that … This character trait becomes apparent when …
- … seems to be …
- The body language / The action reveals that …
- His/Her statement "…" shows/proves/reveals that … / From this one can conclude that …
- It is quite apparent that …
- When saying that … he/she reveals that he/she is/feels …
- Proof of this can be found in/when …
- This is an example of …
- He/She has many positive personality traits/traits of character/characteristics.
- His/Her behaviour is marked by … He/She shows … behaviour.
- A positive/negative aspect of his/her behaviour is …
- He/She reacts …
- He/She gradually develops into … / In the course of the film he/she undergoes a development.
- … remains unchanged.
- … is/reacts/shows/seems to be/feels …
- The motive/reason for his/her action … is …
- … is influenced by …
- The relationship can be described as / characterized by …

Positive character traits

active	conscientious	proud		
affectionate	courageous	reliable		
ambitious	dedicated	sensitive		
brave	glamorous	sophisticated		
caring	honourable	talkative		
charismatic	humble	tenacious		
charming	mature	virtuous		
compassionate	patriotic	warm-hearted		
confident	perseverant	witty		

Negative character traits

bad-tempered	obnoxious
cold-hearted	old-fashioned
deceitful	petty-minded
grouchy	rude
hypocritical	self-centred
ignorant	stubborn
impolite	
jealous	
malicious	
narrow-minded	

Useful linking words

giving examples	adding information	sequencing ideas	summarizing
for example for instance such as	and as well as too in addition also furthermore, moreover, apart from, in addition to, besides	the former, the latter firstly, secondly, finally the first point is lastly the following last but not least	in short, in brief, to summarize, to sum up, in a nutshell, to put it in a nutshell, to conclude, in conclusion, all in all, on the whole
giving reasons	**giving a result**	**contrasting ideas**	**comparing ideas**
due to/due to the fact that owing to/owing to the fact that because/because of since/as	therefore so/consequently this means that as a result/the result is this/that is why hence/thus	but, however, although/even though, despite/despite the fact that, in spite of/in spite of the fact that, nevertheless, nonetheless, while, whereas, in contrast (to)	similarly equally likewise in the same way

Boy Erased | **Film**

4

Language support

relating information	reformulating	giving opinions	emphasizing facts
with regard to, with respect to, referring to, regarding, according to, when it comes to	in other words, to put it another way	in my/his/her opinion, my opinion is, I think, I believe, in my view, from my point of view, to my mind	in fact, obviously, undoubtedly, for this reason, again, fortunately, unfortunately, indeed

4 CHALLENGE → **Workshop:** Ananalysing characters → **S8:** How to improve your text

Write a characterization of your assigned character.

Practices of conversion therapy

5

a) While watching the film, take notes on how the conversion therapy program Love In Action works. Focus on the following aspects:

Love In Action	
Circumstances	*staff wear uniforms and use walkie-talkies, …*
Rules	*no mobile phones, no talking about the therapy with parents, …*
Routines and methods	*genograms, …*
Forms of therapy	*12 days (from 9:00 am to 5:00 pm), …*

b) Comment on the emotional, psychological and physical abuse as carried out by Love In Action.

6 CHALLENGE → **S16:** Checklist: Analysis of a film scene → **Workshop:** Analysing a feature film

Analyse how cinematography and film music contribute to the depiction and atmosphere of Love In Action (0:04:45–0:08:35). (You can use "Revisiting cinematography" on pp. 83–85.)

Film — Boy Erased

7

John Smid (cf. task 11 on p. 75, **Webcode** DSW-73684-03) reports that conversion therapy practices are similar to Alcoholics Anonymous (AA). Look at the Twelve Steps of the AA program and compare them to your findings about the conversion therapy Love In Action.

1. We admitted we were powerless over alcohol – that our lives had become unmanageable.
2. Came to believe that a Power greater than ourselves could restore us to sanity.
3. Made a decision to turn our will and our lives over to the care of God as we understood Him.
4. Made a searching and fearless moral inventory of ourselves.
5. Admitted to God, to ourselves and to another human being the exact nature of our wrongs.
6. Were entirely ready to have God remove all these defects of character.
7. Humbly asked Him to remove our shortcomings.
8. Made a list of all persons we had harmed, and became willing to make amends to them all.
9. Made direct amends to such people wherever possible, except when to do so would injure them or others.
10. Continued to take personal inventory and when we were wrong promptly admitted it.
11. Sought through prayer and meditation to improve our conscious contact with God as we understood Him, praying only for knowledge of His will for us and the power to carry that out.
12. Having had a spiritual awakening as the result of these steps, we tried to carry this message to alcoholics and to practice these principles in all our affairs.

Portrayals of homosexuality

8

Watch the scene about Jared outing himself again (0:40:23–0:50:09).
a) Outline the plot.
b) Examine how the plot is supported by cinematography. Pay close attention to the use of light and shadow.
c) **CHALLENGE** Why does Jared finally out himself? In class, discuss whether the trauma of the rape confirmed Jared's idea that homosexuality was sinful and destructive and might have been a catalyst.

9

Watch the scene at Dr. Muldoon's office again (0:50:12–0:52:01).
a) Read Dr. Muldoon's diagnosis below and state why she is "in a bit of a bind".
b) Explain what Dr. Muldoon is aiming at.
c) Comment on why Jared seems unable to take her advisory diagnosis.

> "Your father's asked me to take some of your blood. He wants me to check for testosterone levels. I'm in a bit of a bind here, Jared, and I said this to your mother too. Now, I'm a religious woman, there's no question, but I have also been to medical school. And, well, you can say that I hold science in one hand and God in the other, and that is not always an easy balance. And I know that everybody would like for me to say otherwise and send you down to the pharmacy for a pill that would magically fix you, but that's not going to happen. But I'm going to take your blood, and I know what it's going to show me. That you are a perfectly normal, very healthy teenage boy. Jared, it's not my place to tell you that your parents are wrong, but let's say that they are wrong. I understand your father signed you up for a program next month. Whatever happens next, it is still your choice. It may not feel that way, but it is. You're eighteen. Do you have anything that you'd like to say to me? Any questions?"

10

Watch the scene with Gary giving advice to Jared again (1:09:16–1:11:01).
a) State what Gary advises Jared to do.
b) Imagine you are Gary. Write a blog post for the website "Survivors of Conversion Therapy". Report on your experiences with Love In Action and give advice on how to "survive" to people who are obliged to take part in conversion therapy. → **S7:** Checklist: Writing a blog post
c) **CHALLENGE** Do you think conversion therapy has worked for anyone doing it? Discuss in class.

11

Read and rewatch Sarah's and Gary's moral inventory scenes.

Moral inventory	
Sarah (0:26:50–0:28:27)	**Gary (0:54:45–0:55:51)**
"I would look at other girls in the changing rooms before gym and in the showers. My biggest sin is one that I am also thankful for, because it has led me to Love in Action. [...] I had run away from my uncle's house and stayed with some girls I knew whose parents were away. It was there that I finally acted on my homosexual thoughts. [...] I let a girl touch my ... kiss m-my ... my vagina ... [...] ... and put her fingers inside me, and I did the same. I renounce these sinful thoughts and actions, and ask God to forgive me all these things."	"Dear Heavenly Father, today I ask your forgiveness for my sins. For a year, we lived together under the cover of being roommates. But in reality, the whole time, I was committing the sin of sodomy. And then my family discovered the truth and brought me back to my senses. They helped me realize that I was fooling myself. That I was being fooled. That I was seduced into a life of sin by all sorts of sinful people. And I knew in my heart that I had forsaken Jesus for Satan. But now ... I am awake to my sins. I'm enlightened. I'm here with all of you. And I am disgusted at the person that I once was. I want to ask God for his forgiveness, and I want to thank all of you guys, especially you, Mr. Sykes, for helping me get back on the path to righteousness."

a) Outline each moral inventory.
b) Compare Sarah's and Gary's moral inventory.
c) **CHALLENGE** Imagine you are either Sarah or Gary. After having presented your moral inventory, you decide to put down your thoughts and feelings by writing a diary entry. Write one diary entry reflecting on your moral inventory.
- Start with "Dear Diary, ...".
- Write in the first person.
- Be honest and reflective.
- Ponder on and express your feelings.

12

Watch the scenes with Brandon Ellis again (0:22:14–0:26:16).
a) When is a man a man? Examine and outline how concepts of masculinity are portrayed by the program Love In Action.
b) Discuss the validity of masculinity as portrayed by Love In Action.

13 Group work **CHOOSE**

Form groups and choose one of the following tasks. Present your results to the class.
a) Rewatch the scene where Mr. Sykes advises Jared to stay in the program for a year instead of going to college (0:52:02–0:54:45).
- Explain why Mr. Sykes thinks that college is not a good idea at all.
- Research the book titles from the reading list that Mr. Sykes names. Why does Mr. Sykes consider these books dangerous for Jared?

OR

b) Rewatch the scene where Jared goes jogging in the evening, destroys an advertising sign and swears (0:57:30–0:58:32).
- Outline the scene.
- Explain what is going on inside Jared and why he is so enraged.

OR

c) Rewatch Jared's encounter with Brandon in the bathroom (1:07:40–1:09:15).
- Outline what is being said and done. Comment on the humiliation carried out by Brandon in this scene.
- Do some research on gay bashing. Evaluate whether Brandon's words and actions can be considered to be gay bashing.

OR

d) "Love In Action meets exorcism": Rewatch the scenes where Cameron is being harmed physically (1:13:01–1:15:50).
- Analyse the scenes.
- **CHALLENGE** Comment on the violence used by Love In Action and its members as well as by Cameron's family.

OR

e) Rewatch Jared's attempt to deliver his moral inventory (1:19:00–1:26:22).
- Summarize the scenes around Jared's moral inventory and his intention to quit the program and go home by outlining reasons why Jared is getting more and more angry, frustrated and fearful.
- Examine how the intensity of these scenes is underscored by cinematographic and musical means (cf. "Revisiting cinematography" on pp. 83–85).

Homosexuality as God's test?

14 Pair work

In Xavier's studio room Jared talks about Job (1:02:25–1:03:01):

> "I imagine I'm him sometimes. And that God and the Devil are having a bet over me. That one day God will let me in on the experiment he was having to test me."

Read the information on Job and discuss if Jared's comparison is fitting.

Info

Job

Job is a figure from the Bible. A book of the Old Testament named after him tells his story: In essence, Job's story says that you should keep your faith in God even in difficult times.

Job is a wealthy man who has a big family and lives a good life. He firmly believes in God and wants to obey him unconditionally. One day Satan speaks to God and claims that Job only serves God because of his blessed life and God's protection; if God stopped protecting Job, Job would stop serving him. God is certain that Job will remain devout, so he allows the Devil to test Job.

A lot of terrible things happen: Job loses his livestock and all of his possessions, his servants and even his children die, and Job himself suffers from bad pain. Job is desperate and complains about his suffering, but despite all that he does not lose his faith in God. As a reward for his faithfulness, Job finally gets back prosperity and health; God gives him a new family and a long and happy life.

Time and symbolism

15

Jared's hand in the wind during car rides is a reoccurring symbol in the film.
a) Read the information on the symbolism of wind below.
b) Rewatch the following scenes:
0:04:05–0:04:25 | 0:13:06–0:17:06 | 0:55:52–0:57:07 | 1:32:11–1:33:31 | 1:42:46–1:43:46
c) Analyse this reoccurring symbol against the background of your knowledge about the plot.

Wind

Wind surrounds people and it is also in them as breath. Breath means life. Through wind and draughts, people can hear vibrations and perceive smells.

Whoever tries to grasp at wind reaches into a void. Wind is volatile and can appear in different forms: welcomed as a mild breeze on hot summer days or feared as the persistent force of a hurricane.

Wind is not only a meteorological phenomenon, but also a supernatural manifestation: the intentions of the gods. On the one hand, wind can be unpredictable and unreliable – on the other hand, it has tangible effects despite its invisibility. In many cultures, wind is understood as the breath of God. Wind is also associated with indomitable powers. In the Old Testament the Spirit of God is spoken of as "ruach", the breath of wind. At the creation of man, God breathed into man the breath of life.

16
a) Read the information on screen vs. plot duration below.
b) Analyse how in the film the plot duration has been compressed to the screen duration. You may rewatch the following scenes:
0:03:24–0:04:00 | 0:30:18–0:52:02 | 1:00:25–1:04:12 | 1:16:35–1:18:03 | 1:30:58–1:31:06

Screen duration vs. plot duration

Screen duration is the time that passes until a story is fully told. For a film it is simply its length or its time duration, so for *Boy Erased* it is 110 minutes.

The time that passes within that story is called **plot duration**. For example, from Jared's time at Love In Action to living in New York City: About five years of Jared's life (5 years = 2,628,000 minutes = plot duration) are told in 110 minutes (= screen duration).

Usually, films compress the plot duration, i.e. it is much shorter than the time span in which the story takes place. This is possible with the help of editing: Employing fades, time lapse and slow motion, directors and editors can create a new, cinematic time within the framework of editing – beyond the possibilities of the camera. Here are some examples:

fade-in / fade-out	If a film frame fades in smoothly from darkening to the first film frame, the fade-in opens our field of vision to something that was already there before and in which the action will now take part. Conversely, the slowly darkening image as a fade-out symbolizes the passage of time in a shot.
crossfade	A crossfade merges two shots together: The previous shot fades – and the following shot appears almost simultaneously.
flashback	A flashback is the insertion of a scene into a storyline which shows earlier events. Flashbacks can be memories, but also explanations for the viewer. With a flashback, the viewer gets a head start in knowledge compared to the characters appearing in the film.
flash-forward	A flash-forward is a short scene in which the action jumps ahead to the future. It takes a narrative forward in time from the current point of the story.
jump cut	A jump cut is an unusual alternative to time compression. It is a cut between two images that are identical in terms of camera distance and framing, but make a jump in the action.
durative time lapse	In the case of durative time lapse, time sequences that have no connection with the characters in the plot are cinematically condensed, for example the change of seasons or the growth of plants.

4 Film — Boy Erased

Info

iterative time lapse	Iterative time lapse shows sequences of images of characters doing recurring, regular activities – such as driving to work every day: in this example, the change of clothes indicates that not one, but several car trips to work are shown.
cinematic time lapse	Cinematic time lapse can be visualized by speeding up or slowing down the time depicted.
music	Music may be employed for connecting different scenes that occur over time as a musical montage; a piece of music may help the viewer to understand the totality of all the scenes in a montage, and what is trying to be expressed.

POST-VIEWING

17 CHALLENGE

Research the real people represented in the film *Boy Erased* and compare the film characters with the real, authentic people and their stories.

- Jared Eamons – Garrard Conley
- Victor Sykes – John Smid

Garrard Conley and Lucas Hedges (as Jared Eamons)

18 CHOOSE

a) Rewatch the scene where Jared's father asks for information about Henry Wallace to take (legal) action (0:42:54–0:44:34). Imagine you are the script writer. Develop and write a short screenplay about Henry being confronted with allegations against him.

OR

b) **Pair work**
After Jared's dramatic leave from the camp, it remains hidden from the viewer what happens at Love In Action after Nancy "rescued" her son. Discuss with a partner what camp leader Mr. Sykes might do to calm down the situation and what he might do to Cameron, who helped Jared. Imagine you are the script writer. Develop and write a screenplay.

Info

How to write a screenplay

- Write your screenplay based on what you know about the characters and the plot of the film as well as plausible deductions.
- Before you start writing, answer the following questions: Who? What? When? Where? Why?
- Indicate the setting, camera operations, action lines (the equivalent of stage directions in a theatre play) and props.

19

After Jared has heard about Cameron's suicide (1:29:20–1:30:45), he retires to his room. As Jared loves writing, he might write down his feelings in a diary. Imagine you are Jared. Write his diary entry.
- Start with "Dear Diary, …".
- Write in the first person.
- Be honest and reflective.
- Ponder on and express your feelings.

Boy Erased | **Film** | **4**

20
After having dealt with Joel Edgerton's film *Boy Erased* in detail, write a film review for an online audience. Use the following guidelines to structure your text.

Info

How to write a film review

A film review offers information on a film. It is usually a recommendation for a film or informs its readers why it might not be worth watching.
- Start with a catchy introduction in which you give essential information about the film (title, director, genre, release date, actors, characters, setting and plot).
- Then, give a brief summary of what the film is about, but avoid spoilers.
- Afterwards, state your personal impression of the film.
- Finally, point out the purpose of the film and come up with a convincing conclusion as to why the reader should or should not watch the film.

Language support

Writing a film review

Useful phrases:
- The film "…" is a drama/action film/thriller/…
- The film was directed/produced by … and released in …
- The film was well-directed by …
- Starring … (actor's name)
- The main character is played …
- … is absolutely remarkable as …
- The acting is remarkable/convincing/too melodramatic …
- The film won … / was awarded …

Characters/Plot:
- The main character is called …
- The story is about/deals with/focuses on …
- The film tells the story of …
- The film opens/begins with …
- As the story continues/unfolds/develops …
- The plot is multi-dimensional/complicated/thrilling/ captivating / arouses curiosity / is full of tension …
- The plot has a surprising twist. / The plot is incoherent/mediocre/appalling …
- One of the best moments in the film is when …
- It's a non-linear/fragmented narrative.
- The characters show an exceptional performance when …
- The characters are believable/shallow/ unconvincing …

Setting:
- It is set in …
- The story takes place in / unfolds in …
- The film begins in …
- The film creates a … atmosphere/mood …

Cinematography:
- The camera work is impressive/spectacular/ unrealistic/confusing …
- The camera operations draw attention to …
- The special effects are stunning/impressive/poor/ amateurish …
- The music is profound/clichéd/conveys a … atmosphere …
- The music underlines emotions/connects scenes …

Opinion
- I believe …
- He/She does a very god job as …
- I (highly/strongly/definitely) recommend/don't recommend this film because …
- A 'must-see'/box-office success/failure! / Don't miss it!
- A very impressive portrayal of …
- On a scale of 1–10, I give this film a …
- The best/worst thing is …
- If you like … this film is for you.
- The film is a worthwhile watch. / I'm afraid the film is a complete waste of time and money. Only watch this film if you have plenty of time to spare.
- … is well worth seeing / not to be missed / a truly great piece of filmmaking.
- The film is exciting/realistic/over-complicated/confusing/far-fetched …
- The film is thought-provoking/touching/moving …

4 Topic — Boy Erased

Coming of age

1 Read the information about the coming-of-age genre below. Transfer the given information into a suitable form of visualization (e.g. graphic organizer, mind map/concept map, flow chart, plot diagram, fish-bone graphic, etc.).

Info

Coming of age – or: The crises of adolescence

The transition between childhood and adulthood, becoming an adult or entering maturity, is referred to as 'coming of age'.

Coming-of-age as a genre refers to literature and films in which older children and adolescents[1] as the protagonists encounter for the first time fundamental issues of growing up or intense emotions that call for maturing[2] socially and psychologically. The focus is on the confrontation with the adult world, the parental home, school and society. The plot usually revolves around family, social or individual conflicts, sexuality, gender roles, rebellion, opinion formation, and other moral as well as emotional challenges that young people face during puberty. The protagonist will encounter[3] loss or discovery, or an internal or external conflict, making him/her suffer from arduous[4] trials and misfortunes and personal development, change and growth. However, these crucial[5] experiences will eventually lead to life-altering adulthood despite scarification[6]. The protagonist will find himself/herself clashing with their traditional culture and societal standards while progressing. Courses of self-discovery, identity formation and emancipation are characteristic of this genre. It is the protagonist's psychological or sometimes even physical journey from being a child to being an adult: from naive to wise, from idealist to realist, and from immature to mature. Dialogues and emotional responses are more in focus than the action itself, and often the story is told in the form of flashbacks. Both provide deep insights into the protagonist.

The typical plot pattern of a coming-of-age story is as follows: At the beginning, the exposition, the protagonist is in a childhood stage. He/She is young, immature, naive, and feels alienated[7] and alone. As his/her story proceeds, the action rises to a conflict. Here the protagonist encounters a challenge or a problem. The plot continues with the protagonist's struggle to overcome his/her challenge. At one turning point, comparable to a climax, there is a sudden realization of the truth about himself/herself or the world, an "epiphany"[8]. The protagonist makes a tough decision regarding his/her problem and starts changing because of this decision. With falling action comes the story's conclusion, in which the protagonist displays evidence of change. He/She has found a sense of belonging or self-realization reaching maturity. He/She is now seen as different or changed and the significance of the change is revealed. The protagonist finally enters the adulthood stage. Because of the universal, relatable and dramatic nature of these coming-of-age narrative motifs, the genre belongs to the most popular genres of literary fiction. Mark Twain's *The Adventures of Tom Sawyer*, the *Harry Potter* series by J.K. Rowling, Stephenie Meyer's *Twilight*, or Lois Lowry's *The Giver* are some prominent examples of coming-of-age stories: fictional texts in which the process of growing up is portrayed.

Annotations
[1] **adolescent** = a young person who is developing from a child into an adult
[2] to **mature** = to develop emotionally and start to behave like a sensible adult
[3] to **encounter** = to experience something, especially something unpleasant or difficult, while you are trying to do something else
[4] **arduous** = involving a lot of effort and energy, especially over a period of time
[5] **crucial** = extremely important or necessary
[6] **scarification** = the result of scarifying (making small cuts in somebody's skin), a scratch or scratches
[7] **alienated** = feeling of not belonging and being separated
[8] **epiphany** = a sudden and surprising moment of understanding

COMING OF AGE IN *BOY ERASED*

2
Examine in what way the film *Boy Erased* can be seen as a coming-of-age story by focusing on and exemplifying Jared's journey through conversion therapy and ending up as a journalist.

3 CHOOSE → **S8:** How to improve your text
Right at the beginning of the film, Jared states (0:02:08–0:02:15):

> "I wish none of this had ever happened. But sometimes, I thank God that it did."

Using this quote, give a two-minute presentation **OR** write an argumentative essay in which you justify why *Boy Erased* can be classified as a coming-of-age story.

4
The German title of the film *Boy Erased* is "Der verlorene Sohn" ("The Lost Son"), which is an allusion to the Parable of the Prodigal Son in the New Testament of the Bible, appearing in Luke 15:11–32.
a) Research the Parable of the Prodigal Son and outline it.
b) Compare the biblical parable to the film.
c) CHALLENGE Write a blog post in which you make a reasoned case for the film title that you think is more appropriate. Justify your opinion. → **S7:** Checklist: Writing a blog post

Sexual diversity – Tolerance and discrimination

MEDIATION: CONVERSION THERAPY IN GERMANY

1 → **Workshop:** Mediation → **S19:** How to improve your mediation skills → **S8:** How to improve your text
At the end of the film *Boy Erased*, we get to know that Jared publishes articles on conversion therapy. Imagine that Jared has asked his international online community to help him with his research on gay conversion therapy in other countries. Read the following interview from Deutschlandfunk Kultur on a new German law banning conversion therapy. Write an e-mail to Jared in which you explain to him what the German law prohibits and why.

Gesetz gegen „Homoheiler"– Ein Meilenstein für Deutschland

Markus Kowalski im Gespräch mit Stephan Karkowsky • 07.05.2020

„Homoheilern" soll das Handwerk gelegt werden. Der Bundestag stimmt über ein Verbot von „Konversionstherapien" ab, die Homosexuelle oder Transgender „umdrehen" sollen. Ein gutes Signal, findet der Journalist Markus Kowalski.

Stephan Karkowsky: Der Bundestag will heute über ein Gesetz abstimmen, das sogenannte Konversionstherapien erschweren soll, also Angebote von selbst ernannten „Homoheilern", die Sexualität als Krankheit betrachten und deshalb behandeln wollen. Der Lesben- und Schwulenverband kritisiert das Gesetz als nicht weitgehend genug. Über die Details sprechen möchte ich mit dem Journalisten Markus Kowalski, der das Thema seit Jahren verfolgt. Was genau wird heute verboten und was bleibt erlaubt?

Markus Kowalski: Es wird verboten, dass man Homosexuellen und Transgendern anbietet, geheilt zu werden, wie auch immer das passieren soll, also heterosexuell zu werden oder cisgeschlechtlich zu werden. Das heißt, zum Beispiel Transgendern anzubieten, wieder in das von Geburt an biologische Geschlecht zurückzukehren.

Darf man das, im juristischen Sinne, verbieten?

Karkowsky: Ist denn nur das Angebot verboten und die Werbung dafür?

Topic: Boy Erased

Kowalski: Genau, es ist beides verboten. Zum einen ist es verboten, dafür zu werben, dafür droht einem 30.000 Euro Geldstrafe. Und wenn man die Therapie wirklich durchführt, dann droht einem bis zu einem Jahr Haft. Das ist schon eine ordentliche Abschreckung, die da heute im Gesetz beschlossen wird.

Karkowsky: Die Haft betrifft diese Pseudo-„Homoheiler", aber nicht verboten werden die Pseudobehandlungen generell für Erwachsene, die sich freiwillig einer solchen Therapie unterziehen wollen. Warum nicht?

Kowalski: Da gibt es juristische Fragen, also Detailfragen, ob man das überhaupt verbieten kann, weil natürlich trotzdem jeder Erwachsene mit seinem Leben machen kann, was er will. Aber in dem Gesetz gibt es eben diese folgende Regelung, dass, wenn man sagt, okay, Erwachsene dürfen trotzdem nicht diese Konversionstherapie bekommen, wenn ihr Wille beeinträchtigt ist, das heißt, wenn sie genötigt wurden oder gezwungen wurden, das zu tun.
Ich glaube, das ist eine ganz intelligente Lösung, weil genau das ja in der Gesellschaft passiert. Homosexuelle werden dazu gezwungen oder genötigt, sich anzupassen, heterosexuell zu werden oder sich zu verhalten, und deswegen ist diese Ausnahme trotzdem im Gesetz eingebaut.

[...]

Karkowsky: Wie groß ist denn das Problem überhaupt, dass der Bundestag heute da ein eigenes Gesetz zu beschließen muss, wie viele gehen diesen selbst ernannten Homoheilern auf den Leim, mit dem Versprechen, Schwule und Lesben angeblich heilen zu können? Weiß man das?

Kowalski: Ja, es gab eine Studie von der Bundesstiftung Magnus Hirschfeld, die sich jetzt damit beschäftigt hat im Zuge dieses Verfahrens, die hat gesagt, sie schätzen, ungefähr 1000 Betroffene pro Jahr gibt es in Deutschland. Das heißt, das sind vor allem Heranwachsende, Jugendliche oder junge Erwachsene in den religiösen Gemeinden, die da aufwachsen und in diesen Strukturen verstrickt sind und da einfach beeinflusst werden in ihrem Heranwachsen und da sich nicht frei äußern können, sich nicht frei zu ihrer sexuellen Orientierung bekennen können.

Depressionen bis hin zu Selbstmord

Karkowsky: Nun weiß man ja, dass diese Pseudotherapien nicht funktionieren, da könnte man sagen, na, lasst die doch machen, oder gibt es Probleme bei Leuten, die die durchgeführt haben?

Kowalski: Das Problem ist, dass zum einen für die Betroffenen das ganz schwierig ist, weil die Betroffenen ja einem enormen Druck ausgesetzt werden, was zu machen, was sie nicht sind, also als lesbische Frau plötzlich auf Männer zu stehen. Das ist natürlich extrem belastend und führt bei den Betroffenen zum einen zu einer Angst, aber auch zu Depressionen bis hin zum Selbstmord, dafür gibt es immer wieder Beispiele. Das führt natürlich auch in unserem Land zu einer Ausgrenzung und zu einem vergifteten gesellschaftlichen Klima, dass man eben zulässt, dass Leute diese falschen Theorien verbreiten und sagen, Homosexualität sei krank.

Karkowsky: Sie haben das Thema lange begleitet jetzt, jahrelang als Journalist mit Artikeln immer wieder auf das Problem aufmerksam gemacht. Das Gesetz, so wie es jetzt verabschiedet werden soll, ist das für Sie okay?

Kowalski: Ja, ich glaube, dieses Gesetz ist wirklich ein Meilenstein für dieses Land. Wir dürfen nicht vergessen, dass die wichtigen Errungenschaften für die queere Community, also für die Lesben, Schwulen, Bisexuellen und Transgender, dass die alle schon in den letzten Jahren kamen: 2017 die Ehe für alle, die dritte Geschlechtsoption für Intersexuelle, das sind wichtige Meilensteine, und heute kommt einer dazu, weil das einfach ein wichtiges Zeichen ist, dass diese Gesellschaft sagt, dieses Land sagt, wir wollen diese Konversionstherapie nicht, wir wollen dieses Klima des Hasses nicht, sondern wir wollen auch die queere Community schützen und entsprechend abschreckende Strafen in diesem Gesetz einbauen.

Der Bundestag hat am Donnerstag, 7. Mai 2020, den Gesetzentwurf der Bundesregierung „zum Schutz vor Konversionsbehandlungen" in der vom Gesundheitsausschuss geänderten Fassung angenommen. CDU/CSU, SPD und FDP stimmten für den Gesetzentwurf, die übrigen Fraktionen enthielten sich, es gab eine Gegenstimme aus der AfD-Fraktion. Unser Gespräch war bereits am Morgen gelaufen, bevor diese Entscheidung der Bundestagsabgeordneten am Abend fiel. Nähere Informationen über die Abstimmung finden Sie auf der Webseite des Deutschen Bundestages.

TOLERANCE AND DISCRIMINATION IN *BOY ERASED*

2
Throughout the film, Nancy Eamons, Jared's mother, undergoes a development: She finds her voice and emancipates herself. Outline her development using a flow chart.
You may rewatch the following scenes:
0:03:24–0:04:00 | 0:04:34–0:05:55 | 0:19:35–0:22:06 | 0:40:12–0:42:41 | 0:44:57–0:46:03 | 0:46:55–0:49:20 | 0:55:52–0:57:07 | 0:58:32–1:00:05 | 1:24:39–1:28:18 | 1:32:11–1:34:50 | 1:36:43–1:37:37

Mediation

3 → **Workshop:** Mediation   → **S19:** How to improve your mediation skills   → **S8:** How to improve your text

In the film, the viewer can see some of the articles Jared has written. Read the article from the German online magazine *ZEITjUNG* below. Use the given information to write one of Jared's articles ("My mother became my personal ally"). Explain what an ally is and illustrate on the basis of Nancy's actions and statements in the film in what way Jared's mother became his ally.

Was ist ein Ally?

11/08/2020 / By Salomé Kofler

Gerade im Zusammenhang mit der #blacklivesmatter-Bewegung ist der Begriff Ally in letzter Zeit immer wieder gefallen. Aber auch in der LGBTQA+-Community kennt man den Begriff. Aber woher kommt der Begriff eigentlich und was heißt er denn jetzt ganz genau? Denn hinter dem Wort „Ally" steckt viel mehr als nur ein*e Verbündete*r.

Was ist denn nun ein Ally?
Der Begriff Ally kommt aus dem Englischen und bedeutet direkt übersetzt so viel wie „Verbündete*r". Damit sind Menschen gemeint, die ihre Privilegien nutzen, um Minderheiten zu unterstützen. Sie verbünden sich also mit einer diskriminierten Gruppe, obwohl sie selbst kein Teil davon sind. Bekannt ist der Begriff vor allem in der LGBTQA+-Szene und durch die #blacklivesmatter-Bewegung. Ein Ally der LGBTQA+-Community nutzt zum Beispiel seine vorteilhaftere Position als hetero- und cisnormatives Individuum, um anderen Geschlechtsidentitäten zu helfen, in der Gesellschaft anerkannt zu werden.

Wer kann ein Ally sein?
Prinzipiell kann jede*r, der*die möchte und genug Bereitschaft zeigt, ein Ally sein. Allerdings geht es eben darum, diskriminierte Gruppen aktiv zu unterstützen, nur darüber zu reden, dass Unterdrückung falsch ist, reicht nicht. Um ein Ally zu sein, kann man logischerweise auch nicht selbst zur diskriminierten Gruppe gehören, mit der man sich verbünden möchte. In der Regel besitzt man eine vorteilhaftere Position in der Gesellschaft, die man gegen Ungerechtigkeit einsetzt.

Was genau macht ein Ally?
Verständnis und Mitleid zeigen ist schön und wichtig, das allein macht einen Ally allerdings noch nicht aus. Es ist ausschlaggebend, dass von selbst die Initiative ergriffen wird, um eine Minderheit zu unterstützen. Man kämpft den Kampf gegen die Ungerechtigkeit, als ob es sein eigener wäre. Aktiv statt passiv sein ist also ein wichtiger Punkt. Ein Ally setzt sich nicht nur für Gerechtigkeit ein, sondern akzeptiert, dass er*sie als privilegierte Mehrheit ein Teil des Problems sein kann und geht bewusst dagegen vor, indem er*sie diese Privilegien nutzt, um Menschen mit einer schwächeren Position zu helfen. Privilegiert sein heißt in dem Fall übrigens nicht, besonders reich zu sein oder ein einfaches Leben zu haben, sondern eine bestimmte Art von Benachteiligung aufgrund struktureller Ungleichheiten nie zu erleben. Ein Ally setzt sich regelmäßig mit aktuellen Themen auseinander und bleibt so gesellschaftskritisch.

Wie kannst du ein guter Ally werden?
Um ein guter Ally zu sein, muss man bereit sein, mit anderen und für andere zu handeln, um Unterdrückung endgültig zu beenden und Gleichheit zu schaffen. Für einen guten Ally gibt es einige Richtlinien, an die man sich halten kann. Zum einen sollte man sich über verschiedene Identitäten und Erfah-

rungen weiterbilden, die marginalisierte Gruppen gemacht haben (können). Zum anderen sollte man sich seine eigenen Vorurteile immer wieder bewusst machen und auch unangenehme Erkenntnisse reflektieren, um gegen unterbewusste und diskriminierende Ansichten vorgehen zu können. Aktives Engagement gegen Benachteiligung und Ungleichheit sind unerlässlich. Das heißt eben nicht nur, dagegen zu reden, wenn sich jemand rassistisch oder homophob äußert, sondern auch ohne Anstoß von außen selbst Dinge in die Hand zu nehmen. Man muss bereit sein, große persönliche, aber auch soziale, institutionelle und gesellschaftliche Veränderungen zu schaffen. [...]

Woher kommt der Begriff Ally?
Ursprünglich aus dem Militär übernommen wurde der Begriff von der LGBTQA+-Szene für Menschen, die sie unterstützen, selbst aber nicht Teil der Community sind und deshalb nicht diese Art von Diskriminierung erfahren haben. Mittlerweile ist der Begriff aber auch vielen Menschen bekannt durch #blacklivesmatter, besonders in Amerika hat sich der Ausdruck etabliert, aber auch im deutschsprachigen Raum wird er immer mehr genutzt. [...]

4
Read the information on tolerance vs. acceptance below.

Info

Tolerance vs. acceptance

To **tolerate** someone or something means to have a fair and objective attitude towards people that differ from you in terms of sexual orientation, religious beliefs, nationality, race, etc. You neither want to harm them nor want to be close friends with them. Tolerance can be seen as the most basic step to a functional society as it implies that you can live with a certain circumstance. It is possible to tolerate something or someone without accepting it or them.

To **accept** someone or something goes one step further and needs tolerance as a basis. It means to welcome or even endorse the reality of differences without having any intentions to change it. It can be described as an act of assenting: You cannot only live with a certain circumstance, but you even judge it favourably.

5
a) Using your knowledge from the info box above, draw a developmental line for Marshall Eamons, Jared's father. Show if and when he rejects, tolerates or accepts Jared's sexual orientation. Support your ideas with examples from the film (situations, gestures, etc.).
b) Discuss your results in class.

Boy Erased — Topic 4

The development of Jared's father in *Boy Erased*

acceptance

tolerance

rejection

Jared's outing　　　　　　　　　　　　　　　　　　　　Christmas invitation

Examples from the film:

_____
_____
_____
_____
_____
_____
_____
_____
_____

5 Play — seven methods of killing kylie jenner

PRE-READING

1

Read the title and the PREMEDIATION. Speculate on what the play will be about.

2

a) Read the article about the dramatist Jasmine Lee-Jones.
b) Find out more about her:
- age
- family background
- motivation for writing the play
- ideals
- personal experiences with theatre
- ...

Jasmine Lee-Jones interview: I want people to come to the theatre like they watch Netflix

by Jessie Thompson

[...] Jasmine Lee-Jones's debut play, exploring female friendship, cultural appropriation and the internet, became one of the most talked-about plays of the year after a triumphant run at the Royal Court, picking up a trail of awards and an ecstatic stream of social media appreciation. [...]

It's immediately obvious when talking to Lee-Jones IRL, [...] that she is a deep and impressive thinker, often pausing for several seconds before she answers a question. [...] Born in North London, Lee-Jones became interested in theatre because of a strong connection she felt with words and language. "I always wanted to read things out loud," she says. "When I found theatre, I started to realise: oh, you can do a job where you're actually paid to speak words aloud, to really interrogate language." [...]

The play's text is written in gifs, online acronyms, merging the IRL-world with the social media-sphere. It's the most original and successful way any writer has ever managed to capture the internet on stage, but Lee-Jones didn't do it on purpose – she just wanted it to feel real. "I think theatre can sometimes feel quite isolating like, oh, this is for someone else. We have a prestige about theatre and what should be on stage, like it's just for Shakespeare. And then you put something in from the internet that feels very casual and personal to people, and people are willing to give you more license," she says.

[...] The online reaction to seven methods made it clear that the play was reaching new, more diverse audiences, something that matters greatly to Lee-Jones. "I want people to come to the theatre like they watch Netflix," she says. "I like watching reality TV and all of that as much as the next person. But one thing I find super interesting about TV is everyone will watch good, really thoroughly written, well-plotted TV. [...] But when there's something really good in theatre on, people still feel like it's not for them. There's a universality to TV and film that theatre just hasn't created yet. It's still like, oh, it's meant for those people."

Having been nurtured as a writer by the Royal Court from the age of 17, Lee-Jones has always felt more comfortable there than at other theatres. But she had an experience a few years ago that shook that. She was watching a play with a friend, also a black woman, and they were waiting at the bar to get a drink. "This group of white people, I think maybe husband and wife, just went in front of us. I looked at my friend and was like, did you see that? And she just nodded, but eventually I realised they just didn't see us. They didn't think we were there to do something important or watch a show. They thought we were kind of just loitering," she tells me. "I think that was the first experience I had in this theatre where I realised – not because of the theatre, necessarily – but there's an audience that thinks this space belongs to them more than other people."

In the post-pandemic era, Lee-Jones thinks the theatre world will only bring in new audiences if it's really committed to doing so. "They have to keep programming the plays until people feel safe enough to come to the work. And what happened to me in the bar downstairs doesn't keep happening, because people realise: oh, this space is for everyone, it's not just for us." As she's telling me this, just behind her is the Royal Court's building; on the front of it, her name is written in neon lights. How thrilling that, right now, that one belongs to her. [...]

100

seven methods of killing kylie jenner — Play 5

3

Pair work State what you know about Kylie Jenner, the American media celebrity. Find out on the Internet and then decide whether the statements are true or false (if it is false, correct the statement).

	true	false	correction
1. Kylie Jenner is the daughter of Caitlyn and Kris Jenner.			
2. Kylie Jenner belongs to the generation alpha.			
3. She was part of the reality TV series "Keeping up with the Kardashians" because she was adopted by Robert Kardashian.			
4. Jenner launched her own cosmetics line called *Kylie's BW lip kit*.			
5. In 2017, Jenner was placed on the Forbes Celebrity 100 list, making her the youngest person to be featured on the list.			
6. Kylie Jenner beat Mark Zuckerberg by two years when being announced the youngest self-made billionaire in 2019.			
7. Kylie Jenner is black.			

Language

4

a) Users of social media normally don't use formal language. What abbreviations do you use?

CHOOSE

Pair work If you prefer the analogue world you may write the abbreviations down.
OR
Group work You may use the online tool on oncoo.de for this task.

b) Rewrite the following comment in Standard English.

INCOGNEGRO @INCOGNEGRO
Errybody and they aunty need to quit fronting like Kylie killing it! She ain't killing shit! And tbh if I had it my way the only thing geetting kilt would be that bitch! #kyliegjennerfidead (p. 5)

5

Reading social media content in another language can be confusing. All the slang, idioms and abbreviations people use can make even simple sentences tricky to understand.

a) Get acquainted with the abbreviations the protagonists are using by finding the correct partners: which abbreviation means what? Write the matching partners from the box into the table.

5 Play: seven methods of killing kylie jenner

actually | Big man thing / honestly in all seriousness | Don't piss me off! | Go on! | I don't care! | Kiss my teeth! | Never mind! | Not gonna lie. | Oh my days! | Say no more! | Swear to god! | to be honest | What are you doing? | What the hell!

abbreviation	meaning
LEWL	similar to LOL
DPMO	
OMDS	
BMT	
IDC	
SNM	
S2g	
Nvm	
wyd	
KMT	
ngl	
acc	
WTH	
tbh	
gwarn	

b) Now compare your entries with the list of the most important abbreviations used in the play. You can find a link to the list here: **Webcode** DSW-73684-04

c) While reading the play add more abbreviations to the list that are used by the protagonists.

d) Rewrite the following e-mail as a tweet by using as many abbreviations as possible.

> Hello my best friend in the twitter world!
> How are you today? I can't believe we're finally meeting each other. Have I told you that my mom believes you don't exist? That's extremely funny!!!!! However, I can't wait to meet you in real life. I'll see you in Berlin next week!
> Bye for now,
> your dearest friend.

e) **CHALLENGE** You may add content to make the tweet more realistic.

f) **OPTIONAL** Rewrite the following hypothetical tweet into Standard English.

> Look @ her DP. What a QT! tbh, that's only in TL – never IRL! Check YT 4 more lies!

seven methods of killing kylie jenner — Play 5

WHILE READING
Keeping notes

6

> Tip Keeping a reading journal with the focus of summarizing the content as well as adding information about place and time and the relevant page numbers can be one option for remembering the content of a play. Taking notes with a specific focus (e.g. on one of the characters, topics, langauge etc.) is another option to structure the content of a play.

CHOOSE

Focus on one character's perspective: What aspects of Kylie's life are making Cleo furious? Take notes while reading.

OR

Focus on language: The playwright uses words from the black community, like "kiking" (p. 14) "bredrin" (p. 8) etc. Find more examples and explain their meanings.

OR

Focus on language: The play deals with serious topics but in a comical tone. Find examples from the text and evaluate the author's decision to make use of comic elements. Finally fill in your results in the following table:

quotation	topic	effect
1.		
2.		
3.		
4.		

THE PREMEDIATION (PP. 1-3)

7

a) Fill in the table.

1. **Who** are the characters?	
2. **When** do the scenes take place?	
3. **Where** does the action take place?	
4. **What** action is described?	
5. **What** references are made to the world outside the stage?	

103

5 Play — seven methods of killing kylie jenner

b) In the newest version of her play from 2021, Jasmine Lee-Jones makes considerable changes to the PREMEDIATION from the original version from 2019 (see below). If you were Jasmin Lee-Jones and were asked by journalists why you made those changes to the play, apart from "A work of art is never finished" what would you answer?

The present.
In the most present sense of the present tense.
5th March 2019.
Early morning. Outside. A park. Dark.

KARA and CLEO drag something resembling a body onto the platform. They open the traps and throw it in. Cover it with earth. Suddenly they stop, standing over the body.

Blackout.

PART 1 (PP. 4-9): THE START

8

a) Cleo retweets a tweet by Forbes. Describe the "Forbes-tweet" in your own words.

_____

b) Cleo is angry about the tweet's hypocrisy. Explain why.

_____

c) Cleo creates the hashtag #kyliejennerfidead as a response to the Forbes tweet and tweets hypothetical death threat at Kylie Jenner. Describe Cleo's methods in your own words.

Method # 1: _____

Method # 2: _____

d) Complete the sentence: With tweeting the first two methods of killing, Cleo wants to point out / criticize / make aware of the facts / aim at …

_____

e) Fill in the summary with the appropriate adjectives from the box:

> angry | crazy | happy | hypothetical | ingenious | real | surprise | worried

The first part of the plot describes developments in the Twitter world as well as in real life. When the action takes place in _____ life, Cleo gets a _____ visit from Kara. Kara had seen Cleo's tweets and wants to know why she is _____. Cleo plays down the seriousness of her _____ death threats and therefore wants to calm her _____ friend.

seven methods of killing kylie jenner — Play 5

PART 2 (PP. 10-27): TL AND IRL

9

Social media users are responding to Cleo's tweets (pp. 10-13).

Pair work

a) List the words they are using.

_____

_____

b) Read the infobox. Describe the tweets' tone.

Language support

Talking about the tone
accusatory | admiring | aggressive | ambivalent | amused | appreciative | colloquial | concerned | critical | defensive | dis-/respectful | dis-/approving | judgmental …

Info

Tone

Tone refers to an author's use of words and writing style to convey his or her attitude towards a topic. Tone is transported through diction (choice of words), viewpoint, syntax (grammar, how you put words together) and level of formality.

_____

_____

c) Explain the following quote in the play's context:

"Inside that tweet is hundreds of years of anti-blackness, positive affirmations of capitalism, cultural appropriation […]" (p. 15)

d) Name and describe Method # 3 in your own words.

_____

e) Describe the tone of the responses to Method # 3.

_____

f) **CHOOSE**

Pair work Kara and Cleo are not of the same opinion on various matters. They are having an argument about the tweets' importance (p. 15). List their arguments.

topic of discussion: "It's (just) a tweet"	
Kara	Cleo

105

Play: seven methods of killing kylie jenner

OR
Kara and Cleo are having an argument about the application of violence as an answer to oppression (p. 21). List their arguments.

topic of discussion: "violence is the answer to oppression"	
Kara	Cleo

g) Cleo has broken up with her boyfriend. Explain why his new girlfriend upsets Cleo.

h) **OPTIONAL**
Pair work Act out the scene in which the two girls talk about Cleo's boyfriend, the breakup and the new girlfriend.
OR
Group work (4) Create a freeze frame in which the relationships between the following characters become apparent: Cleo, Cleo's boyfriend, the new girlfriend and Kara. You may also add up to three sentences that each character is saying.

The protagonists

10 **CHOOSE**

Group work What do you get to know about Cleo when reading the play? Write down her profile. Note down the pages, e.g. university student (p. 9).

Age: _____

Education: _____

Family and friends: _____

Topics of interest: _____

Political views: _____

Sexual orientation: _____

Black identity (appearance, language etc.): _____

Character traits: _____

OR
Group work What do you get to know about Kara when reading the play? Write down her profile. Note down the pages.

Age: _____

Education: _____

seven methods of killing kylie jenner — Play 5

Family and friends: _____

Topics of interest: _____

Political views: _____

Sexual orientation: _____

Black identity (appearance, language etc.): _____

Character traits: _____

PART 3 (PP. 28-53): BACKGROUND

11

a) Name and describe Method # 4 in your own words.

_____

b) Describe the tone of the twitter responses to Method # 4.

_____

LISTENING

12

Dr. Kathomi Gatwiri, a senior Academic, psychotherapist and the founder of Healing Together Psychotherapy is talking about the term "gaslighting". You can find a link to the video here: **Webcode** DSW-73684-05

a) Listen to the first part of episode 1: "Racial gaslighting" (00:00-3:28). Decide whether the following sentences are right or wrong. Correct the statements when they are wrong.

	right	wrong	correction
1. Gaslighting is a form of physical abuse.			
2. People who are being gaslighted know that they are being manipulated and are therefore content about their knowledge.			
3. The term refers to a movie in which a husband convinces his wife that she is just imagining the dimming of lights.			
4. Racial gaslighting is when people of colour are told that their experiences are acknowledged.			
5. Racial gaslighting is deliberately used to maintain white supremacy.			
6. The more black people resist to this racial hierarchy the more acceptance they are experiencing in society.			

b) "My own bredrin gaslighting me" (p. 32). Explain Cleo's accusation.

5 Play — seven methods of killing kylie jenner

13
Which sentences about Kara's and Cleo's past are correct? Give proof from the text. → **S23:** How to quote

- The primary school teachers admired Cleo's curly hair.
- Cleo was always in Kara's shadow.
- Cleo had many boyfriends when she was young.
- Kara is satisfied with her appearance.
- Cleo accuses Kara of not having helped her at a party.

14
a) Name and describe Method # 5.

_____

b) Describe the tweets responding to Cleo's method # 5. What historical references are made? (twitterludes 4 and 5)

_____

PART 4 (PP. 54-78): CHANGES

15
a) Cleo's tweets get out of hand when one of her older tweets is re-tweeted by someone else.
- What gets re-tweeted and why?

_____

- How does Cleo respond?

_____

b) **Pair work** Both Cleo and Kara share stories from the past to explain when they felt misunderstood by each other.
- Partner A: Outline Cleo's story of #wiggate (pp. 45-48).
- Partner B: Outline Kara's story of T'Sharn's 13th birthday party (p. 66).
- Give feedback on how well the summary was performed by your partner.

c) **CHALLENGE**
Comment on the following statement: "If they had acted differently in the past their relationship now would be a different one". Justify your answer.

d) Name and describe Method #6.

_____

e) Put these events into the right order:
- [ ] Her identity in real life is revealed on Twitter.
- [ ] Cleo's IRL and TL identities merge into one.
- [ ] Cleo and Kara have a fight about Cleo's behaviour at T'sham's birthday party.
- [ ] Cleo is blocked from following Kara's Twitter account.
- [ ] Someone on TL re-tweets a comment by Cleo accusing her of being homophobic.
- [ ] Cleo apologizes for the two homophobic tweets from 2014.

f) In Method # 7, Cleo wants Kylie Jenner to experience the same mistreatments that Saartjie must have gone through. Which mistreatments does Cleo mean? Describe the historical context Cleo is referring to.

___

___

___

PART 5 (PP. 79-83): THE END

16

a) With the sentence "I just don't wanna feel heavy no more" (p. 79) Cleo describes a burden she is carrying. From what burden does Cleo need to be freed?

___

b) Saartjie's spirit is appearing. What are Kara and Cleo praising her for?

___

c) The image from the PREMEDIATION of Cleo and Kara standing over a body reappears in the POST-MORTEM.

> **Info**
> The post mortem interval is the time that has elapsed since a person has died. The term can also be applied to the post mortem examination of a corpse in order to determine the cause of death.

Why do you think Jasmine Lee-Jones chose this title for the last scene?

POST-READING

Relationships

17

a) Describe the friendship between Kara and Cleo.

> **Help** Look at the following pages: 7-9, 21-25, 32-40, 48-49, 59-60, 66, 69-73, 79ff.
> Then draw a table like the one below.

section	content	description of their friendship / relationship

b) In the following quote Cleo makes a reference to slaverey on a plantation:
"Back in the old days I'd be the field nigger out shucking corn and you'd be in the house beating the master." (p. 39)
- Explain the parallels she is drawing.
- What does the quote reveal about the friendship between Cleo and Kara?

c) Kara is blocking Cleo from following @KARA and viewing her tweets. Describe Cleo's reaction. How would you feel if your best friend did that to you?

d) **Pair work** At the end of the play, Cleo and Kara share a spiritual encounter with Snaartjie.
- Does this experience strengthen their friendship?
- Discuss: Will they stay friends?

Play: seven methods of killing kylie jenner

18 CHOOSE
Group work Create five freeze frames in which you show the development of Kara and Cleo's relationship. You may act between the freeze frames.
OR
Choose a part of Cleo and Kara's conversation described on the pages 32 to 35, l. 3. Act out the scene.

19
Pair work Talk for five minutes about the question in the bubble and come to a conclusion.

Characterization

20 CHOOSE
Write a characterization of Cleo (including her online and offline identity)
OR
Kara.
Consider if Cleo's and / or Kara's character develop throughout the play. Illustrate and proove it with the text.

→ **Workshop:** Analysing characters   → **S23:** How to quote

> **Tip** You can find language support for writing a characterization in *Camden Town Oberstufe* on page 353.

Illustrations and graphic layout of the play's script

21
a) On social media, words are often flanked by photos, emojis, cartoons etc. Look at the following pages: 4, 10, 12, 13, 17, 44.
b) Explain the combined use of language and illustrations in TL. Draw a box like the one below and fill in your findings.
- Define the type of illustration. Is it a photo, a film still, an emoji, a gif, a meme, a cartoon etc?
- What are the illustrations showing?
- How are illustrations used to transport meaning?

	type of illustration (photo, gif, emoji, cartoon, film still ...)?	What does it show?	Why is it used? What is the meaning?
1. p. 4			

c) Find more examples and add them to the list.
d) **CHALLENGE** Describe the layout of words and the way some words are written. What could be the reason people use such a layout?

_____

_____

e) **CHALLENGE** There are parts in the play where the TL seems to intersect with the IRL, e.g. pictures are shown IRL (pp. 22, 34, 45, 71-73). What could be the playwright's intention?

Putting the play on stage

22

The director of a play decides how elements of the play script can be transferred to the stage.
a) **Group work** Come up with an option for how TL can be staged. Consider how light, sound, actors, stage and audience can play a role.
b) Watch the video of a scene from a production and note down how TL is staged. Explain the effect on the audience. You can find a link to the video here: **Webcode** DSW-73684-06
c) Take a look at the production photos from the version staged at the Royal Court Theatre in London in 2021. Considering the elements on stage (cables, purple-blue cloud, dark background) and the actors' gestures, what part of the play could be shown? You can find a link to the photo gallery here: **Webcode** DSW-73684-07

VIPs

23

Cleo and Kara are making references to various famous people existing in IRL.

> Joanne The Scammer | Cardi B | Angela Davis | Maxine Water | MLK | Saartjie (Sarah Baartman)

a) **Group work** Placemat: Get into groups using the placemat method:
- Each member finds out about one historical figure.
- Write your findings into your section of the placemat.
- Turn the placemat clockwise so that you can read your teammates' findings.
- Discuss and agree on a result, which you write into the group section in the middle.
- Present your results in front of the class.

b) Discuss: To what extent are these people important for the context of the play?

Body images

24

a) **CHOOSE** Choose a country: Iran, Japan, New Zealand, Brazil, France, Kenya, South Korea, Mauritania, Oman or United States and prepare a two minute talk on the beauty standard of this country as it is described in the video "How Beauty standards differ around the world". You can find a link to the video here: **Webcode** DSW-73684-08

Info

Body image

Body image refers to a person's emotional attitudes, beliefs, and perceptions of their own body. […]
Body image relates to
- what a person believes about their appearance
- how they feel about their body, height, weight, and shape
- how they sense and control their body as they move

A person's body image will range from positive, or satisfaction with their body, to negative, or dissatisfaction with their body.

---

b) Who defines what beauty is? Explain the following quote in the context of body image as it is described in the info box:

"[…] and even Miss Fitzgerald always said how pretty your hair was, and the only time she came remotely close to commenting on how nice my hair was, was when my Mum straightened it for the Year 5 pictures." (p. 35)

Play: seven methods of killing kylie jenner

25 Pair work

Now take a look at the following photo by Carrie Mae Weems of a woman in front of a mirror. You can find a link here: **Webcode** DSW-73684-09. What does she want to show the viewer about black body image / ethnic identity? Explain.

a) Read the quote by Jasmine Lee-Jones.

> I keep a scrapbook with pictures for everything that I write. The main image is currently [art by Carrie Mae Weems] of a black woman looking in the mirror saying "Mirror, mirror on the wall, who's the fairest of them all?" and the mirror's response is "Snow White, you black bitch." That's very much this play.

Elements and structure of a play

26

a) Label the following elements of a play script: stage directions, scene, characters, title, setting, playwright, text and cast.

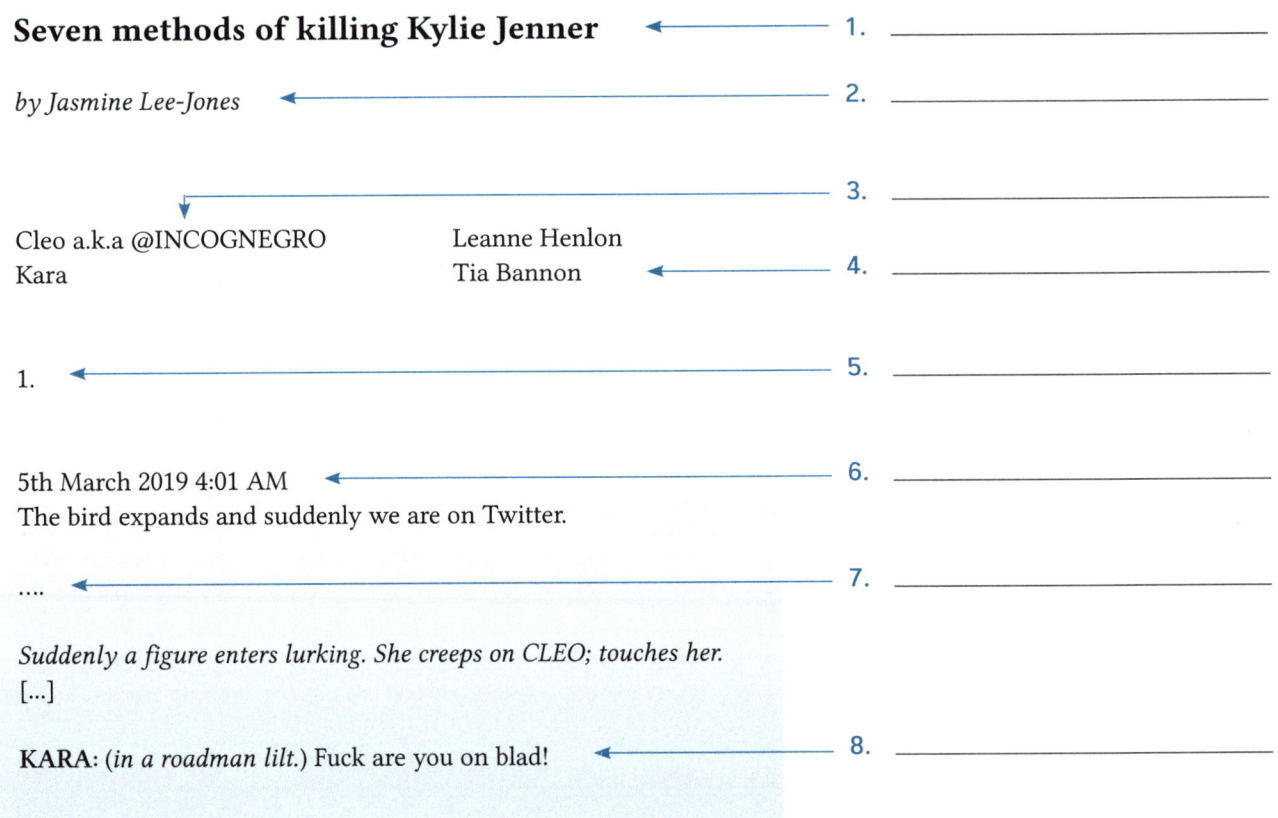

b) Normally, the development of the plot follows a certain structure as shown below.
- Does the play meet this scheme?
- Where can you see contemporary elements?

> **Tip** You can find an explanation of the different terms in *Camden Town Oberstufe* on page 350.

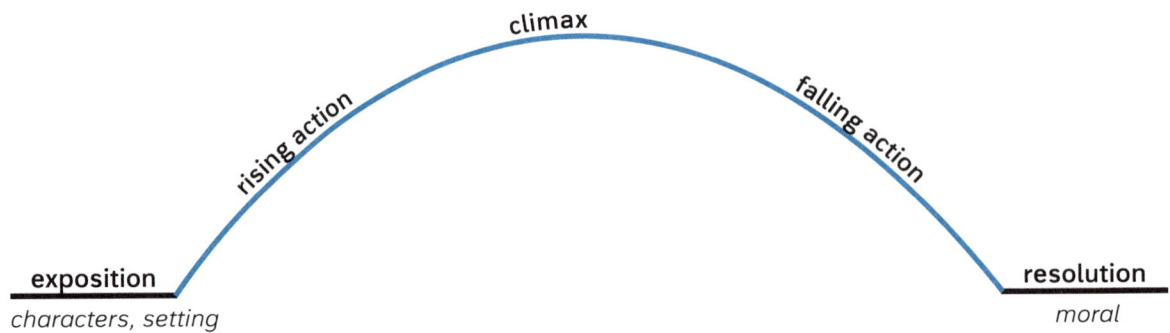

seven methods of killing kylie jenner — Play

Reviews

27

a) Lee-Jones created a contemporary theatre play that has been widely reviewed. Compare the two opinions by Kate Wywer (1.) and Natasher Beecher (2.).

> 1. Although the physicalisation of the internet is imaginative, the Twitter-interlude structure feels a little trapped towards the end, as if it's stopped inventing. The arguments begin to circle and the finale can't quite hold the weight of history it attempts to. Nevertheless, Henlon and Bannon are gripping throughout. Jones is a brilliant, dynamic writer, and this is a striking debut.

> 2. For us black women '*Seven methods of killing kylie Jenner*' with its blend of nostalgia and heart, is us being seen and being heard in a way that's almost too difficult to watch, our collective trauma laid bare. […]
>
> For anyone who isn't black, and white people, in particular, this play will resonate with you in a magical way that you won't quite understand. But one thing is for sure, this poignant play that goes beyond just the zeitgeist is for everyone. It's a play for now and for after – a cultural marker of the way the world is changing and needs to change. Everyone should go see it.

b) **CHOOSE**

Write a review as a tweet.
OR
Write a review for a broadsheet newspaper.

| Topic | seven methods of killing kylie jenner |

The influence of social media on young people's identity

1
a) **Pair work** Brainstorming: list advantages and disadvantages of using social media.
b) Explain the chart. → **S18:** How to analyse statistics

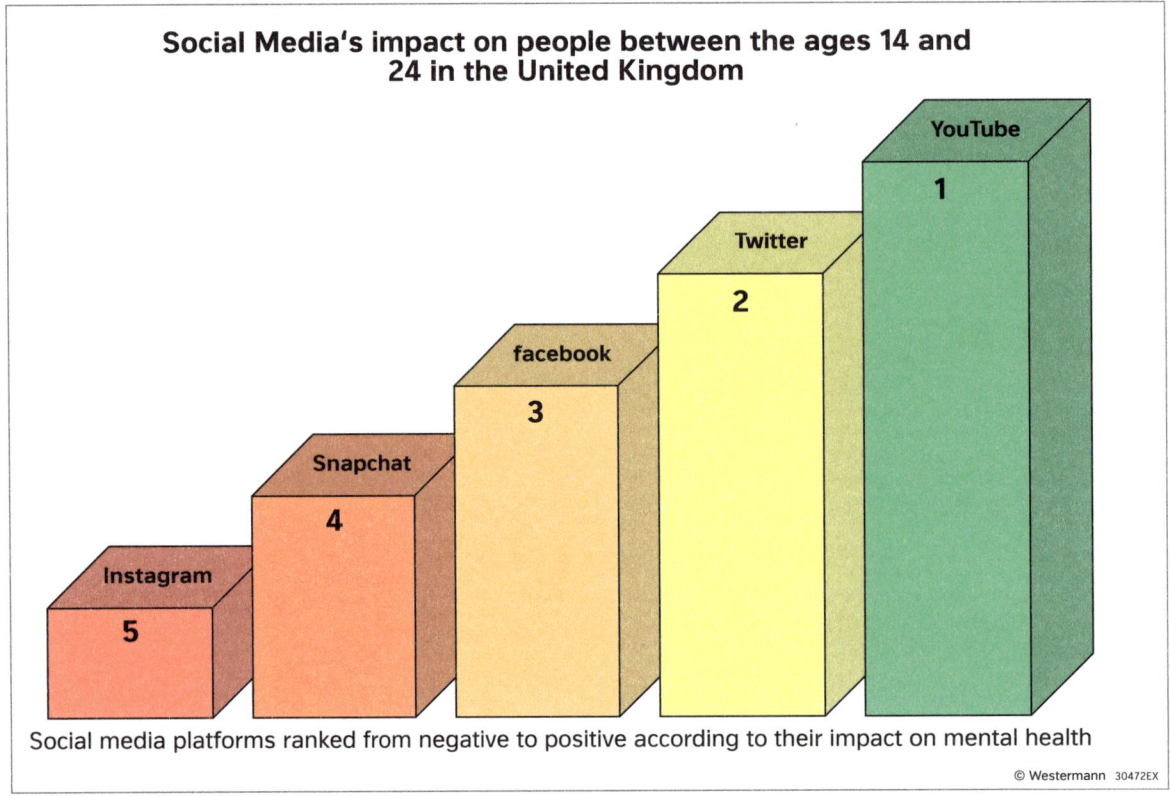

c) **Pair work** Discuss: Would you take part in a school challenge of a social media free week?

2
Tweets play a major role in *seven methods of killing kylie jenner* and are responsible for the play's development.
a) Examine to what extent the twitter comments are changing in the course of the play. Fill in the table with keywords.

content twitterludes	Who is writing?	scale of factual information (1 true to 9 false)	scale of humour (1 little to 9 the most)	scale of hatred (1 little to 9 the most)
1				
2				

seven methods of killing kylie jenner — Topic 5

content twitterludes	Who is writing?	scale of factual information (1 true to 9 false)	scale of humour (1 little to 9 the most)	scale of hatred (1 little to 9 the most)
3				
4				
5				
6				
7				
8				
9				
10				
11				

Topic: seven methods of killing kylie jenner

b) Choose from the following adjectives to describe the development: use a timeline / graph / colour scheme to illustrate.

> accusing | amused | conspirational | funny | homophobic | inflammatory | international | irritated | misogynist | racist | sexist | shocked | surprised

c) With the increasing usage of digital technologies, a new form of bullying has emerged: "cyberbullying". Have you or your friends ever experienced cyberbullying? Illustrate (topics, feelings, consequences).

d) **Pair work** At what point in the development of the twitterludes do you think cyberbullying starts? Give reasons.

3

Cleo and Kara are having a discussion about the reactions to the death threats against Cleo that are announced in TL (pp. 43-44).

a) List their arguments. Give your opinion.
b) Cleo describes the following humiliating incident. What is happening?

> "Cameras flashing without my consent
> Over and over
> Images posted all over socials
> Me a meme
> A silent, unconsenting gif
> Like I was some sort of spectacle
> Or a fucking freak
> I've never felt so ugly in my life." (p. 48)

c) Taking photos – now and fifty years ago: what has changed? What role does social media play today compared to then?
d) Internet research: Find out about the rules of taking photographs in public and private areas in Germany.

The role of ethnic identity on (social) media

4

a) Cleo is a black woman having an identity in real life and in twitter life ("incognegro") and for both identities, her ethnic identity seems to play a role. How are these identities connected?
b) **CHOOSE** Take one of the quotes concerning the topic "skin colour" and explain it in the context of the conversation between Cleo and Kara.

- "You don't own blackness just because you're dark-skinned!" (p. 37)

OR

- "You are a lightie" (p. 33)

OR

- "All the BW considered universally beautiful are lighties" (p. 34)

seven methods of killing kylie jenner — Topic 5

Stating your opinion

5 → **S6:** How to write a discussion / comment → **S9:** How to structure a text → **S8:** How to improve your text

Cleo shows her anger by creating hypothetical death threats to Kylie Jenner.

a) **CHOOSE**

Write a comment on the question of whether you think social media is a good channel to state your opinion.

OR

Pair work Write an electronic text together with a partner in a collaborative document.

> **Help** Alternative options to state your opinion and make it public:
> - going on a strike
> - talking to people face-to-face
> - sending emails or letters to the government
> - starting a petition

b) Why did the playwright choose to include twitter in her play?

MEDIATION

6 → **S19:** How to improve your mediation skills

a) Read the article.
b) Write an email to the playwright Jasmine Lee-Jones in which you describe the latest development in Germany concerning the influence of social media on politics. Refer to her play by pointing out parallels.

Anfeindungen gegen Sarah-Lee Heinrich
Medienexpertin: Koordinierte Twitter-Kampagnen als Methode

Immer häufiger werden Akteure aus Politik und Medien im Netz mit fragwürdigen Aussagen aus ihrer Vergangenheit konfrontiert. Dabei gerate aus dem Blick, aus welchen Kreisen diese Enthüllungen stammen, sagte Tajana Graovac vom „No Hate Speech Movement" im Dlf.

Ein paar Tweets können reichen, damit bei Twitter und darüber hinaus innerhalb weniger Stunden eine große Debatte in Gang kommt. So war das zuletzt zum Beispiel im Fall der neuen Bundessprecherin der Grünen Jugend.

Sarah-Lee Heinrich geriet in den Fokus wegen mehrerer alter Nachrichten, in denen sie im Jahr 2015 zum Beispiel „Heil" unter einen Tweet mit Hakenkreuz geschrieben hatte. Die heute 20-Jährige schrieb, sie könne sich nicht daran erinnern, als Jugendliche jemals einen solchen Tweet abgesetzt zu haben. „Das war maximal dumm und unangebracht", schrieb Heinrich. Die Sozialwissenschafts-Studentin betonte aber auch, dass sie sich „jetzt nicht zu allem erklären" wolle, „was ich mal so mit 14 gedacht und gesagt habe".

Erst Tweets, dann Morddrohungen

Heinrich beklagte außerdem, seit ihrer Wahl ver-

The German politician Sarah-Lee Heinrich

suchten Rechte, Shitstorms gegen sie hochzuziehen: „Haben wohl Bammel vor einer schwarzen, linken Frau", schrieb Heinrich. Nach diesen Tweets zog sich Heinrich vorerst aus der Öffentlichkeit zurück. Der Grünen-Jugendorganisation zufolge hatte sie Mord- und Gewaltandrohungen erhalten. Es gehe „jetzt erst einmal darum, alles für ihre Sicherheit zu tun", sagte der scheidende Bundessprecher der Grünen Jugend, Georg Kurz.

„Das ist koordiniert"

Dass der Fall eine solche Entwicklung genommen hat, sei typisch, sagte Tajana Graovac vom „No Hate Speech Movement" im Deutschlandfunk „Was wir feststellen können, dass es große Accounts sind, die meistens eher in der rechten Ecke zu finden sind, die große Reichweite haben", sagte Graovac.

Accounts aus rechten und rechtsextremen Kreisen würden dann dafür sorgen, dass sich die entsprechenden Nachrichten weit verbreiten. „Das ist koordiniert. Und es ist tatsächlich auch immer das gleiche Schema und das geht fast immer nach der gleichen Dynamik", so Graovac weiter.

Topic: seven methods of killing kylie jenner

Manipulierte Kampagnen erkennen

Zudem würden zum Teil Screenshots verbreitet, 55 die nachträglich manipuliert worden seien. „Man schneidet die Zeit und das Datum ab, damit die irgendwie auch aktuell aussehen. Es werden teilweise Wörter weggelassen, damit die Tweets noch schlimmer klingen. Und das zieht dann wirklich 60 Kreise."

Aufgabe von Journalistinnen und Journalisten sei es, dies zu erkennen und nicht auf eine Kampagne hereinzufallen. Sie müssten offenlegen, „dass es eine gezielte, koordinierte Attacke ist gegen eine 65 schwarze Person".

Cartoon analysis – images of black female identity

7 → **S17:** How to work with cartoons

a) Study the woman's depiction in the cartoon carefully, then describe it.

b) Explain the cartoon's message by referring to its individual elements.
c) Come up with a possible title and give reasons for your decision.
d) Black women are regularly depicted in the media and society as 'angry', 'aggressive' and 'sassy'. Imagine in which situations black women could be seen as behaving in an "angry" way?
e) Read the following Wikipedia entry on this stereotype. You can find a link to the text here:
   Webcode DSW-73684-10
   Pair work
   • Sum up the text in keywords and compare your result with a partner.

f) Discuss how it is possible for black women to escape the vicious circle of being referred to as an "angry black woman" when they show anger about being called this term.
You may refer to M. Obama's reactions described in the following newspaper excerpt:

Language support

index finger | megaphone | speech bubble

seven methods of killing kylie jenner — Topic 5

Michelle Obama: 'I'm no angry black woman'

The Obamas, by New York Times reporter Jodi Kantor, portrays her as a behind-the-scenes force in the White House.

[...] Mrs Obama did not deny being an important voice to her husband.

"I am his biggest ally," Mrs Obama said. "I am one of his biggest confidants. But he has dozens of really smart people who surround him. That's not to say that we don't have discussions and conversations."

"I guess it's more interesting to imagine this conflicted situation here and a strong woman. But that's been an image that people have tried to paint of me since the day Barack announced [he would run for president] – that I'm some angry black woman," she said.

"I just try to be me. And my hope is that over time people get to know me," she told CBS. "And they get to judge me for me." [...]

8

a) Read the article.
b) Outline Ritu Prasad's view on the myth of the "angry black woman" as presented in this article.

Serena Williams and the trope[1] of the 'angry black woman'

by Ritu Prasad

Mammies, jezebels, Sapphires. Black women in America have long been dogged by negative stereotypes, rooted in a history of racism and slavery. In the aftermath of Serena Williams' controversial US Open loss, it's the trope of the "angry black woman" that has once again re-emerged.

During the US Open final, Williams received a code violation for coaching[2], a penalty point for breaking her racket and a game penalty for calling the umpire a "thief". And later, a fine of $17,000 (£13,000).

Her reactions to the referee's calls – which the Women's Tennis Association has since decri[b]ed as "sexist" – were no different from how many top players react in the heat of a championship game. But it was the way she was punished for her anger that has sparked further outrage.

[...] The law professor and tennis fan Prof Trina Jones has studied racial stereotyping and how it plays into the lives of African-American women.

"Black women are not supposed to push back and when they do, they're deemed to be domineering. Aggressive. Threatening. Loud." Similar words have been levelled at[3] Serena Williams more than once, as well as former First Lady Michelle Obama and top Democrat Maxine Waters in recent years. Prof Jones says some have compared the referee's calls to speeding tickets: many people speed and sometimes a few are caught. But that analogy, she says, misses the point that African Americans are disproportionately pulled aside. In the case of Williams, she was first dinged[4] on a coaching violation that happens often but is rarely called out as the player's fault. "Why would a black woman in a championship match therefore be called on it?" Prof Jones says, adding that an attack on one's integrity is only natural to be angry about. "[Williams] is outraged because she knows the context."

The myth of the 'angry black woman'

The "angry black woman" trope has its roots in 19th Century America, when minstrel shows, which

Annotations
[1] **trope** = *Tropus, bildlicher Ausdruck*
[2] **coaching** = Players aren't allowed to be coached in Grand Slam matches. Violations lead to warnings or penalties.
[3] to **be levelled at** = thrown at / labels given to her without much consideration or thought
[4] to **be dinged** = sharp ringing sound; here: held to account

Topic: seven methods of killing kylie jenner

Annotations
5 **comic skit** = a comedy sketch
6 **sassy** = frech
7 **pervasive** = common
8 **to grapple** = to fight with or to continually discuss a difficult issue
9 **clarion call** = appeal

involved comic skits⁵ and variety acts, mocking African Americans became popular. Blair Kelley, associate professor of history at North Carolina State University, says black women were often played by overweight white men who painted their faces black and donned fat suits "to make them look less than human, unfeminine, ugly". "Their main way of interacting with the men around them was to scream and fight and come off angry, irrationally so, in response to the circumstances around them," she says. "The real problem in their everyday life was not the structural things that black people faced, but the mouth of the black woman – her tone, her irrationality and her anger," Prof Kelley says of Sapphire's role.

As segregation laws known as Jim Crow laws saw black Americans assaulted, jailed and killed, popular culture pushed ideas of "sassy⁶ mammies" and "Sapphires" – an archetype depicting black women with iron-fists, yelling at everyone from children to white men. [...] This trope of the "angry black woman" has endured, and has been pervasive⁷ in modern media even without more overtly racist portrayals, says Brandi Collins, senior campaign director at the racial justice organisation Color of Change.

On screen, it is easy to push sass for laughs. But black women in America see these depictions translate differently in real life. For Ms Collins, the picture of the "hyperemotional" black woman has become more commonplace as Americans grapple⁸ with issues of polarised politics and civility. Black women, she says, are often faced with people responding to their emotions "from a place of perceived fear. There's almost a paranoia around it. A feeling that you have to go above and beyond to make people feel comfortable around you."

Robin Boylorn, an intercultural communications professor at the University of Alabama told the BBC it seems impossible to be a black woman and not be angry, after "generations of oppression, discrimination and erasure". "Black women should be celebrated for not being completely consumed by anger," she says.

"Men are allowed to be angry as a performance of masculinity. White women are allowed to be angry as a clarion call⁹. So black women should be encouraged to express their anger as well, particularly in the face of injustice."

[...] Ms Collins notes that fixing the problem is not just about eliminating the "angry black woman" trope. "For every type of white man you can imagine, there's a movie about his story and his experience and his journey. Black women in media aren't afforded that diversity of experience," she says. Instead, understanding the diversity of a black woman's experience – and not just her anger – is the key.

For Williams, that's a lesson she hopes her fans will learn from her US Open upset. "I'm here to fight for women's rights and women's equality. The fact that I have to go through this is an example," she told reporters after the match. "Maybe it didn't work out for me, but it's going to work out for the next person."

9

Explain why it is inadequate to refer to an African American woman as an "angry black woman".

Looking back at the play

10

Pair work Cleo is being criticized for her behaviour in the TL, e.g. "I for one can't believe @INCOGNEGRO acting like dis. U ain't the next civil rights activist." (p. 19).

Are there any more parallels between Serena Williams' depiction as an angry woman and the comments in TL that describe Cleo as hysterical and over-reacting?

11

Group work Your school is planning a project week with the topic "school for the future" and is asking students to send in podcasts, videos, posters, etc. with ideas of how schools can address and eliminate racism. What would be your contribution?

A Midsummer Night's Dream — Play 6

Pre-reading

1

A Midsummer Night's Dream is one of William Shakespeare's most popular plays. The comedy was written around 1594–1596 and is set in Athens.

To get some ideas about the setting and atmosphere of the play, carefully study the photos below. Then choose the adjectives from the box that best describe the atmosphere the photos convey. Give reasons for your choice.

> convivial | dreamlike | eccentric | electric | emotional | happy | heady | illusory | irrational | lively | romantic | stifling | strange | tense | unreal

1

2

3

4

2

a) As you have gained some insight into the setting, find out about the characters in *A Midsummer Night's Dream*. Read the short descriptions of the characters. Then start a character map in which you show the relationships between them. Add additional information to your map while you read the play.

Theseus	Hippolyta
Duke of Athens; he has conquered the Amazons	the conquered Queen of the Amazons; she is about to get married to Theseus

Egeus	Philostrate
father of Hermia, who wants his daughter to get married to Demetrius	Master of the Revels at Theseus's court

6 Play — A Midsummer Night's Dream

Hermia	Lysander
daughter of Egeus, who is in love with Lysander	a young man who is in love with Hermia

Helena	Demetrius
Hermia's friend, who is in love with Demetrius	a young man who courts Hermia

Oberon	Titania
King of the fairies	Queen of the fairies

Puck	Peaseblossom, Cobweb, Mote and Mustardseed
a mischievous sprite who serves Oberon	fairies

Quince, Bottom, Flute, Snout, Snug and Starveling
a group of workmen who want to rehearse a play in the woods for the wedding of Theseus and Hippolyta

b) Having caught a first glimpse at the characters involved, outline what you expect from the play.

> **Language support**
>
> I expect the play to be full of emotional entanglements / confusion / mischief-making / lovesickness / …
> I think that … will try to win (back) … / avenge … / make mischief / …
> From what I have read, I assume the play will be fast-paced / action-packed / a love story / a comedy / …

c) Watch a video by the Royal Shakespeare Company and check if your assumptions from the previous tasks were correct. Add new information to your character map from a). **Webcode** DSW-73684-11

3

Shakespeare seems to have taken some of his ideas for the play from various literary sources. Among these are Ovid's *Metamorphoses*, Plutarch's *Parallel Lives*, and Geoffrey Chaucer's *The Canterbury Tales*.

a) Group work (3)
Research the following works of literature and share the information with your group members.
- Ovid, *Metamorphoses: Pyramus and Thisbe*
- Plutarch, *Parallel Lives: Theseus*
- Geoffrey Chaucer, *The Canterbury Tales: The Knight's Tale*

b) Use the charts on the next page to illustrate the plots of these works of literature.

A Midsummer Night's Dream — Play 6

Ovid: Pyramus and Thisbe

    Pyramus   Thisbe

                             mulberry tree

    lioness   cloak

                               sword

                             metamorphosis:
                             mulberry tree

Plutarch: Theseus

                Phaedra   Theseus

                                                 Athens

                             Amazons

    Hippolytus   Hippolyta

Chaucer: The Knight's Tale

    Theseus   Hippolyta

                    Palamon   Arcite

                               Emily

                             tournament

                           three prayers:

    Arcite   Emily   Palamon

Play — A Midsummer Night's Dream

While reading: Act I

SCENE 1

The play opens with Theseus and Hippolyta entering the stage. They have been at war with each other, but now prepare to get married. The setting is Athens, Theseus's palace.
Read the opening scene of the play and try to understand as much as possible. You don't need to understand every single word.

Extract 1 (Act I, Scene 1)

Athens, the palace of THESEUS:
Enter THESEUS, HIPPOLYTA, PHILOSTRATE, *with others*
THESEUS. Now, fair Hippolyta, our nuptial hour
Draws on apace; four happy days bring in
Another moon – but O, methinks, how slow
This old moon wanes! She lingers my desires,
5 Like to a step-dame or a dowager
Long withering out a young man's revenue.
HIPPOLYTA. Four days will quickly steep themselves in night;
Four nights will quickly dream away the time;
And then the moon, like to a silver bow
10 New bent in heaven, shall behold the night
Of our solemnities.
THESEUS.   Go, Philostrate,
Stir up the Athenian youth to merriments,
Awake the pert and nimble spirit of mirth;
Turn melancholy forth to funerals;
15 The pale companion is not for our pomp.
    Exit PHILOSTRATE
Hippolyta, I woo'd thee with my sword,
And won thy love doing thee injuries;
But I will wed thee in another key,
With pomp, with triumph, and with revelling.

> **Tip** Don't get confused by the line numbers. Sometimes a single verse line is divided up between two characters (for example, the verse in line 11:
> HIPPOLYTA: "Of our solemnities." –
> THESEUS: "Go, Philostrate,").

Annotations
l. 1 **our nuptial hour** = the time of our wedding
l. 2 **apace** = quickly
ll. 2–3 **four … moon** = there will be a full moon in four days
l. 3 **methinks** = I think
l. 4 to **wane** = to fade
     to **linger** = *here:* to make me wait for
l. 5 **step-dame** = step-mother
     dowager = widow
l. 6 **long withering … revenue** = growing old and spending a young man's inheritance (which he can only claim when she dies)
l. 7 to **steep** = to drown
l. 11 **solemnities** = wedding ceremonies
l. 12 **youth** = young people
l. 13 **pert** = lively, cheeky
      nimble = moving quickly and easily
l. 14 to **turn … forth** = to send away
l. 15 **the pale … pomp** = we can't have miserable guests at our celebrations
ll. 16–17 **I woo'd thee … injuries** = In Greek mythology, Theseus was a legendary ruler of Athens who defeated an invasion of the Amazons and married their Queen, Hippolyta, afterwards.
l. 18 **in another key** = *here:* in a different way
l. 19 **triumph** = public festivities
      revelling = noisy celebrations

a) Tick (✓) the summary that fits best. Explain your choice.
  ❑ 1. Whereas Theseus complains that time is passing so slowly, Hippolyta seems rather relaxed about their wedding day. Theseus promises that he will make up for the suffering Hippolyta has had to endure by providing public festivities on their wedding day.
  ❑ 2. Theseus can't wait to get married to Hippolyta and instructs his master of the revels to see to the wedding preparations. He discloses that he will now make amends to her for having won her by force.
  ❑ 3. Theseus is impatient to get married to Hippolyta and tells his master of the revels to make sure the celebration will be a success.

b) Describe your first impression of the relationship between Theseus and Hippolyta. Give evidence from the text.

> **Language support**
> Their relationship can be described as …
> caring | close | cold | formal | fragile | harmonious | intimate | love-hate | loving | stormy | troubled | violent | …

c) Speculate why Shakespeare opens his play with two prominent figures from a classical myth that was well-known in Shakespeare's days.

A Midsummer Night's Dream — Play

5
Egeus enters with Hermia and her two suitors, Lysander and Demetrius, to see Theseus about a legal matter. Read the following extract.

Extract 2 (Act I, Scene 1)

EGEUS. Happy be Theseus, our renowned duke!
THESEUS. Thanks, good Egeus. What's the news with thee?
EGEUS. Full of vexation come I, with complaint
Against my child, my daughter Hermia.
5 Stand forth, Demetrius! – My noble lord,
This man hath my consent to marry her.
Stand forth, Lysander! – And, my gracious duke,
This man hath bewitch'd the bosom of my child.
Thou, thou, Lysander, thou hast given her rhymes,
10 And interchang'd love-tokens with my child.
Thou hast by moonlight at her window sung
With feigning voice verses of feigning love,
And stolen the impression of her fantasy,
With bracelets of thy hair, rings, gauds, conceits,
15 Knacks, trifles, nosegays, sweetmeats – messengers
Of strong prevailment in unharden'd youth;
With cunning hast thou filch'd my daughter's heart,
Turn'd her obedience, which is due to me,
To stubborn harshness. And, my gracious duke,
20 Be it so she will not here, before your grace,
Consent to marry with Demetrius,
I beg the ancient privilege of Athens;
As she is mine, I may dispose of her;
Which shall be either to this gentleman
25 Or to her death, according to our law
Immediately provided in that case.
THESEUS. What say you, Hermia? Be advis'd, fair maid.
To you your father should be as a god,
One that compos'd your beauties; yea, and one
30 To whom you are but as a form in wax
By him imprinted, and within his power
To leave the figure, or disfigure it.
Demetrius is a worthy gentleman.
HERMIA. So is Lysander.
THESEUS.   In himself he is;
35 But in this kind, wanting your father's voice,
The other must be held the worthier.
HERMIA. I would my father look'd but with my eyes.
THESEUS. Rather your eyes must with his judgement look.
HERMIA. I do entreat your grace to pardon me.
40 I know not by what power I am made bold,
Nor how it may concern my modesty
In such a presence here to plead my thoughts;
But I beseech your grace that I may know
The worst that may befall me in this case,
45 If I refuse to wed Demetrius.
THESEUS. Either to die the death, or to abjure
For ever the society of men.
Therefore, fair Hermia, question your desires,
Know of your youth, examine well your blood,

Annotations
l. 3   **vexation** = worry or anger
l. 8   **bosom** = *here:* heart
l. 10 **token** = sign, symbol
l. 12 **feigning** = pretending to be sincere
l. 14 **gauds** = silly toys
       conceits = fancy things
l. 15 **knacks** = knick-knacks, useless little things
       nosegays = bunches of flowers
       sweetmeats = sweets
l. 16 **prevailment** = power
       unharden'd = inexperienced
l. 17 to **filch** = to steal
l. 18 **due** = owed
l. 20 **be it so** = if
l. 22 **privilege** = *here:* special right
l. 23 **I may dispose of her** = I may have her at my command; I may get rid of her
l. 29 **compos'd your beauties** = made you beautiful
l. 32 to **disfigure** = to destroy
l. 35 **kind** = *here:* matter
       wanting = *here:* lacking
       voice = *here:* approval
l. 37 **I would** = *here:* I wish
l. 39 to **entreat** = to beg
l. 42 to **plead** = *here:* to express
l. 43 to **beseech** = to beg
l. 46 to **abjure** = to give up officially
l. 49 to **know of** = *here:* to think of

6 Play — A Midsummer Night's Dream

50 Whether, if you yield not to your father's choice,
You can endure the livery of a nun,
For aye to be in shady cloister mew'd,
To live a barren sister all your life,
Chanting faint hymns to the cold fruitless moon.
55 Thrice blessed they that master so their blood
To undergo such maiden pilgrimage;
But earthlier happy is the rose distill'd
Than that which, withering on the virgin thorn,
Grows, lives, and dies in single blessedness.
60 **HERMIA.** So will I grow, so live, so die, my lord,
Ere I will yield my virgin patent up
Unto his lordship, whose unwished yoke
My soul consents not to give sovereignty.
THESEUS. Take time to pause, and by the next new moon,
65 The sealing-day betwixt my love and me
For everlasting bond of fellowship,
Upon that day either prepare to die
For disobedience to your father's will,
Or else to wed Demetrius, as he would,
70 Or on Diana's altar to protest
For aye austerity and single life.
DEMETRIUS. Relent, sweet Hermia; and, Lysander, yield
Thy crazed title to my certain right.
LYSANDER. You have her father's love, Demetrius;
75 Let me have Hermia's – do you marry him.
EGEUS. Scornful Lysander, true, he hath my love,
And what is mine my love shall render him;
And she is mine, and all my right of her
I do estate unto Demetrius.

Annotations
l. 50 to **yield** = to give in, to surrender
l. 51 **livery** = habit (a special piece of long clothing worn by nuns)
l. 52 **aye** = ever
 mew'd = shut up
l. 54 **fruitless moon** = reference to Diana, goddess of the moon and of chastity
l. 55 to **master** = to discipline
 blood = *here*: passions
l. 56 **maiden pilgrimage** = *here*: a life of celibacy
l. 57 **earthlier happy** = happier on earth
 the rose distill'd = the rose that is plucked and whose scent is distilled to make perfume
l. 61 **ere** = before
 yield my virgin patent up = give up my right to remain a virgin
l. 62 **his lordship** = the domination of this man
 yoke = *Joch*
l. 65 **sealing-day** = the day on which they will seal their vows
 betwixt = between
l. 70 to **protest** = *here*: to vow
l. 71 **aye** = ever
 austerity = strict simplicity (i.e. the life of a nun)
l. 73 **crazed title** = uncertain claim
l. 79 **I do estate unto** = I give to (as a legal act)

a) Tick (✓) the correct answers. Give evidence from the text.

1. Egeus wants …
   ☐ a) Hermia to get married to Demetrius.
   ☐ b) Hermia to get married to Lysander.
   ☐ c) Lysander to court Hermia.

2. According to Egeus, Lysander …
   ☐ a) only pretends to be in love with her.
   ☐ b) is sincere in his wooing.
   ☐ c) is a good-for-nothing.

3. Lysander has given Hermia …
   ☐ a) books and jewellery.
   ☐ b) flowers and a strand of his hair.
   ☐ c) toys and pets.

4. Egeus complains about Hermia's …
   ☐ a) insolence.
   ☐ b) disloyalty.
   ☐ c) disobedience.

5. According to the Athenian law, Hermia must …
   ☐ a) either obey her father or die.
   ☐ b) leave Athens with Demetrius.
   ☐ c) stay unmarried until her death.

6. Theseus tries to …
   ☐ a) find out what Hermia really wants.
   ☐ b) understand Hermia's wish.
   ☐ c) convince Hermia to obey her father.

7. Hermia …
   ☐ a) rather wants to die or become a nun than obey her father.
   ☐ b) wants to reconsider Theseus's proposal.
   ☐ c) happily accepts Theseus's decision.

8. Lysander suggests that …
   ☐ a) Demetrius courts Helena.
   ☐ b) Demetrius marries Egeus.
   ☐ c) Hermia should obey her father.

b) Outline Egeus's and Hermia's conflict.

c) Collect information on how the women are presented in the scene. Start a table like the one below. Add new information as you read on.

Women in the play	
Quotation	Analysis/Interpretation
"I woo'd thee with my sword" (extract 1, l. 16) ...	the Queen of the Amazons, Hippolyta, is defeated → "subjected" ...

6

a) First impressions: Explain how Theseus, Egeus and Hermia come across. Give evidence from the text.

Language support

appeasing | conciliatory | domineering | gentle | headstrong | irreconcilable | meek | peace-making | relentless | remorseless | strong-minded | submissive | uncompromising | ...

b) **Group work (4)**
Show their relationship in a tableau: Each student slips into the role of one character: Theseus, Egeus and Hermia. The fourth student serves as the director and presenter.
- First discuss a typical pose, mood or gesture of the characters.
- Then display in a still a particular gesture, expression or movement that shows each character's attitude towards the other characters.
- The fourth student invites other students to interpret the still and leads the talk.

Info

Tableau

In a tableau, still images of characters from a play are presented. This method can be used to show the relationship between characters or to point out important moments in a scene.

c) Step into the shoes of one of the characters – Theseus, Egeus or Hermia – and write a soliloquy, in which you reflect upon the meeting.

Info

Soliloquy

Soliloquy is the act of talking to oneself. This can be done silently or aloud. In drama, the term describes the practice by which a character, alone on stage, utters his or her thoughts for the audience to hear. Soliloquies serve as a dramatic device to let the audience know about the character's intentions and state of mind, and also to give additional information about the action of the play.

Soliloquies are often used to
- set the scene
- make the audience part of the play
- explicate the character's feelings
- clarify matters
- introduce further information.

Play — A Midsummer Night's Dream

7 Lysander and Hermia are alone hatching a plan. Read the following extract.

Extract 3 (Act I, Scene 1)

LYSANDER. How now, my love? Why is your cheek so pale?
How chance the roses there do fade so fast?
HERMIA. Belike for want of rain, which I could well
Beteem them from the tempest of my eyes.
5 **LYSANDER.** Ay me! For aught that I could ever read,
Could ever hear by tale or history,
The course of true love never did run smooth;
But either it was different in blood –
HERMIA. O cross! too high to be enthrall'd to low.
10 **LYSANDER.** Or else misgraffed in respect of years –
HERMIA. O spite! too old to be engag'd to young.
LYSANDER. Or else it stood upon the choice of friends –
HERMIA. O hell, to choose love by another's eyes!
LYSANDER. Or, if there were a sympathy in choice,
15 War, death, or sickness did lay siege to it,
Making it momentany as a sound,
Swift as a shadow, short as any dream,
Brief as the lightning in the collied night,
That in a spleen unfolds both heaven and earth,
20 And, ere a man hath power to say 'Behold!',
The jaws of darkness do devour it up.
So quick bright things come to confusion.
HERMIA. If then true lovers have been ever cross'd
It stands as an edict in destiny.
25 Then let us teach our trial patience,
Because it is a customary cross,
As due to love as thoughts, and dreams, and sighs,
Wishes, and tears – poor fancy's followers.
LYSANDER. A good persuasion. Therefore hear me, Hermia:
30 I have a widow aunt, a dowager,
Of great revenue, and she hath no child.
From Athens is her house remote seven leagues;
And she respects me as her only son.
There, gentle Hermia, may I marry thee;
35 And to that place the sharp Athenian law
Cannot pursue us. If thou lov'st me, then
Steal forth thy father's house tomorrow night,
And in the wood, a league without the town,
Where I did meet thee once with Helena
40 To do observance to a morn of May,
There will I stay for thee.
HERMIA.   My good Lysander,
I swear to thee by Cupid's strongest bow,
By his best arrow with the golden head,
By the simplicity of Venus' doves,
45 By that which knitteth souls and prospers loves,
And by that fire which burn'd the Carthage queen
When the false Trojan under sail was seen,
By all the vows that ever men have broke –
In number more than ever women spoke –
50 In that same place thou hast appointed me,
Tomorrow truly will I meet with thee.
LYSANDER. Keep promise, love. Look, here comes Helena.

Annotations

- l. 2 **how chance** = why
- l. 3 **belike** = probably
  for want of = for lack of
- l. 4 to **beteem** = to allow
- l. 5 **aught** = anything
- l. 8 **blood** = *here:* social class
- l. 9 **enthrall'd** = fascinated
- l. 10 **misgraffed** = badly matched
- l. 11 **spite** = the desire to upset or hurt sb
- l. 12 to **stand upon** = *here:* to depend on
- l. 14 **sympathy** = *here:* agreement
- l. 15 to **lay siege to** = to make war on
- l. 18 **collied** = blackened
- l. 19 **spleen** = sudden impulse of anger
  to **unfold** = *here:* to light up
- l. 20 **ere** = before
  to **behold** = to see or look at
- l. 23 **cross'd** = *here:* annoyed, frustrated
- l. 24 **edict** = *Erlass, Anordnung*
- l. 25 **trial** = test
- l. 26 **customary** = usual, traditional
- l. 27 **due to** = belonging to
- l. 28 **fancy** = *here:* love
- l. 29 **persuasion** = *here:* advice
- l. 30 **dowager** = widow
- l. 31 **revenue** = income, money
- l. 32 **remote** = far away
  league = a unit of distance (usually about 3 miles)
- l. 36 to **pursue** = to follow and try to catch
- l. 38 **without** = *here:* outside
- l. 40 **observance** = a ritual or ceremony to celebrate a religious event
  morn = morning
- l. 41 to **stay** = *here:* to wait
- l. 42 **Cupid** = In classical mythology, Cupid (also known as Amor) is the god of love and desire. He is often depicted with a bow and two arrows.
- l. 44 **the simplicity of Venus' doves** = Venus is the Roman goddess of love. Her chariot used to be drawn by white doves, a symbol of the innocence of pure love.
- l. 45 to **knit** = *stricken, verknüpfen*
- l. 46 **the Carthage queen** = Dido was the legendary Queen of Carthage. According to the story in Virgil's *Aeneid*, she fell in love with the Trojan Aeneas and was so heartbroken when he sailed away from her that she killed herself.

A Midsummer Night's Dream — Play

a) "The course of true love never did run smooth; […]." (l. 7) Tick (✓) the obstacles lovers must overcome according to Lysander and Hermia.

	Possible obstacles	✓	Evidence
1	The lovers are from different social classes.	✓	"different in blood" (l. 8)
2	The lovers have a different financial background.		
3	The lovers differ in age.		
4	The lovers are advised against the relationship by family members, friends, guardians, etc.		
5	Other people fancy them.		
6	War tears them apart.		
7	They are from different ethnic groups.		
8	One lover dies or becomes ill.		
9	One lover changes his / her mind.		

b) Outline Lysander's plan.

c) In class, talk about the obstacles that lovers might need to overcome today.

8

Helena enters and pours out her heart to Hermia. Read the following extract.

Extract 4 (Act I, Scene 1)

HERMIA. God speed, fair Helena! Whither away?
HELENA. Call you me fair? That 'fair' again unsay.
Demetrius loves your fair: O happy fair!
Your eyes are lodestars, and your tongue's sweet air
5 More tuneable than lark to shepherd's ear
When wheat is green, when hawthorn buds appear.
Sickness is catching. O, were favour so,
Yours would I catch, fair Hermia, ere I go;
My ear should catch your voice, my eye your eye,
10 My tongue should catch your tongue's sweet melody.
Were the world mine, Demetrius being bated,
The rest I'd give to be to you translated.
O, teach me how you look, and with what art
You sway the motion of Demetrius' heart.
15 **HERMIA.** I frown upon him; yet he loves me still.
HELENA. O that your frowns would teach my smiles such skill!
HERMIA. I give him curses; yet he gives me love.
HELENA. O that my prayers could such affection move!
HERMIA. The more I hate, the more he follows me.

Annotations
l. 1 **God speed** = may God be with you
　　fair = *here:* beautiful, lovely
　　Whither away? = Where are you going?
l. 3 **your fair** = your beauty
l. 4 **lodestar** = guiding star
　　air = *here:* sound, song, melody
l. 5 **tuneable** = melodious, with a pleasant tune
l. 6 **hawthorn** = *Weißdorn*
l. 7 **catching** = infectious, able to be given to sb else
　　favour = *here:* beauty, charm
l. 8 **ere** = before
l. 11 **bated** = *here:* excepted
l. 12 **translated** = *here:* transferred
l. 14 **to sway** = to cause sth to move or change, to influence

6 Play — A Midsummer Night's Dream

20 **HELENA.** The more I love, the more he hateth me.
HERMIA. His folly, Helena, is no fault of mine.
HELENA. None but your beauty; would that fault were mine!
HERMIA. Take comfort: he no more shall see my face;
Lysander and myself will fly this place.
25 Before the time I did Lysander see,
Seem'd Athens as a paradise to me.
O then, what graces in my love do dwell,
That he hath turn'd a heaven unto a hell?
LYSANDER. Helen, to you our minds we will unfold:
30 […]

Annotations
l. 21 **folly** = stupidity, foolishness
l. 22 **would** = *here:* I wish
l. 24 **to fly** = *here:* to leave, to escape from
l. 27 **grace** = *here:* quality
 to dwell = to live or stay
l. 29 **mind** = *here:* thought, plan

a) Describe Helena's problem and Hermia's reaction.
b) Analyse the language Shakespeare uses to show the complications of love.
 → **Workshop:** Analysing a Shakespearean sonnet
c) **Pair work** Dramatic reading: Read out the dialogue. One student takes Hermia's role, the other student Helena's role. Try several different ways of delivering Helena's lines. How does she come across? You can find some ideas in the box.
d) Describe your first impression of Helena.

Literary devices: alliteration | anaphora | antithesis | epiphora | inversion | parallelism

Language support

admiring | desperate | infatuated | intimidated | respectful | servile | timid | …

9

Hermia and Lysander have disclosed their plan to Helena: They want to elope and meet in the woods the following night. Then Helena is left alone on stage. Read the following extract.

Extract 5 (Act I, Scene 1)

HELENA. How happy some o'er other some can be!
Through Athens I am thought as fair as she.
But what of that? Demetrius thinks not so;
He will not know what all but he do know.
5 And as he errs, doting on Hermia's eyes,
So I, admiring of his qualities.
Things base and vile, holding no quantity,
Love can transpose to form and dignity.
Love looks not with the eyes, but with the mind,
10 And therefore is wing'd Cupid painted blind.
Nor hath love's mind of any judgement taste;
Wings, and no eyes, figure unheedy haste;
And therefore is love said to be a child
Because in choice he is so oft beguil'd.
15 As waggish boys in game themselves forswear,
So the boy Love is perjur'd everywhere;
For, ere Demetrius looked on Hermia's eyne,
He hail'd down oaths that he was only mine,
And when this hail some heat from Hermia felt,
20 So he dissolv'd, and showers of oaths did melt.
I will go tell him of fair Hermia's flight:
Then to the wood will he, tomorrow night,
Pursue her; and for this intelligence,
If I have thanks it is a dear expense;
25 But herein mean I to enrich my pain,
To have his sight thither, and back again.

Annotations
l. 1 **o'er** = over
l. 2 **fair** = *here:* beautiful, lovely
l. 5 **to dote on** = to love very much, to admire
l. 7 **base** = *here:* having no honour or morals
 vile = bad, evil
 quantity = *here:* value
l. 8 **to transpose** = to transform
l. 12 **to figure** = to cause
 unheedy = thoughtless
 haste = speed, the act of hurrying
l. 14 **beguil'd** = deceived
l. 15 **waggish** = playful, mischievous
 themselves forswear = break promises
l. 16 **perjur'd** = *eidbrüchig, meineidig*
l. 17 **ere** = until
 eyne = eyes
l. 18 **to hail down** = *niederhageln, niederprasseln*
l. 19 **hail** = small balls of ice that fall from the sky
l. 21 **flight** = *here:* escape
l. 23 **intelligence** = *here:* information
l. 24 **dear** = beloved; precious; highly priced
 expense = cost
l. 26 **sight** = view
 thither = to that place, there

A Midsummer Night's Dream — Play 6

What ideas does Helena express? Match the correct sentence halves.

1. It's a surprise
2. It's of no use that
3. Demetrius refuses to accept
4. Demetrius is as wrong about adoring Hermia
5. Love can make worthless things
6. When we are in love,
7. Before Demetrius fell in love with Hermia,
8. I'm going to tell him about Hermia and Lysander's elopement so that
9. I will pay a high price
10. At least I will be able to

a) as I am wrong about loving him.
b) we don't use our eyes, but our mind.
c) he courted me and promised he was mine.
d) for making him grateful for this information.
e) how much happier some people can be than others.
f) he will follow them into the forest.
g) see him come and go.
h) people think I am as beautiful as Hermia.
i) what other people know.
j) look beautiful.

1	2	3	4	5	6	7	8	9	10

10

a) Helena refers to the Roman god of love, Cupid, when she explains what she thinks about love. Describe how Cupid is portrayed in the painting and find references in Helena's passage that match the description.

_____

_____

_____

_____

_____

Piero della Francesca: Cupid Blindfolded (1452–66)

b) Explain to what extent the message of the portrayal is true.

11

a) **Group work (3)** Should Helena disclose her friends' plan to elope? Collect arguments for and against disclosing Hermia and Lysander's plan to Demetrius. Then have one student (Helena) sit on a chair. Two other students (her conscience) stand behind her and take turns to tell her why she should or shouldn't disclose her friends' plan.

b) Comment on Helena's plan. Do you think it will work out? Explain why you think or don't think so.

Play — A Midsummer Night's Dream

SCENE 2

The craftsmen have gathered at the house of Peter Quince, the carpenter, to prepare a play, which they want to perform at the Duke's wedding. Read the following extract.

Extract 6 (Act I, Scene 2)

QUINCE. Is all our company here?
BOTTOM. You were best to call them generally, man by man, according to the scrip.
QUINCE. Here is the scroll of every man's name, which is thought fit
5 through all Athens to play in our interlude before the duke and the duchess on his wedding day at night.
BOTTOM. First, good Peter Quince, say what the play treats on; then read the names of the actors; and so grow to a point.
QUINCE. Marry, our play is 'The most lamentable comedy and most
10 cruel death of Pyramus and Thisbe'.
BOTTOM. A very good piece of work, I assure you, and a merry. Now, good Peter Quince, call forth your actors by the scroll. Masters, spread yourselves.
QUINCE. Answer as I call you. Nick Bottom, the weaver?
15 BOTTOM. Ready. Name what part I am for, and proceed.
QUINCE. You, Nick Bottom, are set down for Pyramus.
BOTTOM. What is Pyramus? A lover or a tyrant?
QUINCE. A lover that kills himself, most gallant, for love.
BOTTOM. That will ask some tears in the true performing of it. If I do
20 it, let the audience look to their eyes: I will move storms, I will condole, in some measure. To the rest – yet my chief humour is for a tyrant. […]
QUINCE. Francis Flute, the bellows-mender?
FLUTE. Here, Peter Quince.
QUINCE. Flute, you must take Thisbe on you.
25 FLUTE. What is Thisbe? A wandering knight?
QUINCE. It is the lady that Pyramus must love.
FLUTE. Nay, faith, let not me play a woman: I have a beard coming.
QUINCE. That's all one: you shall play it in a mask, and you may speak as small as you will.
30 BOTTOM. And I may hide my face, let me play Thisbe too. I'll speak in a monstrous little voice: 'Thisne, Thisne!' – 'Ah, Pyramus, my lover dear; thy Thisbe dear, and lady dear.'
QUINCE. No, no; you must play Pyramus; and Flute, you Thisbe.
BOTTOM. Well, proceed.
35 QUINCE. Robin Starveling, the tailor?
STARVELING. Here, Peter Quince.
QUINCE. Robin Starveling, you must play Thisbe's mother. Tom Snout, the tinker?
SNOUT. Here, Peter Quince.
40 QUINCE. You, Pyramus' father; myself, Thisbe's father; Snug, the joiner, you the lion's part; and I hope here is a play fitted.
SNUG. Have you the lion's part written? Pray you, if it be, give it me; for I am slow of study.
QUINCE. You may do it extempore; for it is nothing but roaring.
45 BOTTOM. Let me play the lion too. I will roar that I will do any man's heart good to hear me. I will roar that I will make the duke say 'Let him roar again, let him roar again!'
QUINCE. And you should do it too terribly, you would fright the duchess and the ladies that they would shriek; and that were enough to hang us
50 all.

Annotations

- l. 2 **generally** = Bottom sometimes confuses similar sounding words. Here he means 'separately'.
- l. 3 **scrip** = list
- l. 4 **scroll** = list
- l. 5 **interlude** = play
- l. 8 **grow to a point** = reach a conclusion
- l. 9 **marry** = *here:* an exclamation used for emphasis or to express an emotion
- ll. 12–13 **spread yourselves** = sit down
- l. 14 **weaver** = *Weber*
- l. 18 **gallant** = brave
- l. 20 to **condole** = to lament
- l. 21 **my chief humour is for ...** = I would prefer ..., I am best suited for ...
- l. 22 **bellows-mender** = *Blasebalgflicker*
- l. 28 **that's all one** = that doesn't matter
- l. 29 **small** = *here:* high-pitched (like a woman's voice)
- l. 31 **monstrous** = *here:* unnatural
- l. 35 **tailor** = *Schneider*
- l. 38 **tinker** = *Kesselflicker*
- l. 40 **joiner** = *Tischler*
- l. 41 **fitted** = cast
- l. 44 **extempore** = spontaneously
- l. 48 **and** = *here:* if
  fright = frighten

ALL. That would hang us, every mother's son.
BOTTOM. I grant you, friends, if you should fright the ladies out of their wits they would have no more discretion but to hang us; but I will aggravate my voice so that I will roar you as gently as any sucking dove. I will roar you and 'twere any nightingale.
QUINCE. You can play no part but Pyramus; for Pyramus is a sweet-faced man, a proper man as one shall see in a summer's day, a most lovely, gentlemanlike man: therefore you must needs play Pyramus.
BOTTOM. Well, I will undertake it. What beard were I best to play it in?
QUINCE. Why, what you will. […] But, masters, here are your parts, and I am to entreat you, request you, and desire you to con them by tomorrow night, and meet me in the palace wood, a mile without the town, by moonlight; there will we rehearse, for if we meet in the city we shall be dogged with company, and our devices known. In the meantime I will draw a bill of properties, such as our play wants. I pray you, fail me not.
BOTTOM. We will meet, and there we may rehearse most obscenely and courageously. Take pains, be perfect: adieu!
QUINCE. At the duke's oak we meet.
BOTTOM. Enough; hold, or cut bowstrings.

Annotations
- l. 52 **fright** = frighten
- l. 53 **no more discretion** = Here Bottom means 'no other choice'.
- l. 54 to **aggravate** = to intensify
  sucking dove = Here Bottom mixes up two expressions of gentleness, 'sucking lamb' and 'sitting dove'.
- l. 55 **and 'twere** = as though it were
  nightingale = Nachtigall
- ll. 56–57 **sweet-faced** = good-looking
- l. 58 **needs** = here: certainly
- l. 61 to **entreat** = to beg
  to **con** = to learn
- l. 62 **without** = here: outside
- l. 64 **dogged** = here: followed
  device = here: plan
- l. 65 **bill of properties** = list of stage equipment
- l. 66 **obscenely** = Here Bottom probably means 'unseen' or 'properly'.
- l. 67 **take pains** = work hard
- l. 69 **hold, or cut bowstrings** = The exact meaning of this phrase is unknown. Bottom probably means that the actors must keep their promises so as not to be disgraced.

a) Match the different roles to the characters. Use the middle column in the grid below.
b) Collect information about the craftsmen: character traits, outer appearance, etc. Use the right-hand column of the grid for your notes.
c) The title of the craftsmen's play is "The most lamentable comedy and most cruel death of Pyramus and Thisbe" (ll. 9–10). Comment on this title.

Character	Role	Information
Peter Quince		
Nick Bottom		
Francis Flute		
Robin Starveling		
Tom Snout		
Snug		

Play — A Midsummer Night's Dream

13 Group work (6)
a) The craftsmen provide a striking contrast to the mythical world of Theseus and Hippolyta. In your group, discuss why Shakespeare might have chosen the group of craftsmen.
b) Identify humorous lines in the scene. Talk about how you would speak the lines to make the most of the humorous situations. Example:
"The most lamentable comedy …" (ll. 9–10) → to emphasize the paradox: stress the two words
c) Each group member chooses a craftsman and establishes a role card for him. Present your character to the other group members. Then act out the scene together.

LOOKING BACK AT ACT I

14
a) Who is in love with whom? Create a diagram to show the love entanglements and the problems that the following characters have.
• Demetrius • Egeus • Helena • Hermia • Hippolyta • Lysander • Theseus

b) **Pair work** Stage an interview: Partner A takes on the role of one of these characters. Partner B is an interviewer, who wants to find out what the character thinks about love, his or her relationship, the problems love can cause and possible solutions.
c) Present your interview to the class.

15
a) Read the information about verse and prose in Shakespeare's time.

Info

Verse and prose in Shakespeare's time

In the 16th century, playwrights often used verse, rhymed or unrhymed, in their plays. This style was particularly suitable for characters such as kings, or important topics such as war and peace or tragic events. Characters spoke in prose, too, but this often mirrored their social position or petty matters. Therefore, noble characters often spoke in verse whereas their subjects or comic characters used prose.

It was a stage convention to use **blank verse**, an unrhymed verse with a five-beat rhythm (**iambic pentameter**). Each line has five feet (= pentameter) which consist of one unstressed (x) syllable and one stressed (/) syllable. Example:

   x / x / x /x / x /
"The course of true love never did run smooth"

As stage technology such as curtains or light did not exist in Shakespeare's time, a lot of scenes and acts as well as long speeches in blank verse often end with a **rhyming couplet** (two lines) to mark their end. Shakespeare also made use of four-stress lines (= tetrameter). For example, the lines spoken by the fairies are mostly written in catalectic (= incomplete) **trochaic tetrameter**. A trochee consists of a stressed (/) syllable followed by an unstressed (x) syllable. Example:

   / x /x / x /
"Through the forest have I gone"

---

b) Find examples of
• blank verse (unrhymed) • rhyme in verse • rhyming couplets • prose
in the play and analyse the use: Who uses verse (rhymed or unrhymed)? Who uses prose? What is the context?

A Midsummer Night's Dream — Play 6

While reading: Act II

SCENE 1

16

Act II of the play is set in a forest near Athens. Read the following extract.

Extract 7 (Act II, Scene 1)

A wood near Athens:
Enter a FAIRY *at one door, and* PUCK *at another*
PUCK. How now, spirit; whither wander you?
FAIRY. Over hill, over dale,
   Thorough bush, thorough briar,
   Over park, over pale,
5 Thorough flood, thorough fire;
   I do wander everywhere
   Swifter than the moon's sphere;
   And I serve the Fairy Queen,
   To dew her orbs upon the green.
10 […]
   Farewell, thou lob of spirits; I'll be gone.
   Our queen and all her elves come here anon.
PUCK. The king doth keep his revels here tonight.
   Take heed the queen come not within his sight,
15 For Oberon is passing fell and wrath,
   Because that she as her attendant hath
   A lovely boy stol'n from an Indian king;
   She never had so sweet a changeling,
   And jealous Oberon would have the child
20 Knight of his train, to trace the forests wild.
   But she perforce withholds the loved boy,
   Crowns him with flowers, and makes him all her joy.
   And now they never meet in grove or green,
   By fountain clear or spangl'd starlight sheen,
25 But they do square, that all their elves for fear
   Creep into acorn cups and hide them there.
FAIRY. Either I mistake your shape and making quite,
   Or else you are that shrewd and knavish sprite
   Called Robin Goodfellow. Are not you he
30 That frights the maidens of the villagery,
   Skim milk, and sometimes labour in the quern,
   And bootless make the breathless housewife churn,
   And sometime make the drink to bear no barm,
   Mislead night-wanderers, laughing at their harm?
35 Those that 'Hobgoblin' call you, and 'Sweet Puck',
   You do their work, and they shall have good luck.
   Are not you he?
PUCK.   Thou speakest aright;
   I am that merry wanderer of the night.
   I jest to Oberon, and make him smile
40 […].
   But room, fairy: here comes Oberon.
FAIRY. And here my mistress. Would that he were gone!

Annotations
l. 2 **dale** = valley
l. 3 **thorough** = *here:* through
     briar = thorn
l. 4 **pale** = gated bit of land
l. 5 **flood** = *here:* water
l. 7 **swifter** = quicker
     sphere = orbit
l. 9 **dew her orbs** = place the dew
     green = *here:* grass
l. 11 **lob** = unsophisticated peasant
l. 12 **anon** = soon
l. 13 **doth keep his revels** = is having a party
l. 14 **take heed** = be careful
l. 15 **is passing fell and wrath** = is extremely angry
l. 16 **attendant** = servant
l. 18 **changeling** = human child
l. 20 **to trace** = to wander
l. 21 **perforce withholds** = refuses to give over
l. 23 **in grove or green** = in the forests or the fields
l. 24 **fountain clear** = clear river
     spangl'd starlight sheen = under the stars
l. 25 **to square** = to argue
l. 27 **I mistake … quite** = I am totally wrong
l. 28 **shrewd** = mischievous
     knavish = naughty
l. 31 **to skim** = to take the cream from milk
     labour in the quern = block up the flour mill
l. 32 **bootless … churn** = prevent the milk from becoming butter, so that they are exhausted from the effort
l. 33 **make the drink to bear no barm** = make the beer flat
l. 38 **merry** = *here:* mischievous
l. 39 **to jest** = to joke
l. 41 **room** = *here:* make some space
l. 42 **would that** = if only

Put the sentences below into the correct order and give line references.

6 Play — A Midsummer Night's Dream

No.	Contents	References
	Titania refuses to hand the boy over to Oberon.	
	Puck admits his identity and describes himself.	
	Oberon is angry about Titania having taken a little boy from India.	
	The fairy describes some of the mischievous tricks Puck plays on people.	
	Puck announces the arrival of Oberon in the forest and warns the fairy to make Titania stay away from Oberon.	
	The fairy recognizes Oberon's attendant as Robin Goodfellow, better known as Puck.	
1	Two fairies meet by chance: one belongs to Titania's train, the other is Oberon's attendant, Puck.	ll. 1, 8, 39
	He is so beautiful that Oberon wants to make him his knight.	

17

a) The fairy and Puck create vivid images of things that happen in the fairy world in the audience's mind. Collect examples that illustrate the world of the fairies. Use a grid like the one on the right.

The fairy	Puck
The fairy flies quickly through the landscape. (ll. 2–7)	…

b) Some of the examples you have listed might be difficult to put on stage. In class, talk about how you would stage the scene. Consider the following aspects:
 • costumes   • props   • scenery   • masks   • light

18

Oberon and Titania enter the stage from opposite sides with their royal trains and immediately start to quarrel. Read the following extract.

Extract 8 (Act II, Scene 1)

OBERON. Ill met by moonlight, proud Titania!
TITANIA. What, jealous Oberon? Fairies, skip hence.
I have forsworn his bed and company.
OBERON. Tarry, rash wanton! Am not I thy lord?
5 **TITANIA.** Then I must be thy lady. But I know
When thou hast stol'n away from Fairyland,
And in the shape of Corin sat all day
Playing on pipes of corn, and versing love
To amorous Phillida. Why art thou here
10 Come from the farthest step of India? –
But that, forsooth, the bouncing Amazon,
Your buskin'd mistress and your warrior love,
To Theseus must be wedded; and you come
To give their bed joy and prosperity.
15 **OBERON.** How canst thou thus, for shame, Titania,
Glance at my credit with Hippolyta,
Knowing I know thy love to Theseus?

Annotations
l. 1 **ill met by moonlight** = I am unhappy to see you tonight
l. 2 **skip hence** = let's go
l. 3 **forsworn** = promised to give up
l. 4 **to tarry** = to wait
   rash wanton = impulsive creature
   lord = *here:* husband
l. 5 **lady** = *here:* wife
l. 6 **stol'n away** = sneaked away
l. 7 **shape of Corin** = disguised as a shepherd (Corin is a shepherd from a famous story)
l. 8 **versing love** = reciting love poetry
l. 9 **to amorous Phillida** = to a loving shepherdess
l. 10 **step** = *here:* hill
l. 11 **forsooth** = of course
   the bouncing Amazon = reference to Hippolyta
l. 12 **buskin'd** = wearing a type of high boots
l. 14 **bed** = *here:* marriage
l. 16 **to glance at** = *here:* to scorn
   credit = relationship

A Midsummer Night's Dream — Play 6

Didst not thou lead him through the glimmering night
From Perigenia, whom he ravished,
20 And make him with fair Aegles break his faith,
With Ariadne, and Antiopa?
TITANIA. These are the forgeries of jealousy:
And never since the middle summer's spring
Met we on hill, in dale, forest, or mead,
25 By paved fountain or by rushy brook,
Or in the beached margent of the sea
To dance our ringlets to the whistling wind,
But with thy brawls thou hast disturb'd our sport.
Therefore the winds, piping to us in vain,
30 As in revenge have suck'd up from the sea
Contagious fogs; which, falling in the land,
Hath every pelting river made so proud
That they have overborne their continents.
The ox hath therefore stretch'd his yoke in vain,
35 The ploughman lost his sweat, and the green corn
Hath rotted ere his youth attain'd a beard.
The fold stands empty in the drowned field,
[…]
And thorough this distemperature we see
40 The seasons alter; hoary-headed frosts
Fall in the fresh lap of the crimson rose,
And on old Hiems' thin and icy crown
An odorous chaplet of sweet summer buds
Is, as in mockery, set. The spring, the summer,
45 The childing autumn, angry winter change
Their wonted liveries, and the mazed world
By their increase now knows not which is which.
And this same progeny of evils comes
From our debate, from our dissension.
50 We are their parents and original.
OBERON. Do you amend it, then: it lies in you.
Why should Titania cross her Oberon?
I do but beg a little changeling boy
To be my henchman.
TITANIA. Set your heart at rest.
55 The fairy land buys not the child of me.
His mother was a votress of my order,
And in the spiced Indian air by night
Full often hath she gossip'd by my side,
[…].
60 But she, being mortal, of that boy did die,
And for her sake do I rear up her boy;
And for her sake I will not part with him.
OBERON. How long within this wood intend you stay?
TITANIA. Perchance till after Theseus' wedding day.
65 If you will patiently dance in our round,
And see our moonlight revels, go with us:
If not, shun me, and I will spare your haunts.
OBERON. Give me that boy, and I will go with thee.
TITANIA. Not for thy fairy kingdom! Fairies, away.
70 We shall chide downright if I longer stay.
Exeunt TITANIA *and her train*
OBERON. Well, go thy way. Thou shalt not from this grove
Till I torment thee for this injury.

Annotations
l. 19 to **ravish** = to abduct and rape
l. 22 **forgeries** = lies
l. 23 **middle summer's spring** = beginning of midsummer
l. 24 **dale** = valley
mead = meadow, field
l. 25 **paved fountain** = spring surrounded by rocks
rushy = rushing, flowing
l. 26 **beached margent** = beach next to
l. 28 **brawls** = quarrels, arguing
sport = *here:* fun
l. 29 **piping** = calling
in vain = without response
l. 31 **contagious** = disease-carrying
l. 32 **pelting** = measly, inferior
proud = *here:* powerful
l. 33 **overborne their continents** = flooded over into the fields
l. 34 **the ox … in vain** = there was no point in ploughing the fields
l. 35 **lost his sweat** = wasted his efforts
l. 36 **ere … beard** = before it grew ripe
l. 37 **fold** = animal enclosure
l. 39 **distemperature** = disturbance
l. 40 to **alter** = to change
hoary-headed = bitter, extreme
l. 41 **fall in the fresh lap of** = descend upon
l. 42 **old Hiems** = a personification of winter and the cold
l. 43 **odorous chaplet** = scented decorative crown
l. 44 **as in mockery** = like some sort of prank
l. 45 **childing** = fruitful
l. 46 **wonted liveries** = usual uniforms
mazed = confused
l. 47 **by … which** = cannot use the produce that grows to know what season they are in
l. 48 **progeny of evils** = set of bad outcomes
l. 49 **dissension** = arguing
l. 50 **original** = *here:* origin
l. 51 **Do you amend it, then** = So are you going to fix it?
it lies in you = it is up to you
l. 52 to **cross** = to disobey
l. 54 **henchman** = assistant
set your heart at rest = calm down
l. 56 **votress** = priestess
l. 60 **of that boy** = when giving birth to that boy
l. 61 to **rear up** = to raise
l. 62 to **part with** = to be separated from
l. 64 **perchance** = maybe
l. 65 **dance in our round** = dance in a circle with us
l. 66 **moonlight revels** = midnight celebrations
l. 67 to **shun** = to stay away from
spare your haunts = keep out of your lands
l. 70 **chide downright** = fight for real
l. 72 **torment thee for this injury** = make you suffer for this behaviour

6 Play — A Midsummer Night's Dream

a) Tick (✓) the summary that fits best. Explain your choice.

☐ 1. Titania and Oberon blame each other for the havoc in the world of the mortals and fight over an Indian boy.
☐ 2. Titania and Oberon are jealous of each other and begrudge each other's happiness with the mortals.
☐ 3. Titania and Oberon accuse each other of feeling attracted to the mortals: Titania blames Oberon for loving Hippolyta. Oberon accuses Titania of showing an interest in Theseus. Titania then claims that her conflict with Oberon has changed the climate in the world of the mortals.

b) Describe what – according to Titania – has changed in nature as well as in the seasons.
c) Explain what reasons Titania gives why she will not hand over the Indian boy.

19

Titania hints at the disorder the world of the mortals is in. What did the Elizabethans think about disordered states? Read the information below to find out what the Elizabethans believed in. Explain how this relates to the situation in *A Midsummer Night's Dream*.

Info

The Elizabethan world picture

Most people believed that everything, from the lowest grain of sand to the highest angel, had its set position in a great hierarchy. This concept was called "the great chain of being". When things were in their proper place, harmony was the result. When order was violated, the entire structure was shaken. Any break in the chain, such as a marriage across social classes, was believed to result in chaos. Accordingly, marriage was usually arranged to bring wealth and prestige to the family – regardless of the feelings of the bride. In fact, women were quite powerless under the law.

Many Elizabethans were convinced that analogous relations existed in the universe and the political world. They believed, for example, that the king was as important to the state as the sun was to the sky. As the chosen representative of God on earth, the king had a supreme position. It was his responsibility to enforce and uphold the order in the world. Any violation of his position would destroy the perfect order of the universe and lead to intense problems, conflicts and chaos on earth. Therefore, any act of treachery against the king was considered to be a mortal sin against God and thus was punished severely.

The concept of microcosm and macrocosm rests upon the idea that there is a corresponding similarity between human beings and the universe: Man is seen as a smaller representation of the universe.

20

Analyse Titania and Oberon's relationship. Choose adjectives that best describe their relationship. Then give evidence from the text to explain your choice.

electric | emotional | gloomy | heady | heated | highly charged | hostile | lively | oppressive | passionate | …

21

Oberon tells Puck about his plan and sends him to get a magic flower. Read the following extract.

Extract 9 (Act II, Scene 1)

OBERON. […]
My gentle Puck, come hither. […]
Fetch me that flower, the herb I show'd thee once;
The juice of it on sleeping eyelids laid
5 Will make or man or woman madly dote
Upon the next live creature that it sees.
Fetch me this herb, and be thou here again
Ere the leviathan can swim a league.

Annotations
l. 2 **hither** = here
l. 4 **laid** = put on (passive)
ll. 5–6 to **dote upon** = to be in love with
l. 8 **ere … league** = as quick as you can

PUCK. I'll put a girdle round about the earth
10 In forty minutes!
    Exit
OBERON.   Having once this juice
I'll watch Titania when she is asleep,
And drop the liquor of it in her eyes:
The next thing then she, waking, looks upon –
Be it on lion, bear, or wolf, or bull,
15 On meddling monkey, or on busy ape –
She shall pursue it with the soul of love.
And ere I take this charm from off her sight –
As I can take it with another herb –
I'll make her render up her page to me.
20 But who comes here? I am invisible,
And I will overhear their conference.

Annotations
l. 9 **put a girdle round** = circle
l. 10 **having once** = once I have
l. 16 **pursue it with the soul of love** = fall in love with it
l. 19 **render her page** = give the boy
l. 21 **conference** = *here:* conversation

a) Describe Oberon's plan in your own words.
b) **Pair work** What does his plan reveal about his character? Share your view with a partner.
c) Create an additional scene after Puck has left, in which Oberon reflects his plan. Write Oberon's soliloquy. (You can find more information about soliloquies in the box on p. 127.)

22
Oberon is listening in on the conversation between Demetrius and Helena. Read the following extract.

Extract 10 (Act II, Scene 1)

DEMETRIUS. I love thee not, therefore pursue me not.
Where is Lysander and fair Hermia?
The one I'll slay, the other slayeth me.
Thou told'st me they were stol'n unto this wood,
5 And here am I, and wood within this wood
Because I cannot meet my Hermia.
Hence, get thee gone, and follow me no more.
HELENA. You draw me, you hard-hearted adamant!
But yet you draw not iron, for my heart
10 Is true as steel. Leave you your power to draw,
And I shall have no power to follow you.
DEMETRIUS. Do I entice you? Do I speak you fair?
Or rather do I not in plainest truth
Tell you I do not, nor I cannot love you?
15 HELENA. And even for that do I love you the more.
I am your spaniel; and, Demetrius,
The more you beat me I will fawn on you.
Use me but as your spaniel: spurn me, strike me,
Neglect me, lose me; only give me leave,
20 Unworthy as I am, to follow you.
What worser place can I beg in your love –
And yet a place of high respect with me –
Than to be used as you use your dog?
DEMETRIUS. Tempt not too much the hatred of my spirit;
25 For I am sick when I do look on thee.
HELENA. And I am sick when I look not on you.
DEMETRIUS. You do impeach your modesty too much,
To leave the city and commit yourself
Into the hands of one that loves you not;
30 To trust the opportunity of night,

Annotations
l. 1 to **pursue** = to follow
l. 3 **the one … slayeth me** = I will kill Lysander, but Hermia's beauty is killing me
l. 4 **were stol'n unto** = sneaked off to
l. 5 **wood within** = far in
l. 7 **get thee gone** = go away
l. 8 to **draw** = to attract
     adamant = magnet
l. 10 **leave … draw** = if you give up your powers to attract me
l. 12 **speak you fair** = speak kindly to you
l. 13 **in plainest truth** = very clearly
l. 16 **spaniel** = notoriously loyal dog breed
l. 17 to **fawn on** = to love
l. 18 **use me but as your spaniel** = treat me like a dog
     to **spurn** = to kick
l. 19 **give me leave** = allow me
l. 21 to **beg** = to ask for
     in your love = *here:* in your heart
l. 22 **and yet … with me** = but I would consider it an honour
l. 23 **used** = *here:* treated
l. 24 to **tempt** = to encourage
l. 27 **impeach your modesty** = call your modesty (chastity) into question

6 Play — A Midsummer Night's Dream

And the ill counsel of a desert place,
With the rich worth of your virginity.
HELENA. Your virtue is my privilege: for that
It is not night when I do see your face,
35 Therefore I think I am not in the night;
Nor doth this wood lack worlds of company,
For you, in my respect, are all the world.
Then how can it be said I am alone
When all the world is here to look on me?
40 **DEMETRIUS.** I'll run from thee and hide me in the brakes,
And leave thee to the mercy of wild beasts.
[…] I will not stay thy questions. Let me go;
Or if thou follow me, do not believe
But I shall do thee mischief in the wood.
45 **HELENA.** Ay, in the temple, in the town, the field,
You do me mischief. Fie, Demetrius,
Your wrongs do set a scandal on my sex!
We cannot fight for love, as men may do;
We should be woo'd, and were not made to woo.
    Exit DEMETRIUS
50 I'll follow thee, and make a heaven of hell,
To die upon the hand I love so well.
    Exit
OBERON. Fare thee well, nymph. Ere he do leave this grove
Thou shalt fly him, and he shall seek thy love.
    Enter PUCK
Hast thou the flower there? Welcome, wanderer.
55 **PUCK.** Ay, there it is.
OBERON.   I pray thee, give it me.
[…]
There sleeps Titania sometime of the night,
Lull'd in these flowers with dances and delight;
And there the snake throws her enamell'd skin,
60 Weed wide enough to wrap a fairy in;
And with the juice of this I'll streak her eyes,
And make her full of hateful fantasies.
Take thou some of it, and seek through this grove:
A sweet Athenian lady is in love
65 With a disdainful youth; anoint his eyes,
But do it when the next thing he espies
May be the lady. Thou shalt know the man
By the Athenian garments he hath on.
Effect it with some care, that he may prove
70 More fond on her than she upon her love.
And look thou meet me ere the first cock crow.
PUCK. Fear not, my lord; your servant shall do so.

Annotations
l. 31 **ill counsel** = bad ideas
    desert = deserted
l. 33 **your virtue is my privilege** = your good nature will protect me
l. 37 **in my respect** = to me
l. 40 **brakes** = bushes
l. 41 **beasts** = *here:* animals
l. 42 **to stay** = *here:* to stay and listen to
    thy questions = *here:* your arguments
l. 45 **ay** = just like, as
l. 46 **fie** = curse you
l. 47 **set a scandal on** = insult
    sex = *here:* gender, i.e. all women
l. 49 **to woo** = to pursue romantically
l. 52 **fare thee well** = goodbye
    grove = forest
l. 53 **to fly** = *here:* to run away from
l. 58 **lull'd** = soothed to sleep
l. 59 **to throw** = *here:* to shed
    enamell'd = shiny
l. 60 **weed wide enough** = a piece of clothing wide enough
l. 61 **to streak** = to wet
l. 62 **hateful** = *here:* pathetic
l. 63 **to seek through** = to search
l. 65 **disdainful youth** = rude boy
l. 69 **to effect** = *here:* to do
l. 71 **ere the first cock crow** = before dawn

a) Match the correct sentence halves.

1. Demetrius does not want
2. He is looking for
3. Helena compares herself to
4. Demetrius chides Helena
5. Helena persists in
6. Demetrius wants to
7. Helena is determined to

a) Hermia in the forest.
b) follow him.
c) wooing Demetrius.
d) Helena to follow him any further.
e) run off and leave Helena to the wild beasts.
f) a faithful spaniel.
g) for putting her reputation at risk.

1	
2	
3	
4	
5	
6	
7	

A Midsummer Night's Dream — Play 6

b) Analyse the atmosphere between Demetrius and Helena. Choose adjectives that best describe it, find evidence from the text, and interpret it.

> calm | desperate | emotional | hostile | intimate | romantic | stifling | strained | tense | …

c) Use your results from b) to write the analysis.
d) **Pair work** What are Demetrius and Helena thinking? Write thought bubbles for Demetrius and Helena and present them to the class.

23
Oberon has watched Demetrius and Helena and makes plans.
a) Sum up the plots Oberon has hatched for Titania and Helena.
b) Imagine you are a fortune-teller. Write Titania's or Helena's horoscope.

SCENE 2

24
While Titania is asleep, Oberon sprinkles Titania's eyes with the magic juice of his flower and leaves. Then Lysander and Hermia enter the stage. They have eloped into the forest and have got lost. Read the following extract.

Extract 11 (Act II, Scene 2)

LYSANDER. Fair love, you faint with wandering in the wood,
And, to speak truth, I have forgot our way.
We'll rest us, Hermia, if you think it good,
And tarry for the comfort of the day.
5 **HERMIA.** Be it so, Lysander; find you out a bed,
For I upon this bank will rest my head.
LYSANDER. One turf shall serve as pillow for us both;
One heart, one bed, two bosoms, and one troth.
HERMIA. Nay, good Lysander, for my sake, my dear,
10 Lie further off yet; do not lie so near.
LYSANDER. O take the sense, sweet, of my innocence!
Love takes the meaning in love's conference;
I mean that my heart unto yours is knit,
So that but one heart we can make of it:
15 Two bosoms interchained with an oath,
So then two bosoms and a single troth.
Then by your side no bed-room me deny,
For lying so, Hermia, I do not lie.
HERMIA. Lysander riddles very prettily.
20 Now much beshrew my manners and my pride
If Hermia meant to say Lysander lied.
But, gentle friend, for love and courtesy
Lie further off, in human modesty;
Such separation as may well be said
25 Becomes a virtuous bachelor and a maid,
So far be distant, and good night, sweet friend;
Thy love ne'er alter till thy sweet life end!
LYSANDER. Amen, amen, to that fair prayer say I,
And then end life when I end loyalty!
30 Here is my bed; sleep give thee all his rest.
HERMIA. With half that wish the wisher's eyes be press'd.
They sleep
Enter PUCK

Annotations
l. 1 to **faint** = to get weaker
l. 2 **I have forgot our way** = I am lost
l. 4 to **tarry** = to wait
l. 6 **bank** = small lump in ground
l. 7 **turf** = ground
l. 8 **bosoms** = *here:* bodies
troth = truth; vow, promise
l. 10 **off** = *here:* away
l. 11 **take … my innocence** = understand I meant it innocently
l. 12 **love … conference** = there is room for interpretation of what lovers say to one another
l. 13 **knit** = joined
l. 14 **but one** = only one
l. 15 **interchained** = joined
oath = vow, promise
l. 17 **no bed-room me deny** = let me sleep here
l. 19 to **riddle** = to play with words
prettily = *here:* cleverly
l. 20 **beshrew** = curse, a curse upon
l. 22 **for** = *here:* for the sake of
l. 25 **becomes** = it is suitable for them
maid = young girl
l. 26 **so far** = for now
l. 29 **end life … loyalty** = may I die should I ever be disloyal to you

141

6 Play — A Midsummer Night's Dream

PUCK. Through the forest have I gone,
But Athenian found I none
On whose eyes I might approve
35 This flower's force in stirring love.
Night and silence – Who is here?
Weeds of Athens he doth wear:
This is he my master said
Despised the Athenian maid;
40 And here the maiden, sleeping sound
On the dank and dirty ground.
Pretty soul, she durst not lie
Near this lack-love, this kill-courtesy.
Churl, upon thy eyes I throw
45 All the power this charm doth owe.
    He drops the juice on LYSANDER's *eyelids*
When thou wak'st let love forbid
Sleep his seat on thy eyelid.
So, awake when I am gone;
For I must now to Oberon.

Annotations
l. 34 **to approve** = to deem worthy
l. 36 **night and silence** = (*exclamation*) whoa!
l. 37 **weeds** = garments, clothing
l. 41 **dank** = moist
l. 43 **lack-love** = hard-hearted
    kill-courtesy = rude
l. 44 **churl** = villain
l. 45 **to owe** = *here:* to have, to possess
l. 46 **to forbid** = to prevent
l. 47 **sleep ... eyelid** = you falling asleep

a) Outline Hermia and Lysander's conversation.
b) Shakespeare is a master of word play. Identify the pun in ll. 13–21 and explain its meaning. In class, discuss why Shakespeare uses that word pun there.
c) Contrast Hermia and Lysander's attitude towards spending the night together in each other's company.
d) **Pair work** Partner A takes Lysander's role, Partner B takes Hermia's role. Write down their thoughts when they are falling asleep. Consider the following aspects:
- what has happened so far
- the feelings they have for one another
- the different attitudes towards spending the night together.

> **Info**
> ### Pun – A play on words
> A pun is the humorous use of a word that either has more than one meaning or sounds like another word with a different meaning.

25
Puck has wandered through the forest and has finally come across Lysander and Hermia.

a) Reread Puck's words and explain his thoughts.
b) Read the information about dramatic irony and examine how Shakespeare succeeds in creating suspense at this moment.
c) Discuss in class how you view Puck in this scene.
Is he ... mischievous, naive, serious, or well-intentioned?

> **Info**
> ### Dramatic irony
> This literary device is used when the audience knows more than the characters in the play, thus being able to foresee an outcome different to the characters' expectations.

26
While Helena is following Demetrius into the woods, she stumbles across Lysander. Read the following extract.

Extract 12 (Act II, Scene 2)

HELENA. [...] But who is here? – Lysander, on the ground?
Dead, or asleep? I see no blood, no wound.
Lysander, if you live, good sir, awake!
LYSANDER. (*Waking*) And run through fire I will for thy sweet sake!
5 Transparent Helena, nature shows art
That through thy bosom makes me see thy heart.
Where is Demetrius? O, how fit a word
Is that vile name to perish on my sword!

Annotations
l. 2 **wound** = injuries
l. 4 **and run ... sake** = I would run through fire for you
l. 5 **transparent** = *here:* beautiful
    art = *here:* magic

HELENA. Do not say so, Lysander, say not so.
10 What though he love your Hermia? Lord, what though?
Yet Hermia still loves you; then be content.
LYSANDER. Content with Hermia? No; I do repent
The tedious minutes I with her have spent.
Not Hermia, but Helena I love.
15 Who will not change a raven for a dove?
The will of man is by his reason sway'd,
And reason says you are the worthier maid.
Things growing are not ripe until their season;
So I, being young, till now ripe not to reason.
20 And touching now the point of human skill,
Reason becomes the marshal to my will.
And leads me to your eyes, where I o'erlook
Love's stories written in love's richest book.
HELENA. Wherefore was I to this keen mockery born?
25 When at your hands did I deserve this scorn?
Is't not enough, is't not enough, young man,
That I did never, no, nor never can
Deserve a sweet look from Demetrius' eye
But you must flout my insufficiency?
30 Good troth, you do me wrong, good sooth, you do,
In such disdainful manner me to woo!
But fare you well: perforce I must confess
I thought you lord of more true gentleness.
O, that a lady of one man refus'd
35 Should of another therefore be abus'd!
Exit
LYSANDER. She sees not Hermia. Hermia, sleep thou there,
And never mayst thou come Lysander near.
For, as a surfeit of the sweetest things
The deepest loathing to the stomach brings,
40 Or as the heresies that men do leave
Are hated most of those they did deceive,
So thou, my surfeit and my heresy,
Of all be hated, but the most of me!
And, all my powers, address your love and might
45 To honour Helen, and to be her knight.
Exit
HERMIA. (*Waking*) Help me, Lysander, help me! Do thy best
To pluck this crawling serpent from my breast!
Ay me, for pity! What a dream was here!
Lysander, look how I do quake with fear –
50 Methought a serpent ate my heart away,
And you sat smiling at his cruel prey.
Lysander! What, remov'd? Lysander, lord!
What, out of hearing? Gone? No sound, no word?
Alack, where are you? Speak and if you hear,
55 Speak, of all loves! I swoon almost with fear.
No? Then I well perceive you are not nigh.
Either death or you I'll find immediately.

Annotations
l. 10 **what though** = what does it matter
l. 12 to **repent** = to regret
l. 16 **will** = desires
    sway'd = controlled
l. 18 **things growing** = fruits and vegetables
l. 19 **ripe to reason** = be mature in judgement
l. 20 **touching** = *here:* reaching
    human skill = making good judgements
l. 21 **marshal** = director
l. 22 to **o'erlook** = to read over
l. 24 **wherefore** = why
    keen = cruel
    born = *here:* subjected to
l. 25 **when ... scorn** = what did I do to deserve this mockery
l. 28 **sweet** = *here:* loving
l. 29 to **flout** = to make fun of
    insufficiency = not being good enough
l. 30 **good troth** = honestly
    good sooth = really
l. 32 **perforce** = indeed
l. 33 **gentleness** = courtesy, kindness
l. 35 **abus'd** = mocked
l. 38 **surfeit** = excess
l. 39 **loathing** = *here:* sickness
l. 40 **heresies** = false beliefs
l. 43 **of** = *here:* by
l. 44 **might** = strength
l. 45 **knight** = loyal man
l. 47 to **pluck** = to remove
    serpent = snake
l. 48 **Ay me, for pity!** = Oh my goodness!
l. 49 to **quake** = to shake, to tremble
l. 50 **methought** = I thought
l. 52 **What, remov'd?** = Where have you gone?
l. 53 **What, out of hearing?** = Are you too far away to hear me?
l. 54 **alack** = alas
l. 55 to **swoon** = to faint
l. 56 to **perceive** = *here:* to guess
    nigh = nearby

a) Decide whether the statements below are right or wrong. Correct them if necessary.

Play — A Midsummer Night's Dream

	Statement	Right	Wrong	Correction
1.	Helena finds Lysander dead on the ground.			
2.	Lysander compares Helena to a raven.			
3.	Helena thinks that Lysander makes fun of her.			
4.	Lysander explains how his feelings for Hermia have changed.			
5.	After Hermia wakes up from a nightmare, she finds that Lysander is gone.			

b) Hermia wakes up from a nightmare. Describe the nightmare and interpret its meaning.

c) Discuss to what extent the dream reveals some subconscious fears of hers.

LOOKING BACK AT ACT II

27

a) Read the information about the world of the fairies. Then examine to what extent the fairy world mirrors the world of the mortals in the play. Consider the following aspects:
- characters
- conflicts
- power and control
- language

b) **Group work** Discuss how the fairy world and the world of the mortals reflect the Elizabethan world picture.

Info

The world of the fairies

Before Shakespeare's time, fairies were considered evil or mischievous spirits that made people's lives difficult. It was mainly a rural belief, but Elizabethan playgoers would know the stories about fairies: They played tricks on servants and old women, they stole things, they pinched maids and caused them to drop things, or they led travellers astray. For example, Puck, or Robin Goodfellow, is also a character in English folklore. Despite the many treatises about anti-superstition, the fairy world fascinated the Elizabethans, which is why many authors of the 16th and 17th centuries made use of the fairy world in their works – such as William Shakespeare, John Lyly and Edmund Spenser.

28

a) Study the quotations about Puck. Conclude what they tell the audience about him.

1 "I am that merry wanderer of the night."
(Puck, Act II, Scene 1)

2 "I jest to Oberon, and make him smile [...]."
(Puck, Act II, Scene 1)

3 "My gentle Puck, come hither. [...]"
(Oberon, Act II, Scene 1)

4 "Fear not, my lord; your servant shall do so."
(Puck, Act II, Scene 1)

5 "[...] you are that shrewd and knavish sprite Called Robin Goodfellow."
(Fairy, Act II, Scene 1)

6 "[...] Are not you he
That frights the maidens of the villagery,
Skim milk, and sometimes labour in the quern,
And bootless make the breathless housewife churn,
And sometime make the drink to bear no barm,
Mislead night-wanderers, laughing at their harm?"
(Fairy, Act II, Scene 1)

b) Analyse how Shakespeare refashions Puck's role.
c) Look at some photos of different actors playing the role of Puck. What do you think? Which portrayal captures him best? Explain your choice.

1

2

3

d) In class, discuss why Shakespeare makes use of the fairy world.

While reading: Act III

SCENE 1
29

While Titania is asleep, the craftsmen meet in the forest to talk about some staging problems and rehearse the play of *Pyramus and Thisbe*. Puck, who is watching, decides to play a prank on them: He puts a donkey's head on Bottom. Read the following extract.

Extract 13 (Act III, Scene 1)

Enter PUCK, *and* BOTTOM *with the ass head on*
BOTTOM. (*as Pyramus*) If I were fair, fair Thisbe, I were only thine.
QUINCE. O monstrous! O strange! We are haunted! Pray, masters, fly, masters! Help!
   Exeunt QUINCE, SNUG, FLUTE, SNOUT, *and* STARVELING
   […]
5 **BOTTOM.** Why do they run away? This is a knavery of them to make me afeard.
   Enter SNOUT
SNOUT. O Bottom, thou art changed. What do I see on thee?
BOTTOM. What do you see? You see an ass head of your own, do you?
   Exit SNOUT
   Enter QUINCE
QUINCE. Bless thee, Bottom, bless thee! Thou art translated!
   Exit
10 **BOTTOM.** I see their knavery. This is to make an ass of me, to fright me, if they could; but I will not stir from this place, do what they can. I will walk up and down here, and I will sing, that they shall hear I am not afraid.

Annotations
l. 1 **fair** = handsome
      I were = I would be
l. 2 **monstrous** = *here:* a monster
      to **fly** = *here:* to run away
l. 5 **knavery** = trick, practical joke
l. 6 **afeard** = scared, afraid
l. 7 **on thee** = on your head
l. 8 **ass** = donkey
l. 9 **translated** = transformed

6   Play   A Midsummer Night's Dream

(*Sings*) The ousel cock so black of hue,
15   With orange-tawny bill,
    The throstle with his note so true,
    The wren with little quill –
TITANIA. (*Waking*) What angel wakes me from my flowery bed?
BOTTOM. (*Sings*) The finch, the sparrow, and the lark,
20   The plainsong cuckoo grey,
    Whose note full many a man doth mark
    And dares not answer nay –
for indeed, who would set his wit to so foolish a bird? Who would give a
bird the lie, though he cry 'cuckoo' never so?
25 **TITANIA.** I pray thee, gentle mortal, sing again;
    Mine ear is much enamour'd of thy note.
    So is mine eye enthralled to thy shape,
    And thy fair virtue's force perforce doth move me
    On the first view to say, to swear, I love thee.
30 **BOTTOM.** Methinks, mistress, you should have little reason for that.
And yet, to say the truth, reason and love keep little company together
nowadays; the more the pity that some honest neighbours will not make
them friends. Nay, I can gleek upon occasion.
TITANIA. Thou art as wise as thou art beautiful.
35 **BOTTOM.** Not so neither; but if I had wit enough to get out of this wood,
I have enough to serve mine own turn.
TITANIA. Out of this wood do not desire to go:
Thou shalt remain here, whether thou wilt or no.
I am a spirit of no common rate;
40   The summer still doth tend upon my state,
    And I do love thee. Therefore go with me.
    I'll give thee fairies to attend on thee,
    And they shall fetch thee jewels from the deep,
    And sing, while thou on pressed flowers dost sleep;
45 And I will purge thy mortal grossness so
    That thou shalt like an airy spirit go.
    Peaseblossom, Cobweb, Moth, and Mustardseed!
      Enter four FAIRIES

Annotations
l. 14 **ousel cock** = male blackbird
     hue = colour
l. 15 **tawny** = tan-coloured
     bill = beak
l. 16 **throstle** = *Drossel*
     note so true = beautiful singing voice
l. 17 **wren** = *Zaunkönig*
     quill = high-pitched voice
l. 20 **plainsong** = song that never changes
l. 21 **many a man doth mark** = heard by many men
l. 23 **set his wit to** = argue with
ll. 23–24 **give a lie** = say it was lying
l. 25 **gentle mortal** = noble human
l. 27 **shape** = *here*: looks, appearance
l. 28 **thy fair virtue's force** = the power of your beauty
     perforce = indeed
     to move = *here*: to cause
l. 31 **keep little company together** = have no link
l. 32 **the more the pity** = it is a shame
l. 33 **to gleek** = to tell a joke
l. 35 **not so neither** = also untrue
     to have wit = to be smart
l. 36 **turn** = *here*: needs
l. 39 **no common rate** = no ordinary rank
l. 40 **tend upon my state** = serve me
l. 42 **to attend on** = to serve
l. 45 **to purge** = *here*: to remove
     mortal grossness = human body
l. 46 **airy** = light

a) Explain the situation Bottom finds himself in.
b) Is this a funny or sad scene? Discuss this question in class.

30
a) While the craftsmen rehearse their play, Titania is sleeping on stage. If you were the director, where would you make her sleep on stage? Give reasons for your answer.
b) Titania is woken up by Bottom's singing. Describe Titania's reaction.
c) Examine how reason and love are presented in this extract.

31
a) Describe how Bottom reacts to Titania. Is he … intimidated, flattered, surprised, baffled, or courteous? Explain your choice.
b) Write Bottom's inner monologue after he has met Titania and the fairies.

SCENE 2
32
Puck informs Oberon of his successful deeds. Read the following extract.

A Midsummer Night's Dream — Play

Extract 14 (Act III, Scene 2)

PUCK. [...] When in that moment, so it came to pass,
Titania wak'd, and straightway loved an ass.
OBERON. This falls out better than I could devise.
But hast thou yet latch'd the Athenian's eyes
5 With the love juice, as I did bid thee do?
PUCK. I took him sleeping – that is finished too –
And the Athenian woman by his side,
That when he wak'd, of force she must be ey'd.
    Enter DEMETRIUS and HERMIA
OBERON. Stand close: this is the same Athenian.
10 **PUCK.** This is the woman, but not this the man.
DEMETRIUS. O, why rebuke you him that loves you so?
Lay breath so bitter on your bitter foe.
HERMIA. Now I but chide; but I should use thee worse,
For thou, I fear, hast given me cause to curse.
15 If thou hast slain Lysander in his sleep,
Being o'er shoes in blood, plunge in the deep,
And kill me too.
The sun was not so true unto the day
As he to me. Would he have stol'n away
20 From sleeping Hermia? I'll believe as soon
This whole earth may be bor'd, and that the moon
May through the centre creep, and so displease
Her brother's noontide with th'Antipodes.
It cannot be but thou hast murder'd him:
25 So should a murderer look; so dead, so grim.
DEMETRIUS. So should the murder'd look, and so should I,
Pierc'd through the heart with your stern cruelty;
Yet you, the murderer, look as bright, as clear,
As yonder Venus in her glimmering sphere.
30 **HERMIA.** What's this to my Lysander? Where is he?
Ah, good Demetrius, wilt thou give him me?
DEMETRIUS. I had rather give his carcass to my hounds.
HERMIA. Out, dog! Out, cur! Thou driv'st me past the bounds
Of maiden's patience. Hast thou slain him then?
35 Henceforth be never number'd among men.
O, once tell true; tell true, even for my sake:
Durst thou have look'd upon him being awake?
And hast thou kill'd him sleeping? O, brave touch!
Could not a worm, an adder do so much?
40 An adder did it; for with doubler tongue
Than thine, thou serpent, never adder stung.
DEMETRIUS. You spend your passion on a mispris'd mood.
I am not guilty of Lysander's blood,
Nor is he dead, for aught that I can tell.
45 **HERMIA.** I pray thee, tell me then that he is well.
DEMETRIUS. And if I could, what should I get therefor?
HERMIA. A privilege, never to see me more;
And from thy hated presence part I so.
See me no more, whether he be dead or no.
    Exit
50 **DEMETRIUS.** There is no following her in this fierce vein;
Here therefore for a while I will remain. [...]
    He lies down and sleeps

Annotations

- l. 1 **to come to pass** = to happen
- l. 3 **this ... devise** = this turned out better than I could have hoped
- l. 4 **latch'd** = captured
- l. 5 **to bid** = to instruct
- l. 8 **of force** = certainly
  - **ey'd** = seen
- l. 11 **to rebuke** = to be cruel to
- l. 12 **breath** = *here*: words
  - **bitter foe** = worst enemy
- l. 13 **to chide** = to scold
- l. 15 **slain** = killed
- l. 16 **o'er shoes in blood** = knee-deep in blood (i.e. guilty)
  - **plunge in the deep** = go all the way
- ll. 18–19 **the sun ... to me** = he is more faithful to me than the sun is to the daytime
- l. 19 **stol'n** = sneaked
- l. 21 **bor'd** = *durchbohrt*
- l. 23 **her brother** = reference to the sun
  - **with th'Antipodes** = at the other side of the planet
- l. 27 **stern** = harsh
- l. 29 **yonder** = over there
  - **Venus** = reference to the evening star and the goddess of love
  - **sphere** = orbit
- l. 30 **what's this to** = what does this have to do with
- l. 32 **carcass** = dead body
- l. 33 **cur** = dog
  - **past the bounds** = too far
- l. 35 **number'd among** = counted as
- l. 37 **durst** = dare
- l. 39 **worm** = *here*: snake
- ll. 40–41 **for with ... stung** = for there has never been such a fork-tongued snake as you
- l. 42 **to spend passion** = to waste energy
  - **mispris'd mood** = misunderstanding
- l. 43 **blood** = *here*: murder
- l. 46 **therefor** = for it
- l. 50 **in this fierce vein** = when she is this angry

6 Play — A Midsummer Night's Dream

OBERON. What hast thou done? Thou hast mistaken quite,
And laid the love juice on some true love's sight.
Of thy misprision must perforce ensue
55 Some true love turn'd, and not a false turn'd true.
PUCK. Then fate o'errules, that, one man holding troth,
A million fail, confounding oath on oath.
OBERON. About the wood go swifter than the wind,
And Helena of Athens look thou find.
60 All fancy-sick she is and pale of cheer
With sighs of love, that costs the fresh blood dear.
By some illusion see thou bring her here;
I'll charm his eyes against she do appear.
PUCK. I go, I go, look how I go!
65 Swifter than arrow from the Tartar's bow.
    Exit

Annotations
l. 52 **mistaken quite** = made a big mistake
l. 53 **on some true love's sight** = on someone who is really in love
l. 54 **of thy** = because of your
     misprision = error, mistake
     to **ensue** = consequently happen
l. 56 **o'errules** = *here:* ensures
     holding troth = remaining faithful
l. 57 **confounding oath on oath** = making many promises to many lovers
l. 58 **swifter** = faster
l. 60 **fancy-sick** = heartbroken
     cheer = *here:* complexion
l. 63 **against** = *here:* ready for when
l. 65 **Tartar** = The Tartars (from central Asia) were skilled archers.

a) Decide whether the statements below are right or wrong. Give evidence or correct them if necessary.

	Statement	Right	Wrong	Evidence / Correction
1.	Puck has used the magic spell on the right couple.			
2.	Hermia thinks that Demetrius has killed Lysander.			
3.	Demetrius has fed Lysander to his dogs.			
4.	According to Demetrius, Hermia is mistaken in her belief that he has killed Lysander.			
5.	Hermia wants to see Demetrius again if he tells her where to find Lysander.			

b) Analyse how the language Hermia uses reflects her state of mind.
c) Describe Oberon's reaction. Is he angry or amused?
d) Reread ll. 52–55. Explain what Oberon means when he says these lines.

33
While Demetrius is asleep, Oberon sprinkles his eyes with the magic juice of the flower. Then the other young Athenians arrive one by one and start to quarrel. This is a rather long scene, full of emotions and with a lot of back and forth. Read the following extract.

Extract 15 (Act III, Scene 2)

LYSANDER. Why should you think that I should woo in scorn?
Scorn and derision never come in tears.
Look when I vow, I weep; and vows so born,
In their nativity all truth appears.
5 How can these things in me seem scorn to you,
Bearing the badge of faith to prove them true?
HELENA. You do advance your cunning more and more.
When truth kills truth, O devilish-holy fray!
    […]

Annotations
l. 1 to **woo** = to pursue romantically
    in scorn = as a cruel joke
l. 2 **derision** = mockery
    in tears = with tears
l. 3 to **vow** = to swear love to
l. 4 **nativity** = origin
l. 7 **advance your cunning** = get sneakier and sneakier
l. 8 **truth kills truth** = one true love kills another true love
    O devilish-holy fray! = What a fight it will be!

DEMETRIUS. (*Waking*)
10 O Helen, goddess, nymph, perfect, divine!
   To what, my love, shall I compare thine eyne?
   Crystal is muddy! O, how ripe in show
   Thy lips, those kissing cherries, tempting grow!
   […]   O, let me kiss
15 This princess of pure white, this seal of bliss!
   HELENA. O spite! O hell! I see you all are bent
   To set against me for your merriment.
   If you were civil, and knew courtesy,
   You would not do me thus much injury.
20 Can you not hate me, as I know you do,
   But you must join in souls to mock me too?
   If you were men, as men you are in show,
   You would not use a gentle lady so,
   To vow, and swear, and superpraise my parts,
25 When I am sure you hate me with your hearts.
   You both are rivals, and love Hermia;
   And now both rivals to mock Helena.
   A trim exploit, a manly enterprise,
   To conjure tears up in a poor maid's eyes
30 With your derision! None of noble sort
   Would so offend a virgin, and extort
   A poor soul's patience, all to make you sport.
   LYSANDER. You are unkind, Demetrius: be not so,
   For you love Hermia – this you know I know –
35 And here with all good will, with all my heart,
   In Hermia's love I yield you up my part;
   And yours of Helena to me bequeath,
   Whom I do love, and will do till my death.
   HELENA. Never did mockers waste more idle breath.
40 **DEMETRIUS.** Lysander, keep thy Hermia; I will none.
   If e'er I lov'd her, all that love is gone.
   My heart to her but as guest-wise sojourn'd,
   And now to Helen is it home return'd,
   There to remain.
   LYSANDER.   Helen, it is not so. […]
      Enter HERMIA
45 **HERMIA.** Dark night, that from the eye his function takes,
   The ear more quick of apprehension makes;
   Wherein it doth impair the seeing sense
   It pays the hearing double recompense.
   Thou art not by mine eye, Lysander, found;
50 Mine ear, I thank it, brought me to thy sound.
   But why unkindly didst thou leave me so?
   LYSANDER. Why should he stay whom love doth press to go?
   HERMIA. What love could press Lysander from my side?
   LYSANDER. Lysander's love, that would not let him bide,
55 Fair Helena – who more engilds the night
   Than all yon fiery oes and eyes of light.
   (*To Hermia*) Why seek'st thou me? Could not this make thee know
   The hate I bare thee made me leave thee so?
   HERMIA. You speak not as you think; it cannot be.
60 **HELENA.** Lo, she is one of this confederacy!
   Now I perceive they have conjoin'd all three
   To fashion this false sport in spite of me.

Annotations
l. 11 **eyne** = eyes
l. 12 **muddy** = unclear (in comparison)
      in show = in appearance
l. 15 **seal of bliss** = happiness if he were to marry her
l. 16 **you all are bent** = you have all decided
l. 17 **merriment** = amusement
l. 21 **in souls** = all together
l. 22 **as you are in show** = as you pretend to be
l. 23 **to use** = *here:* to treat
l. 24 **to superpraise** = to praise over the top
      my parts = my appearance
l. 28 **trim exploit** = impressive achievement
      manly enterprise = a manly thing to do
l. 29 **to conjure tears up** = to make cry
l. 30 **derision** = mockery
      of noble sort = noble people
l. 31 **virgin** = *here:* innocent girl
      to extort = to manipulate
l. 32 **make you sport** = entertain you
l. 36 **yield ... my part** = give over
l. 37 **to bequeath** = *here:* to give
l. 39 **mockers** = bullies
      waste idle breath = waste their effort
l. 40 **I will none** = I don't want her
l. 42 **but as guest-wise sojourn'd** = was only visiting her as a guest
l. 47 **to impair** = to block
l. 48 **pays ... double recompense** = makes ... twice as good
l. 52 **Why ... go?** = Why should I stay when love told me to go?
l. 53 **to press** = *here:* to take
      from my side = away from me
l. 54 **to bide** = to stay, to wait
l. 55 **to engild** = to light up
l. 56 **yon fiery ... light** = the stars
l. 57 **make thee know** = show you
l. 58 **I bare thee** = I have for you
l. 59 **you speak not as you think** = you don't mean what you are saying
l. 60 **confederacy** = *here:* group mocking Helena
l. 61 **conjoin'd** = joined together
l. 62 **to fashion** = to create
      false sport = game of lies
      in spite of = in scorn of

6 Play — A Midsummer Night's Dream

Injurious Hermia, most ungrateful maid,
Have you conspir'd, have you with these contriv'd
65 To bait me with this foul derision?
Is all the counsel that we two have shar'd,
The sisters' vows, the hours that we have spent
When we have chid the hasty-footed time
For parting us – O, is all forgot?
70 All schooldays' friendship, childhood innocence?
[…] And will you rent our ancient love asunder,
To join with men in scorning your poor friend?
It is not friendly, 'tis not maidenly.
Our sex, as well as I, may chide you for it,
75 Though I alone do feel the injury.
HERMIA. I am amazed at your passionate words.
I scorn you not; it seems that you scorn me.
HELENA. Have you not set Lysander, as in scorn,
To follow me, and praise my eyes and face?
80 And made your other love, Demetrius,
Who even but now did spurn me with his foot,
To call me goddess, nymph, divine and rare,
Precious, celestial? Wherefore speaks he this
To her he hates? And wherefore doth Lysander
85 Deny your love, so rich within his soul,
And tender me, forsooth, affection,
But by your setting on, by your consent?
What though I be not so in grace as you,
So hung upon with love, so fortunate,
90 But miserable most, to love unlov'd:
This you should pity rather than despise.
HERMIA. I understand not what you mean by this.
[…]
LYSANDER. Stay, gentle Helena: hear my excuse,
95 My love, my life, my soul, fair Helena!
HELENA. O, excellent!
HERMIA. (*To Lysander*) Sweet, do not scorn her so.
DEMETRIUS. If she cannot entreat, I can compel.
LYSANDER. Thou canst compel no more than she entreat;
Thy threats have no more strength than her weak prayers.
100 Helen, I love thee, by my life, I do:
I swear by that which I will lose for thee
To prove him false that says I love thee not.
DEMETRIUS. I say I love thee more than he can do.
LYSANDER. If thou say so, withdraw, and prove it too.
105 **DEMETRIUS.** Quick, come.
HERMIA. Lysander, whereto tends all this?
LYSANDER. Away, you Ethiop!
DEMETRIUS. No, no, sir,
Seem to break loose, take on as you would follow,
But yet come not. You are a tame man, go.
LYSANDER. Hang off, thou cat, thou burr! Vile thing, let loose,
110 Or I will shake thee from me like a serpent.
HERMIA. Why are you grown so rude? What change is this,
Sweet love?
LYSANDER. Thy love? – out, tawny Tartar, out;
Out, loath'd medicine! O hated potion, hence!
HERMIA. Do you not jest?

Annotations
l. 63 **injurious** = hurtful
l. 64 **contriv'd** = schemed
l. 65 to **bait** = to torment
       foul = awful
l. 66 **counsel** = secret conversations
l. 67 **sisters' vows** = promises to each other
l. 68 **chid** = cursed
       hasty-footed time = quickness of time
l. 71 to **rent asunder** = to tear apart
l. 73 **maidenly** = ladylike
l. 74 **sex** = *here:* gender
l. 78 to **set** = *here:* to instruct
l. 81 to **spurn** = to kick
l. 83 **wherefore** = why
l. 85 **your love** = *here:* his love for you
l. 86 to **tender** = to offer
       forsooth = indeed
l. 87 **but by … consent** = unless you told him to
l. 88 **in grace** = lucky
l. 89 **hung upon with love** = loved
l. 94 **hear my excuse** = let me explain
l. 96 **sweet** = my love
l. 97 **If she cannot entreat, I can compel.** = If she can't make you stop, I will.
l. 98 **thou … entreat** = you can't force me to stop anymore than she can beg me to
l. 99 **prayers** = *here:* begging
l. 104 **withdraw** = get out your sword
l. 105 **whereto … this** = What does all this mean?
l. 106 **Ethiop** = blackamoor *(racist)*
l. 107 to **seem** = *here:* to pretend
       to **take on** = to act like
l. 108 **tame man** = coward
l. 109 **hang off** = let go
       burr = *Klette*
l. 112 **out** = *here:* go away
       tawny = dark-skinned
       Tartar = person from the Tartar region
l. 113 **loath'd medicine** = disgusting poison
l. 114 to **jest** = to joke

A Midsummer Night's Dream — Play 6

HELENA. Yes, sooth, and so do you.
115 **LYSANDER.** Demetrius, I will keep my word with thee.
DEMETRIUS. I would I had your bond, for I perceive
A weak bond holds you. I'll not trust your word.
LYSANDER. What? Should I hurt her, strike her, kill her dead?
Although I hate her, I'll not harm her so.
120 **HERMIA.** What? Can you do me greater harm than hate?
Hate me? Wherefore? O me, what news, my love?
Am not I Hermia? Are not you Lysander?
I am as fair now as I was erewhile.
Since night you loved me; yet since night you left me.
125 Why then, you left me – O, the gods forbid! –
In earnest, shall I say?
LYSANDER. Ay, by my life;
And never did desire to see thee more.
Therefore be out of hope, of question, of doubt;
Be certain, nothing truer – 'tis no jest
130 That I do hate thee and love Helena.
HERMIA. (*To Helena*) O me, you juggler, you canker-blossom,
You thief of love! What, have you come by night
And stol'n my love's heart from him?
HELENA. Fine, i'faith!
Have you no modesty, no maiden shame,
135 No touch of bashfulness? What, will you tear
Impatient answers from my gentle tongue?
Fie, fie, you counterfeit, you puppet, you!
[...]

Annotations
l. 114 **sooth** = of course
l. 116 **bond** = *here:* written promise
l. 117 **bond** = *here:* the grasp of Hermia's arms
l. 118 **to strike** = to hit
l. 121 **O me** = poor me
what news = what is going on
l. 123 **erewhile** = before
l. 126 **in earnest** = actually
l. 129 **'tis** = it's
l. 131 **juggler** = trickster
canker-blossom = worm-eaten flower
l. 134 **maiden shame** = decency
l. 135 **bashfulness** = shame, embarrassment
l. 137 **fie** = damn you
counterfeit = *here:* liar

Put the sentences below into the correct order and give line references.

No.	Contents	References
	Hermia wants to know from Lysander why he has left her alone in the forest.	
	The young men take turns in expressing their love to Helena, leaving Hermia completely baffled.	
	Demetrius attempts to woo Helena by praising her beauty.	
	Hermia turns against Helena and accuses her of plotting against her.	
	Helena recounts the change of moods of the young men.	
	Demetrius's love for Hermia was only short-termed.	
	Helena thinks that Hermia has conspired with Lysander and Demetrius against her and reminds Hermia of their happy childhood.	
	Lysander wants to give way for Demetrius's love to Hermia.	
	Helena despises the young men as she thinks they both make fun of her.	
1	Helena thinks that Lysander mocks her in his wooing.	ll. 7-8

6 Play — A Midsummer Night's Dream

34
Describe the overall atmosphere of this scene.
Choose adjectives that you find the most appropriate.

> heady | sad | confusing | explosive | …

35
Read the information about stichomythia. Identify examples of stichomythia in ll. 94–119 and analyse the effect on the audience.

> **Info**
>
> ### Stichomythia
>
> Stichomythia is a dialogue of rapidly alternating lines, a device often used in a play when two characters have a vigorous exchange of words or when the emotional intensity of a scene is emphasized. Characters may take turns stating antithetical opinions, take up the other character's words or use puns on them.

36
Use your results from tasks 33–35 to write an analysis of how the language Shakespeare uses contributes to the atmosphere in this scene.

37
After the four young Athenians have left, Oberon and Puck come forward. Read the following extract.

Extract 16 (Act III, Scene 2)

OBERON. This is thy negligence. Still thou mistak'st,
Or else committ'st thy knaveries wilfully.
PUCK. Believe me, King of Shadows, I mistook.
Did not you tell me I should know the man
5 By the Athenian garments he had on?
And so far blameless proves my enterprise
That I have 'nointed an Athenian's eyes;
And so far am I glad it so did sort,
As this their jangling I esteem a sport.
10 **OBERON.** Thou seest these lovers seek a place to fight:
Hie therefore, Robin, overcast the night;
The starry welkin cover thou anon
With drooping fog as black as Acheron,
And lead these testy rivals so astray
15 As one come not within another's way.
Like to Lysander sometime frame thy tongue,
Then stir Demetrius up with bitter wrong,
And sometime rail thou like Demetrius;
And from each other look thou lead them thus,
20 Till o'er their brows death-counterfeiting sleep
With leaden legs and batty wings doth creep.
Then crush this herb into Lysander's eye,
Whose liquor hath this virtuous property,
To take from thence all error with his might,
25 And make his eyeballs roll with wonted sight.
When they next wake, all this derision
Shall seem a dream and fruitless vision,
And back to Athens shall the lovers wend
With league whose date till death shall never end.
30 Whiles I in this affair do thee employ
I'll to my queen and beg her Indian boy;
And then I will her charmed eye release
From monster's view, and all things shall be peace.
[…]

Annotations
l. 1 **negligence** = fault
still = *here:* continually, always
l. 2 **knavery** = trick, practical joke
willfully = on purpose
l. 6 **blameless … enterprise** = I can't be blamed for what I did
l. 7 **'nointed** = *here:* put love juice in
l. 8 to **sort** = to turn out that way
l. 9 **jangling** = arguing
to **esteem** = to find, to see as
sport = *here:* fun
l. 11 to **hie** = to go quickly
to **overcast** = to make cloudy
l. 12 **welkin** = sky
anon = at once
l. 13 **drooping** = heavy
Acheron = black river in the underworld
l. 14 **testy** = angry
to **lead astray** = to make sb get lost
l. 16 **frame thy tongue** = imitate
l. 17 to **stir up** = to taunt, to provoke
bitter wrong = false accusation
l. 18 to **rail** = to insult
l. 19 **from each other look** = away from each other
l. 20 **death-counterfeiting sleep** = really deep sleep
l. 21 **batty** = bat-like (i.e. silent)
l. 23 **virtuous property** = healing power
l. 25 **eyeballs roll with wonted sight** = see as he used to
l. 26 **derision** = mockery
l. 27 **fruitless** = insignificant
l. 28 to **wend** = to go
l. 29 **league** = union
l. 30 **affair** = task
l. 31 **to** = *here:* go to
to **beg** = to ask for
l. 32 **her charmed eye release** = reverse the spell
l. 33 **from monster's view** = from loving Bottom

A Midsummer Night's Dream — Play 6

35 **PUCK.** On the ground sleep sound.
　　I'll apply to your eye,
　　Gentle lover, remedy.
　　He drops the juice on LYSANDER's *eyelids*
　　When thou wak'st, thou tak'st
　　True delight in the sight
40　Of thy former lady's eye;
　　And the country proverb known,
　　That every man should take his own,
　　In your waking shall be shown.
　　Jack shall have Jill,
45　Naught shall go ill:
　The man shall have his mare again, and all shall be well.
　　Exit PUCK; *the lovers remain on stage, asleep*

Annotations
l. 41 **proverb** = *Sprichwort*
l. 44 **Jack shall have Jill** = the man will get the woman he wants
l. 45 **naught** = nothing
l. 46 **mare** = female horse

a) Explain how Puck justifies his actions in front of Oberon.
b) Compare Puck's attitude towards his deeds with your impressions of him from what you have read so far.
c) Describe the contents of the plan Oberon wants Puck to carry out.

LOOKING BACK AT ACT III

38

a) Read the information about the use of language in Shakespeare's day.

Info

The use of second-person pronouns in Shakespeare's time

In modern-day English the pronouns 'you' and 'your' may refer to one person or several people. However, in Shakespeare's time the use of the pronouns 'thou', 'thee', 'thy' and 'thine' was very common alongside 'you' and 'your' – and people were very sensitive to the different implications these pronouns had.
- 'Thou' might be friendly and familiar, but it could also show contempt for someone socially inferior and even express an insult.
- 'You' was used for a polite, more formal, respectful or distant form of address.

Depending on the social context, speakers would switch from one pronoun to the other. A character in a play might switch from one register to the other to express a change of mood or attitude towards another character.

---

b) Identify the second-person pronouns that the four young lovers use in extract 15 when the characters address each other. Explain what feelings the use of the pronouns reveal. The words and phrases from the box below might help you.

Language support

(to) show contempt / hatred / anger for sb | (to) look down on sb | (to) scorn sb | (to) mock sb | (to) loathe sb | (to) abhor sth | (to) express one's aggression towards | (to) treat sb harshly / respectfully / leniently | (to) accuse sb of sth | (to) chide sb for sth | (to) be bewildered and confused | (to) be honest with sb | (to) dote on sb | (to) be head over heels in love with sb | (to) create intimacy with sb | …

c) **Group work (4)** Dramatic reading: Take parts as Helena, Hermia, Demetrius and Lysander and read out extract 15. Try to emphasize the characters' use of second-person pronouns to express their feelings for each other. Present your dialogue to the class.

6 Play — A Midsummer Night's Dream

While reading: Act IV

SCENE 1

39

Titania and the fairies are attending to Bottom. Read the following extract.

Extract 17 (Act IV, Scene 1)

TITANIA. What, wilt thou hear some music, my sweet love?
BOTTOM. I have a reasonable good ear in music. Let's have the tongs and the bones.
TITANIA. Or say, sweet love, what thou desir'st to eat.
5 **BOTTOM.** Truly, a peck of provender, I could munch your good dry oats. Methinks I have a great desire to a bottle of hay. Good hay, sweet hay, hath no fellow.
TITANIA. I have a venturous fairy that shall seek
The squirrel's hoard, and fetch thee new nuts.
10 **BOTTOM.** I had rather have a handful or two of dried peas. But, I pray you, let none of your people stir me; I have an exposition of sleep come upon me.
TITANIA. Sleep thou, and I will wind thee in my arms.
Fairies, be gone, and be all ways away.
   Exeunt FAIRIES
15 So doth the woodbine the sweet honeysuckle
Gently entwist; the female ivy so
Enrings the barky fingers of the elm.
O, how I love thee! How I dote on thee!
   They sleep
   Enter PUCK
OBERON. (*Coming forward*)
Welcome, good Robin. Seest thou this sweet sight?
20 Her dotage now I do begin to pity;
For, meeting her of late behind the wood
Seeking sweet favours for this hateful fool,
I did upbraid her and fall out with her,
For she his hairy temples then had rounded
25 With a coronet of fresh and fragrant flowers;
And that same dew, which sometime on the buds
Was wont to swell like round and orient pearls,
Stood now within the pretty flowerets' eyes
Like tears that did their own disgrace bewail.
30 When I had at my pleasure taunted her,
And she in mild terms begg'd my patience,
I then did ask of her her changeling child,
Which straight she gave me, and her fairy sent
To bear him to my bower in Fairyland.
35 And now I have the boy, I will undo
This hateful imperfection of her eyes.
And, gentle Puck, take this transformed scalp
From off the head of this Athenian swain,
That, he awaking when the other do,
40 May all to Athens back again repair,
And think no more of this night's accidents
But as the fierce vexation of a dream.
But first I will release the fairy queen.
   He drops the juice on TITANIA's *eyelids*

Annotations
l. 2 **reasonable** = quite
tongs = triangle (instrument)
l. 3 **bones** = sticks hit together for percussion
l. 5 **peck** = bundle
provender = animal feed
to munch = to eat
l. 6 **bottle** = *here:* small bundle
l. 7 **hath no fellow** = nothing is as good as it
l. 8 **venturous** = adventurous
l. 9 **hoard** = pile of food
to fetch = to get
ll. 10–11 **I pray you** = please
l. 11 **to stir** = to disturb
exposition = Here Bottom means 'disposition, or desire to'.
l. 13 **wind ... in my arms** = cuddle
l. 15 **woodbine** = a climbing plant
honeysuckle = a climbing plant
l. 16 **to entwist** = to wrap around
l. 17 **to enring** = to curl around
barky fingers = branches
elm = *Ulme*
l. 18 **to dote on** = to love very much
l. 20 **dotage** = obsessive love
l. 21 **meeting her of late** = having met her recently
l. 22 **sweet favours** = pretty flowers
hateful = intolerable
l. 23 **to upbraid** = to scold
to fall out = to have an argument or disagreement
l. 24 **temple** = *Schläfe*
to round = to circle, to put around
l. 25 **coronet** = crown
l. 26 **sometime** = *here:* formerly
bud = *Knospe*
l. 27 **was wont ... pearls** = decorated like shining pearls
l. 28 **floweret** = small flower
l. 29 **disgrace** = source of shame
to bewail = to express great sadness
l. 30 **to taunt** = to provoke with insulting remarks
l. 31 **in mild terms** = gently
l. 33 **straight** = immediately
l. 34 **to bear** = to carry, to take
bower = chambers
l. 36 **hateful imperfection** = bad spell
l. 37 **transformed scalp** = (Bottom's) changed head
l. 38 **swain** = common man
l. 39 **other** = *here:* others
l. 40 **to repair** = to return
l. 41 **accidents** = *here:* strange events
l. 42 **the fierce vexation of a dream** = *here:* a nightmare

A Midsummer Night's Dream — Play 6

Be as thou wast wont to be;
45　See as thou wast wont to see.
　　Dian's bud o'er Cupid's flower
　　Hath such force and blessed power.
Now, my Titania, wake you, my sweet queen!
TITANIA. (*Starting up*) My Oberon, what visions have I seen!
50　Methought I was enamour'd of an ass.
OBERON. There lies your love.
TITANIA.　　　　　　How came these things to pass?
O, how mine eyes do loathe his visage now!
OBERON. Silence awhile: Robin, take off this head.
Titania, music call, and strike more dead
55　Than common sleep of all these five the sense.
TITANIA. Music, ho, music such as charmeth sleep!
　　Soft music plays
PUCK. (*To Bottom, removing the ass's head*)
Now, when thou wak'st, with thine own fool's eyes peep.
OBERON. Sound, music! Come, my queen, take hands with me,
And rock the ground whereon these sleepers be.
　　They dance
60　Now thou and I are new in amity,
And will tomorrow midnight solemnly
Dance in Duke Theseus' house triumphantly,
And bless it to all fair prosperity.
There shall the pairs of faithful lovers be
65　Wedded, with Theseus, all in jollity.
　　[...]
TITANIA. Come, my lord, and in our flight
　　Tell me how it came this night
　　That I sleeping here was found
70　With these mortals on the ground.

Annotations
l. 44 **wont** = used
l. 50 **enamour'd of** = in love with
l. 52 to **loathe** = to hate
l. 54 to **strike** = *here:* to charm
l. 57 to **peep** = to look
l. 60 **amity** = friendship
l. 65 **jollity** = happiness

a) Answer the following questions.
　1. How does Oberon feel about Titania's obsession with Bottom?
　2. How has nature reacted to Titania's love for Bottom?
　3. What is Titania's reaction when Oberon reproaches her?
　4. How does Oberon take advantage of Titania?
　5. What does Oberon wish for Bottom and the other mortals?
　6. How does Titania react when Oberon wakes her up and she sees Bottom?
　7. What is Oberon and Titania's relationship like after Titania has woken up?
　8. What will happen at Theseus's court according to Oberon?

b) **Pair work**
Partner A: Analyse how Oberon's attitude towards Titania has developed in the course of the play. Consider his language and his behaviour towards Titania.
Partner B: Compare Titania's attitude towards Bottom before and after Oberon has used the magic potion on her the second time.
Then share your results.

40 Group work
Discuss how you would present Bottom in this scene. Consider the following aspects:
- Is Bottom aware of his outer appearance?
- What does his language reveal about his attitude towards the fairies?
- How does he like the situation he is in?

Play — A Midsummer Night's Dream

41

Titania asks Oberon to tell her how she came to sleep with Bottom on the ground. Write Oberon's version of the story.

42

After Puck, Oberon and Titania have left, Theseus, Hippolyta and Egeus arrive in the woods with their attendants and find the young couples sleeping. Read the following extract.

Extract 18 (Act IV, Scene 1)

EGEUS. My lord, this is my daughter here asleep,
And this Lysander; this Demetrius is,
This Helena, old Nedar's Helena.
I wonder of their being here together.
5 **THESEUS.** No doubt they rose up early to observe
The rite of May, and hearing our intent
Came here in grace of our solemnity.
But speak, Egeus; is not this the day
That Hermia should give answer of her choice?
10 **EGEUS.** It is, my lord.
THESEUS. Go, bid the huntsmen wake them with their horns.
   Shout within; wind horns; the lovers all start up
Good morrow, friends. Saint Valentine is past;
Begin these wood-birds but to couple now?
LYSANDER. Pardon, my lord.
THESEUS.   I pray you all, stand up.
15 I know you two are rival enemies:
How comes this gentle concord in the world,
That hatred is so far from jealousy
To sleep by hate, and fear no enmity?
LYSANDER. My lord, I shall reply amazedly,
20 Half sleep, half waking; but as yet, I swear,
I cannot truly say how I came here.
But as I think – for truly would I speak,
And now I do bethink me, so it is –
I came with Hermia hither. Our intent
25 Was to be gone from Athens, where we might
Without the peril of the Athenian law –
EGEUS. Enough, enough, my lord; you have enough –
I beg the law, the law upon his head!
They would have stol'n away, they would, Demetrius,
30 Thereby to have defeated you and me,
You of your wife, and me of my consent,
Of my consent that she should be your wife.
DEMETRIUS. My lord, fair Helen told me of their stealth,
Of this their purpose hither to this wood;
35 And I in fury hither follow'd them,
Fair Helena in fancy following me.
But, my good lord, I wot not by what power –
But by some power it is – my love to Hermia,
Melted as the snow, seems to me now
40 As the remembrance of an idle gaud
Which in my childhood I did dote upon;
And all the faith, the virtue of my heart,
The object and the pleasure of mine eye,
Is only Helena. To her, my lord,
45 Was I betroth'd ere I saw Hermia;

Annotations
l. 3 **old Nedar** = Helena's father
l. 4 **to wonder** = *here:* to be surprised
l. 6 **the rite of May** = May Day festival
l. 7 **in grace of our solemnity** = to honour our wedding ceremony
l. 11 **to bid** = to tell them to
l. 12 **morrow** = morning
   Saint Valentine = Valentine's Day (14 February)
l. 13 **wood-birds** = lovebirds, lovers
   to couple = to form pairs
l. 14 **I pray you** = please
l. 16 **gentle concord** = peacefulness
l. 17 **jealousy** = suspicion
l. 18 **by hate** = by the side of one who hates you
l. 19 **amazedly** = *here:* that I am confused
l. 23 **bethink me** = think about it
l. 24 **hither** = here
l. 26 **peril** = threat
l. 28 **upon his head** = brought down on him
l. 29 **stol'n away** = sneaked off
l. 30 **defeated** = *here:* tricked
l. 33 **stealth** = sneaky plans, secret escape
l. 34 **purpose hither** = reason for going here
l. 35 **fury** = anger
l. 36 **in fancy** = in her love
l. 37 **wot** = know
l. 40 **remembrance** = memory
   idle gaud = worthless toy
l. 41 **to dote upon** = to love very much
l. 43 **object** = focus
   mine = my
l. 45 **betroth'd** = engaged
   ere = before

But like in sickness did I loathe this food.
But, as in health come to my natural taste,
Now I do wish it, love it, long for it,
And will for evermore be true to it.
50 **THESEUS.** Fair lovers, you are fortunately met.
Of this discourse we more will hear anon.
Egeus, I will overbear your will;
For in the temple, by and by, with us
These couples shall eternally be knit.
55 And, for the morning now is something worn,
Our purpos'd hunting shall be set aside.
Away with us to Athens. Three and three,
We'll hold a feast in great solemnity.
Come, Hippolyta.
 Exit THESEUS *with* HIPPOLYTA, EGEUS, *and his train*
60 **DEMETRIUS.** These things seem small and undistinguishable,
Like far-off mountains turned into clouds.
HERMIA. Methinks I see these things with parted eye,
When everything seems double.
HELENA.   So methinks;
And I have found Demetrius, like a jewel,
65 Mine own, and not mine own.
DEMETRIUS.   Are you sure
That we are awake? It seems to me
That yet we sleep, we dream. Do not you think
The duke was here, and bid us follow him?
HERMIA. Yea, and my father.
HELENA.   And Hippolyta.
70 **LYSANDER.** And he did bid us follow to the temple.
DEMETRIUS. Why, then, we are awake. Let's follow him,
And by the way let us recount our dreams.

Annotations
l. 46 to **loathe** = to hate
l. 47 **come** = returned
l. 49 **for evermore** = from now on forever
l. 50 **fortunately met** = lucky
l. 51 **discourse** = conversation
     anon = presently
l. 52 to **overbear** = to overrule
l. 54 **knit** = *here:* married
l. 55 **something worn** = almost over
l. 56 **purpos'd** = planned
     to **set aside** = to cancel
l. 58 **solemnity** = celebration
l. 60 **undistinguishable** = hard to understand
l. 62 **with parted eye** = with blurry vision
l. 63 **everything seems double** = I am seeing double
l. 67 **yet** = still
l. 68 **bid** = told
l. 71 **why** = *here:* well
l. 72 **by the way** = on the way
     to **recount** = to tell each other about

a) Outline what reasons the two young men give to Theseus for being in the woods.
b) Analyse the language Demetrius uses when he talks to Theseus. What does it reveal about Demetrius's attitude towards Hermia and Helena? Consider stylistic devices and his choice of words.
c) The audience already knows basically all the details about why the couples are in the woods. In class, talk about possible reasons why Shakespeare revises the plot here.

43
a) Compare Egeus's and Theseus's reactions to the news.
b) **Group work** What might the characters be thinking at this moment? Write thought bubbles for them and present your ideas to the class.

44 Group work (4)
a) The four young lovers reflect upon their situation. Sketch the ways each character describes their experience by either drawing or briefly outlining them.
b) Talk about which metaphor or simile the characters use you like best. Explain your choice.
c) Each group member chooses one character and writes a recount of his or her experience. Consider the following aspects:
   • what the characters have experienced
   • to what extent they have changed their attitudes towards other people
   • what they have learned about themselves
   • what they think about love.
d) Present their recounts to the class.

Play — A Midsummer Night's Dream

45
Bottom wakes up, alone on stage. Read the following extract.

Extract 19 (Act IV, Scene 1)

BOTTOM. When my cue comes, call me, and I will answer. My next is 'Most fair Pyramus'. Heigh-ho! Peter Quince? Flute the bellows-mender? Snout the tinker? Starveling? God's my life! Stolen hence and left me asleep! I have had a most rare vision. I have had a dream, past the wit
5 of man to say what dream it was. Man is but an ass if he go about to expound this dream. Methought I was – there is no man can tell what. Methought I was – and methought I had – but man is but a patched fool if he will offer to say what methought I had. The eye of man hath not heard, the ear of man hath not seen, man's hand is not able to taste, his
10 tongue to conceive, nor his heart to report what my dream was! I will get Peter Quince to write a ballad of this dream; it shall be called 'Bottom's Dream', because it hath no bottom; and I will sing it in the latter end of a play, before the duke. Peradventure, to make it the more gracious, I shall sing it at her death.

Annotations
l. 1 **cue** = time to be on stage
I will answer = *here:* I will say my lines
l. 2 **Heigh-ho!** = Hey there!
l. 3 **God's my life!** = Oh my god!
stolen hence = all gone somewhere else
l. 4 **rare vision** = weird dream
ll. 4–5 **past the wit of man** = beyond explanation
l. 5 to **go about to** = to try to
l. 6 to **expound** = to explain
no man can tell = no one can describe
l. 7 **patched** = *here:* downright, total
l. 8 to **offer to** = to try to
l. 10 to **conceive** = *here:* to feel
to **report** = to describe
l. 12 **hath no bottom** = has no basis in reality
in the latter end = at the end
l. 13 **peradventure** = perhaps
gracious = pleasing
l. 14 **her** = i.e. Thisbe's

a) Choose the adjective that best describes Bottom. Is he … puzzled, bewildered, philosophical, or witty? Explain your choice.
b) Paraphrase Bottom's monologue in your own words.
c) Compare Bottom's version with that of the Bible:
d) In class, talk about possible reasons why Shakespeare makes Bottom refer to the Bible.

> However, as it is written:
> "What no eye has seen,
> what no ear has heard,
> and what no human mind has conceived" –
> the things God has prepared for those who love him –
> these are the things God has revealed to us by his Spirit.
> – 1 Corinthians 2:9–10

SCENE 2

46
The craftsmen are waiting for Bottom at Quince's house. Read the following extract.

Extract 20 (Act IV, Scene 2)

Enter BOTTOM
BOTTOM. Where are these lads? Where are these hearts?
QUINCE. Bottom! O most courageous day! O most happy hour!
BOTTOM. Masters, I am to discourse wonders – but ask me not what; for if I tell you, I am no true Athenian. I will tell you everything, right as
5 it fell out.
QUINCE. Let us hear, sweet Bottom.
BOTTOM. Not a word of me. All that I will tell you is – that the duke hath dined. Get your apparel together, good strings to your beards, new ribbons to your pumps: meet presently at the palace, every man look o'er
10 his part. For the short and the long is, our play is preferred. In any case, let Thisbe have clean linen; and let not him that plays the lion pare his nails, for they shall hang out for the lion's claws. And, most dear actors, eat no onions nor garlic; for we are to utter sweet breath, and I do not doubt but to hear them say it is a sweet comedy. No more words. Away!
15 Go, away!

Annotations
l. 1 **lads** = my friends
hearts = good people
l. 2 **O most courageous day!** = What a great day!
l. 3 **I am to discourse wonders** = I am going to tell you incredible stories
l. 4 **right** = exactly
l. 5 to **fall out** = to happen
l. 8 to **dine** = to eat dinner
apparel = costumes
good strings to = i.e. fasten them on
l. 9 **pumps** = dancing-shoes
presently = immediately
l. 10 **the short and the long is** = in sum, basically
preferred = recommended
l. 11 **linen** = underwear
to **pare** = to cut down
l. 12 to **hang out** = to stick out
l. 13 to **utter sweet breath** = to have fresh breath and say pleasing words

a) List the pieces of advice and commands Bottom gives his fellow craftsmen for their play.
b) From what you have read so far, how do you expect the craftsmen's play to go? Give reasons.
c) Give further pieces of advice to the actors.

LOOKING BACK AT ACT IV

47

In plays, conflicts are usually resolved in Act V. But in *A Midsummer Night's Dream* this already happens in Act IV. So it's time to take stock. Use a grid like the one below: List the ideas or themes of the conflicts. Describe each conflict in detail, e.g. how it starts, how it develops, etc. Then explain how the conflict is resolved. Give evidence from the text.

Idea / Theme of the conflict	Description of the conflict	Resolution of the conflict
…	…	…

48
a) Identify the most crucial moments in Act IV.
b) **Pair work** Compare your ideas with a partner.

While reading: Act V

SCENE 1

49

The final scene is set at Theseus's palace. After the wedding ceremonies, the craftsmen perform their play in front of the newly-wed couples. Read the following extract.

Extract 21 (Act V, Scene 1)

Flourish of trumpets
Enter QUINCE as Prologue
[…]
Enter with a Trumpeter before them BOTTOM *as Pyramus,* FLUTE *as Thisbe,* SNOUT *as Wall,* STARVELING *as Moonshine and* SNUG *as Lion*
QUINCE. (*as Prologue*) Gentles, perchance you wonder at this show,
But wonder on, till truth make all things plain.
This man is Pyramus, if you would know;
This beauteous lady Thisbe is, certain.
5 This man with lime and rough-cast doth present
Wall, that vile Wall which did these lovers sunder;
And through Wall's chink, poor souls they are content
To whisper – at the which let no man wonder.
This man with lanthorn, dog, and bush of thorn,
10 Presenteth Moonshine; for, if you will know,
By moonshine did these lovers think no scorn
To meet at Ninus' tomb, there, there to woo.
This grisly beast, which Lion hight by name,
The trusty Thisbe, coming first by night,
15 Did scare away, or rather did affright;
And as she fled, her mantle she did fall,
Which Lion vile with bloody mouth did stain.
Anon comes Pyramus, sweet youth and tall,
And finds his trusty Thisbe's mantle slain;

Annotations
l. 1 **gentles** = ladies and gentlemen
perchance = maybe
l. 2 **plain** = clear, evident
l. 3 **would** = *here:* would like to
l. 4 **beauteous** = beautiful
l. 5 **rough-cast** = plaster (walls)
l. 6 **vile** = bad, nasty
to **sunder** = to separate
l. 7 **chink** = gap
l. 8 **let no man wonder** = which shouldn't surprise you
l. 9 **lanthorn** = lantern
l. 11 **think no scorn** = not find shameful
l. 13 **grisly** = scary
hight = is called
l. 14 **trusty** = faithful
l. 15 to **affright** = to frighten
l. 16 **mantle** = cloak
to **fall** = *here:* to drop
l. 17 **Lion vile** = the horrible Lion
l. 18 **anon** = then
l. 19 **slain** = *here:* covered in blood

Play — A Midsummer Night's Dream

20 Whereat with blade, with bloody, blameful blade,
He bravely broach'd his boiling bloody breast;
And Thisbe, tarrying in mulberry shade,
His dagger drew, and died. For all the rest,
Let Lion, Moonshine, Wall, and lovers twain
25 At large discourse, while here they do remain.
    Exeunt QUINCE, BOTTOM, FLUTE, SNUG *and* STARVELING
THESEUS. I wonder if the lion be to speak?
DEMETRIUS. No wonder, my lord; one lion may, when many asses do.
SNOUT. (*as Wall*) In this same interlude it doth befall
That I, one Snout by name, present a wall;
30 And such a wall as I would have you think
That had in it a crannied hole or chink,
Through which the lovers, Pyramus and Thisbe,
Did whisper often, very secretly.
This loam, this rough-cast, and this stone doth show
35 That I am that same wall; the truth is so.
And this the cranny is, right and sinister,
Through which the fearful lovers are to whisper.
THESEUS. Would you desire lime and hair to speak better?
DEMETRIUS. It is the wittiest partition that ever I heard discourse, my
40 lord.

    Enter BOTTOM *as Pyramus*
THESEUS. Pyramus draws near the wall; silence!
BOTTOM. (*as Pyramus*) O grim-look'd night, O night with hue so black,
O night which ever art when day is not!
O night, O night, alack, alack, alack,
45 I fear my Thisbe's promise is forgot!
And thou, O wall, O sweet, O lovely wall,
That stand'st between her father's ground and mine,
Thou wall, O wall, O sweet and lovely wall,
Show me thy chink, to blink through with mine eyne.
    Wall parts his fingers
50 Thanks, courteous wall; Jove shield thee well for this!
But what see I? No Thisbe do I see.
O wicked wall, through whom I see no bliss,
Curs'd be thy stones for thus deceiving me!
THESEUS. The wall, methinks, being sensible, should curse again.
55 **BOTTOM.** No, in truth, sir, he should not. 'Deceiving me' is Thisbe's cue.
She is to enter now, and I am to spy her through the wall. You shall see it
will fall pat as I told you. Yonder she comes.

    Enter FLUTE *as Thisbe*
FLUTE. (*as Thisbe*) O wall, full often hast thou heard my moans,
For parting my fair Pyramus and me.
60 My cherry lips have often kiss'd thy stones,
Thy stones with lime and hair knit up in thee.
BOTTOM. (*as Pyramus*) I see a voice; now will I to the chink,
To spy and I can hear my Thisbe's face.
Thisbe!
FLUTE. (*as Thisbe*) My love! Thou art my love, I think?
65 **BOTTOM.** (*as Pyramus*) Think what thou wilt, I am thy lover's grace,
[…].
O, kiss me through the hole of this vile wall!
FLUTE. (*as Thisbe*) I kiss the wall's hole, not your lips at all.

Annotations

l. 20 **whereat** = because of this
blade = sword
bloody = *here:* bloodthirsty
l. 21 **broach'd** = pierced
boiling bloody breast = beating heart
l. 22 **tarrying** = waiting
in mulberry shade = under a mulberry bush
l. 24 **twain** = both
l. 25 **to discourse** = to explain
l. 26 **be to** = will
l. 27 **no wonder** = it wouldn't be a surprise
ass = *here:* foolish person (wordplay)
l. 28 **interlude** = short play
to befall = to happen
l. 31 **crannied** = cracked
l. 34 **loam** = clay
l. 36 **cranny** = crack
right and sinister = running across from left to right
l. 38 **lime and hair** = materials from which bricks were made
l. 39 **wittiest** = cleverest
partition = dividing wall, or division of a speech
l. 42 **grim-look'd** = dark-looking
hue = colour
l. 43 **art** = *here:* exists
l. 44 **alack** = alas
l. 47 **ground** = *here:* property, land
l. 49 **to blink** = *here:* to look
eyne = eyes
l. 50 **Jove** = Zeus (powerful god)
to shield = to protect
l. 52 **wicked** = evil
bliss = happiness
l. 54 **sensible** = *here:* sensitive, having thoughts and feelings
again = *here:* back at him
l. 55 **cue** = Stichwort
l. 57 **to fall** = *here:* to happen
pat = exactly
yonder = there
l. 59 **parting** = separating
l. 61 **knit up** = made up of
l. 65 **lover's grace** = gracious lover
l. 67 **vile** = awful

BOTTOM. (*as Pyramus*) Wilt thou at Ninny's tomb meet me straightway?
70 **FLUTE.** (*as Thisbe*) Tide life, tide death, I come without delay.
   Exeunt BOTTOM *and* FLUTE *in different directions*
SNOUT. (*as Wall*) Thus have I, Wall, my part discharged so;
And being done, thus Wall away doth go.
   Exit
THESEUS. Now is the mural down between the two neighbours.
DEMETRIUS. No remedy, my lord, when walls are so wilful to hear
75 without warning.
HIPPOLYTA. This is the silliest stuff that ever I heard.
THESEUS. The best in this kind are but shadows; and the worst are no worse, if imagination amend them.
HIPPOLYTA. It must be your imagination then, and not theirs.
80 **THESEUS.** If we imagine no worse of them than they of themselves, they may pass for excellent men. Here come two noble beasts in, a man and a lion.

   Enter SNUG *as Lion and* STARVELING *as Moonshine*
SNUG. (*as Lion*) You, ladies, you whose gentle hearts do fear
The smallest monstrous mouse that creeps on floor,
85 May now, perchance, both quake and tremble here,
When Lion rough in wildest rage doth roar.
Then know that I as Snug the joiner am
A lion fell, nor else no lion's dam;
For if I should as lion come in strife
90 Into this place, 'twere pity on my life.
THESEUS. A very gentle beast, and of a good conscience.
DEMETRIUS. The very best at a beast, my lord, that e'er I saw.
   [...]
STARVELING. (*as Moonshine*) This lanthorn doth the horned moon present –
95 **DEMETRIUS.** He should have worn the horns on his head.
THESEUS. He is no crescent, and his horns are invisible within the circumference.
STARVELING. (*as Moonshine*) This lanthorn doth the horned moon present;
Myself the man i'th'moon do seem to be –
100 [...]
HIPPOLYTA. I am aweary of this moon. Would he would change!
THESEUS. It appears by his small light of discretion that he is in the wane; but yet in courtesy, in all reason, we must stay the time.
LYSANDER. Proceed, Moon.
105 **STARVELING.** All that I have to say is to tell you that the lanthorn is the moon, I the man i'th'moon, this thorn bush my thorn bush, and this dog my dog.
DEMETRIUS. Why, all these should be in the lantern, for all these are in the moon. But silence: here comes Thisbe.

   Enter FLUTE *as Thisbe*
110 **FLUTE.** (*as Thisbe*) This is old Ninny's tomb. Where is my love?
SNUG. (*as Lion*) O!
   Lion roars. Thisbe drops her mantle and runs off
DEMETRIUS. Well roared, Lion!
THESEUS. Well run, Thisbe!
HIPPOLYTA. Well shone, Moon! Truly, the moon shines with a good
115 grace.

Annotations
l. 69 **straightway** = right now
l. 70 **to tide** = *here:* to come
l. 71 **discharged** = *here:* performed
l. 73 **mural** = wall
l. 74 **no remedy** = there's nothing we can do
l. 77 **the best in this kind** = even the best actors in this play
l. 78 **amend them** = make up for their lacking performance
l. 80 **than they of themselves** = than they think they are
l. 85 **to quake** = to shake
l. 88 **fell** = *here:* savage
       dam = mother
l. 89 **in strife** = looking for a fight
l. 90 **pity on my life** = cost my life
l. 92 **best at** = best at playing
l. 93 **horned moon** = crescent moon
ll. 96–97 **within the circumference** = inside the full circle
l. 99 **myself ... be** = I am playing the man in the moon
l. 101 **aweary** = tired, bored
l. 102 **of discretion** = being produced
ll. 102–103 **in the wane** = going away
l. 103 **in courtesy** = to be polite
       stay the time = stay until the end
l. 106 **i'th'moon** = in the moon
l. 108 **why** = *here:* well
ll. 114–115 **with a good grace** = well

Play: A Midsummer Night's Dream

Lion worries Thisbe's mantle
THESEUS. Well moused, Lion!
DEMETRIUS. And then came Pyramus –
Enter BOTTOM as Pyramus
LYSANDER. And so the lion vanished.
Exit Lion
BOTTOM. (*as Pyramus*) Sweet moon, I thank thee for thy sunny beams;
120 I thank thee, moon, for shining now so bright;
For by thy gracious, golden, glittering gleams
I trust to take of truest Thisbe sight.
But stay – O spite!
But mark, poor knight,
125 What dreadful dole is here?
Eyes, do you see?
How can it be?
O dainty duck, O dear!
Thy mantle good –
130 What, stain'd with blood?
Approach, ye Furies fell!
O Fates, come, come,
Cut thread and thrum,
Quail, crush, conclude, and quell.
135 **THESEUS.** This passion, and the death of a dear friend, would go near to make a man look sad.
HIPPOLYTA. Beshrew my heart, but I pity the man.
BOTTOM. (*as Pyramus*) O wherefore, Nature, didst thou lions frame,
Since lion vile hath here deflower'd my dear?
140 Which is – no, no – which was the fairest dame
That liv'd, that lov'd, that lik'd, that look'd with cheer.
Come tears, confound!
Out sword, and wound
The pap of Pyramus,
145 Ay, that left pap,
Where heart doth hop:
Thus die I, thus, thus, thus!
He stabs himself
Now am I dead,
Now am I fled;
150 My soul is in the sky.
Tongue, lose thy light;
Moon, take thy flight.
Exit Moonshine
Now die, die, die, die, die.
He dies
DEMETRIUS. No die, but an ace for him; for he is but one.
155 **LYSANDER.** Less than an ace, man; for he is dead, he is nothing.
THESEUS. With the help of a surgeon he might yet recover, and yet prove an ass.
HIPPOLYTA. How chance Moonshine is gone before Thisbe comes back and finds her lover?
160 **THESEUS.** She will find him by starlight.
Enter FLUTE as Thisbe
Here she comes and her passion ends the play.
HIPPOLYTA. Methinks she should not use a long one for such a Pyramus; I hope she will be brief.
[…]

Annotations
l. 116 **moused** = shaken as a cat would shake a mouse
l. 118 to **vanish** = to disappear
l. 121 **gleams** = beams of light
l. 122 **truest** = faithful
to **take sight of** = to see
l. 123 **stay** = *here:* wait
O spite! = Oh no!
l. 124 **mark** = look
l. 125 **dreadful dole** = awful sight
l. 128 **dainty duck** = *here:* my darling
l. 131 **Furies fell** = vengeance-seeking goddesses from Greek mythology
l. 133 **cut thread and thrum** = end my life
l. 134 to **quail** = to overpower
to **conclude** = to finish
to **quell** = to kill
l. 135 **go near to** = almost
l. 137 to **beshrew** = to curse
l. 138 **wherefore** = why
to **frame** = to create
l. 139 **deflower'd** = ravished, carried off; maybe Bottom meant to say 'devoured' (eaten)
l. 141 **look'd with cheer** = smiled
l. 142 to **confound** = to destroy
l. 144 **pap** = chest
l. 145 **left pap** = left side of chest
l. 146 to **hop** = to beat
l. 151 **lose thy light** = stop being able to see
l. 152 **take thy flight** = leave
l. 154 **die** = *here:* one of a pair of dice
ace = side of a die with one dot
he is but one = he is an original
l. 156 **surgeon** = *here:* doctor
to **prove** = *here:* to become
l. 157 **ass** = donkey
l. 158 **how chance** = how does it happen that
l. 161 **passion** = *here:* crying
l. 162 **use a long one** = cry for a long time
l. 163 **brief** = quick

A Midsummer Night's Dream — Play 6

165 **FLUTE.** (*as Thisbe*) Asleep, my love?
   What, dead, my dove?
   O Pyramus, arise.
   Speak, speak! Quite dumb?
   Dead, dead? A tomb
170 Must cover thy sweet eyes.
   These lily lips,
   This cherry nose,
   These yellow cowslip cheeks
   Are gone, are gone.
175 [...]
   Tongue, not a word!
   Come, trusty sword,
   Come, blade, my breast imbrue!
   She stabs herself
   And farewell, friends.
180 Thus Thisbe ends –
   Adieu, adieu, adieu!
   She dies
THESEUS. Moonshine and Lion are left to bury the dead.
DEMETRIUS. Ay, and Wall, too.
BOTTOM. (*Starting up, as* FLUTE *does also*) No, I assure you, the wall is
185 down that parted their fathers. Will it please you to see the epilogue, or to hear a Bergomask dance between two of our company?
THESEUS. No epilogue, I pray you; for your play needs no excuse. Never excuse; for when the players are all dead, there need none to be blamed. Marry, if he that writ it had played Pyramus and hanged himself in
190 Thisbe's garter, it would have been a fine tragedy: and so it is, truly, and very notably discharged. But come, your Bergomask; let your epilogue alone.
   The company return; two of them dance, then exeunt BOTTOM, FLUTE, *and their fellows*
   The iron tongue of midnight hath told twelve.
   Lovers, to bed; 'tis almost fairy time.
195 I fear we shall outsleep the coming morn
   As much as we this night have overwatch'd.
   This palpable-gross play hath well beguil'd
   The heavy gait of night. Sweet friends, to bed.
   A fortnight hold we this solemnity
200 In nightly revels and new jollity.
   Exeunt

Annotations
l. 166 **my dove** = my darling
l. 167 to **arise** = to wake up
l. 168 **dumb** = mute, unable to talk
l. 173 **cowslip** = *Schlüsselblume*
l. 178 **blade** = sword
   to **imbrue** = to stain with blood
l. 186 **Bergomask dance** = country dance
   company = acting group
l. 187 **I pray you** = please
l. 189 **marry** = in fact
   writ it = wrote the play
l. 190 **garter** = *Strumpfband*
l. 191 **notably discharged** = well performed
l. 193 **iron tongue** = clock hand
   told twelve = struck midnight
l. 195 **outsleep the coming morn** = sleep in late
l. 196 **this night have overwatch'd** = have stayed up late
l. 197 **palpable-gross** = terribly bad
ll. 197–198 **beguil'd the heavy gait of night** = amused us and passed the time
l. 199 **fortnight** = two weeks
   hold we this solemnity = we continue to celebrate
l. 200 **revels** = parties
   jollity = happiness

6 Play — A Midsummer Night's Dream

Put the sentences below into the correct order.

No.	Contents
	Bottom suggests he can deliver an epilogue, which Theseus refuses.
	The audience makes funny remarks on Pyramus's death and Thisbe's reappearance.
	Theseus and Demetrius make fun of the talking wall.
	As soon as Thisbe notices the lion, she runs off leaving her coat behind.
	Pyramus and Thisbe express their love through a space in the wall and arrange a nightly meeting.
	Snout presents himself as Wall, through which the lovers keep in touch.
	Theseus, Hippolyta and Demetrius comment on the play.
	After Thisbe returns to their meeting place and finds Pyramus dead, she stabs herself, too.

No.	Contents
	When Bottom as Pyramus is looking for Thisbe, he happens to find her coat.
	Starveling presents himself as Moonshine and is interrupted by Theseus's and Demetrius's comments.
	Theseus expects to hear the wall speak again, but Bottom explains why this won't happen.
1	Quince as Prologue welcomes the audience and outlines the contents of the play.
	Snout as Wall takes his leave.
	Pyramus thinking that Thisbe was killed by a lion stabs himself.
	Snug introduces himself as Lion, so as not to scare the audience.
	Bottom as Pyramus tries to contact Thisbe through the wall.

50

a) Read the information below and examine the function of the play-within-the-play in *A Midsummer Night's Dream*.

Info

The play-within-the-play

The play-within-the-play is a dramatic convention very popular in Shakespeare's time: A character in a story or play becomes the narrator of or an actor in a second story. As the first permanent theatre in England had only been established some years before in 1576, Elizabethan authors liked to explore the new technical possibilities of the theatre and the nature of entertainment. Besides, the question of the kind of truth that can be told through plays was a point of interest for playwrights. Thus, it is not surprising that Shakespeare used the technique of the play-within-the-play to mirror the play's themes and present different perspectives of them. It also enables the female characters to assume the role of the audience and the critic of male-dominated themes such as male hegemony.

In general, the inset story or play may have various functions. It may simply offer entertainment, provide an example of what is told in the outer story, have symbolic or psychological significance to the characters of the outer story, or reveal the truth about something that has happened in the outer story. Finally, it may also deflect the audience's attention from a plot twist.

b) **Group work** Perform the play-within-the-play: Strip the craftsmen's play to its bare bones and make a two-minute play out of it. Then try to reduce more details and act it out in one minute. Can you do it in 30 seconds? Discuss the effect of this acting method.

51

Hippolyta says: "This is the silliest stuff that ever I heard." (l. 76)
Do you agree? Write a comment in which you express your opinion.

52

Reread ll. 77–81 and explain how Theseus sees the role of one's imagination.

A Midsummer Night's Dream — Play

53
Imagine you are a costume designer and must design the costumes for the play-within-the-play. Create the costumes for Pyramus, Thisbe, Wall, Moonshine and Lion. You can either draw or sketch the costumes for the actors, find magazine cuttings or look for pictures on the Internet.

54
After the mortals have gone to bed, Oberon, Titania, and their fairies appear to bless the newly-wed couples. Then Puck is left alone on stage to address the audience.

Extract 22 (Act V, Scene 1)

PUCK. (*To the audience*) If we shadows have offended,
Think but this, and all is mended:
That you have but slumber'd here
While these visions did appear;
5 And this weak and idle theme,
No more yielding but a dream,
Gentles, do not reprehend;
If you pardon, we will mend.
And, as I am an honest Puck,
10 If we have unearned luck
Now to 'scape the serpent's tongue,
We will make amends ere long,
Else the Puck a liar call.
So, good night unto you all.
15 Give me your hands, if we be friends,
And Robin shall restore amends.
  Exit

Annotations
l. 1 **shadows** = *here:* fairies or actors
l. 2 **mended** = fixed
l. 3 **but** = *here:* only
    slumber'd = slept
l. 5 **this weak and idle theme** = this silly and foolish plot
l. 6 **no more yielding but** = producing no more than
l. 7 **gentles** = ladies and gentlemen
    to **reprehend** = to blame
l. 8 to **pardon** = to forgive
    to **mend** = to make better
l. 10 **unearned luck** = luck we don't deserve
l. 11 **'scape the serpent's tongue** = avoid being booed and hissed at (showing the audience's disapproval)
l. 12 to **make amends** = to fix things
    ere long = soon
l. 15 **your hands** = *here:* a round of applause
l. 16 to **restore amends** = to make it up to you

a) **Pair work** Read out Puck's soliloquy by taking turns with your partner.
b) Sum up Puck's message in one or two sentences.
c) Speculate about the reason why Shakespeare makes Puck end the play.
d) Imagine a different character from the play would speak the final lines. Write his or her soliloquy and present it to the class.

Post-reading: Looking back at the play

AN OVERVIEW

55
Identify the main theme of each scene and explain its function. The first one is given as an example.

Act, Scene	What happens?	What is the function of the scene?
I, 1	wedding preparations; the characters unfold their problems: arranged marriage, elopement	introduction of characters; setting the scene and atmosphere
I, 2	…	…

Film — A Midsummer Night's Dream

THE STRUCTURE OF *A MIDSUMMER NIGHT'S DREAM*

56

a) Look at the diagram. A classical play usually has the following structure:

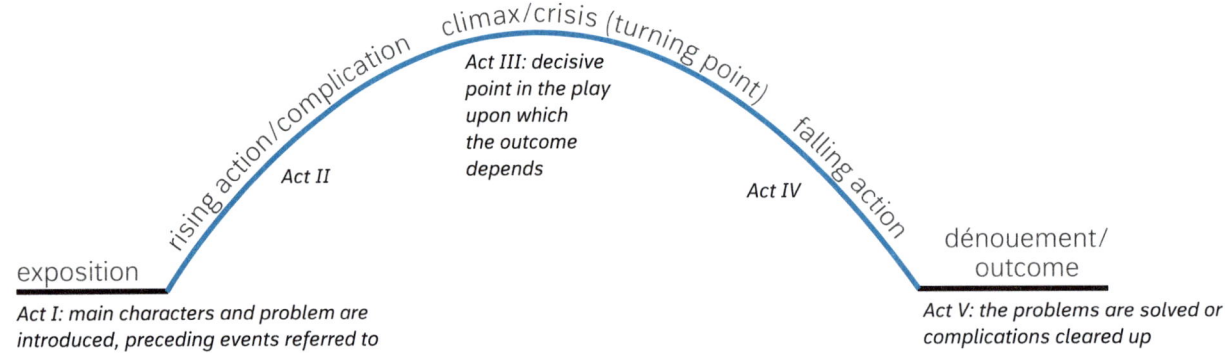

b) Identify the plot developments in *A Midsummer Night's Dream* and give examples from the play to show how they fit into the structure.

c) Group work (4–5) **CHOOSE**
Decide which are the most important passages in the play. Then act out the play in only three minutes (e.g. in a pantomime). One student is the timekeeper. Explain why you chose the passages you did.
OR
Work out a freeze-frame showing the most important moment in a scene. The others must guess what moment is shown in the freeze-frame.

A modern film adaptation: Michael Hoffman's *A Midsummer Night's Dream* (1999)

PRE-VIEWING

In this section, you are going to design your own modern film version of *A Midsummer Night's Dream* and pitch your idea to a production company.

1 Group work (3–4)
Create a poster about the most important scenes or events in the play. Use a symbol to indicate what each scene is about, headline the scene and summarize it in one sentence. Then present your ideas to the class.

2 Group work (4)
Discuss the relevance of the play for modern audiences.

Info

Placemat

Work in groups of four.
1. Fold a big piece of paper twice and draw a square or a rectangle in the middle (look at the example).
2. Each of you writes their ideas in one corner of the paper.
3. Turn the paper round until everyone has read and commented on their neighbours' ideas.
4. Decide on the most important ideas as a group and write them in the middle.
5. One of you presents the results to the class.

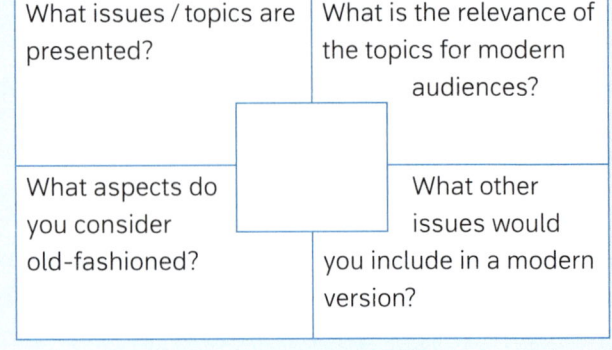

A Midsummer Night's Dream — Film

3
Imagine you are a film director and want to turn Shakespeare's *A Midsummer Night's Dream* into a modern film version.
a) Design your modern film version. Think about the following aspects and make notes.
- title
- genre (e.g. romance, sitcom, horror film, …)
- setting (Where and when does the story take place?)
- cast (actors for the main roles)

b) Present your ideas to the class.

4
a) **Pair work**
Prepare a pitch for your modern film version of *A Midsummer Night's Dream* to convince a production company to fund the project.
- Summarize the original plot.
- Present your reasons for making such a film.
- Talk about the relevance of the story for modern audiences.
- Outline the idea for your film version.

> **Info**
>
> **Pitch**
>
> A pitch is a short oral presentation of an idea. When you make a pitch, you try to persuade someone to support your idea. As time is money, a pitch must be concise and to the point.

b) Present your pitch to the class. The other students function as the board of film producers at the production company. At the end of the presentations, vote for the best pitch.

5 → Workshop: Analysing a feature film → S16: Checklist: Analysis of a film scene

In 1999, a film version of *A Midsummer Night's Dream* by American director Michael Hoffman came out, with Rupert Everett, Calista Flockhart, Kevin Kline, Michelle Pfeiffer, Stanley Tucci, Christian Bale, Anna Friel and Dominic West playing the main roles.

a) Look at the film stills below and match them with the cinematic devices in the box. More than one term might fit.

> medium shot | blurry foreground | establishing shot | close-up | out of focus | blurry background | over-the-shoulder shot | long shot | bird's eye view | full shot | low-angle shot | high-angle shot | superimposed text | point-of-view shot | worm's eye view | eye-level shot | in focus

b) In class, talk about your first impressions that the film stills convey, e.g. the overall atmosphere, the setting and the characters.

6 Film — A Midsummer Night's Dream

WHILE VIEWING

The beginning of the film

6 → **Workshop:** Analysing a feature film → **S16:** Checklist: Analysis of a film scene

a) Read the opening scene of the play again (extract 1, p. 124). Then outline how you would turn it into a film scene if you were a director. Use the middle column in the grid below.
b) Now watch the beginning of Michael Hoffman's version of *A Midsummer Night's Dream* (0:00:00–0:04:59). Note down your first impressions. Compare them to your impressions from task 5b).
c) Watch the scene again and fill in the right-hand column of the grid.
d) **Pair work** Compare your notes with a partner.
e) Explain which version you prefer and give reasons for your choice.

	Your idea	Film version
The setting: Where and when does the story take place?		
Choice of actors for the roles of Theseus and Hippolyta: Describe their physical appearances and personalities.		
Events: What happens in the scene?		
Cinematic devices: field size, camera angle, special effects, music		

The relationship between father and daughter

7

a) Read extract 2 again (p. 125f.). Analyse the relationship between Egeus and his daughter Hermia as depicted by Shakespeare. Choose words from the box that best describe the relationship. Explain your choice and give line references to support it.

> cold-hearted | unloving | unemotional | indifferent | broken | intimate | difficult | love-hate | full of hatred | toxic

b) **Pair work** Choose the most important lines in this extract for Egeus and his daughter. Compare your choice with a partner.
c) Watch the film scene in which the conflict between Egeus and Hermia is presented (0:04:59–0:09:29). Note down your first impression of the father-daughter relationship in the film scene.
d) **Pair work** Watch the film scene again, this time focusing on the lines they speak. Compare your ideas from b) with the lines chosen for the film. If the lines differ, discuss possible reasons for the differences.
e) **EXTRA** Identify some of the cinematic devices the director uses to convey the nature of the father-daughter relationship. → **Workshop:** Analysing a feature film → **S16:** Checklist: Analysis of a film scene

A Midsummer Night's Dream — Film

The play-within-the-play

8 Group work

a) Reread the scene in which *Pyramus and Thisbe* is performed at the Duke's palace (extract 21, p. 159ff.). Then decide how you would adapt this scene for a film. Create a storyboard for your film scene, which includes the following elements:
- sketches of the different shots
- for each shot:
  → the lines to be spoken
  → a short description of the action
  → camera movements, music and sound effects
  → further directions

Kevin Kline (as Nick Bottom) and Michael Hoffman (director)

b) **EXTRA** Film the scene based on your ideas from a).
c) Watch the film scene (1:31:52–1:46:09) and compare it to your ideas.
d) Discuss possible reasons for Michael Hoffman's decision to film the scene in this way.

POST-VIEWING

9

a) **Group work** Read some reviews of the film on the Internet and outline the reviewers' opinions of Michael Hoffman's film version. Exchange the views with your group members.
b) Read what Roger Ebert, a famous American film critic and author, said about *A Midsummer Night's Dream*.

Reviews   Roger Ebert   May 14, 1999

William Shakespeare's A Midsummer Night's Dream

[...] Michael Hoffman's new film of "William Shakespeare's a Midsummer Night's Dream" (who else's?) is updated to the 19th century, set in Italy and furnished with bicycles and operatic[1] interludes. But it is founded on Shakespeare's language and is faithful, by and large, to the original play. [...]

Hoffman, whose wonderful "Restoration"[2] re-created a time of fire and plague, here conducts with a playful touch. There are small gems of stagecraft for all of the actors, including Snout, the village tinker, who plays a wall in the performance for the duke, and makes a circle with his thumb and finger to represent a chink in it. It's wonderful to behold Pfeiffer's infatuation with the donkey-eared Bottom, who she winds in her arms as "doth the woodbine the sweet honeysuckle gently twist"; her love is so real, we almost believe it. Kline's Bottom tactfully humors her mad infatuation, good-natured and accepting. And Tucci's Puck suggests sometimes that he has a darker side, but it not so much malicious as incompetent. [...]

Why is Shakespeare so popular with filmmakers when he contains so few car chases and explosions? Because he is the measuring stick by which actors and directors test themselves. His insights into human nature are so true that he has, as [Harold] Bloom argues in his book, actually created our modern idea of the human personality. Before Hamlet asked, "to be, or not to be?," dramatic characters just were. Ever since, they have known and questioned themselves. Even in a comedy like "Midsummer," there are quick flashes of brilliance that help us see ourselves. "What fools these mortals be," indeed.

Annotations
[1] **operatic** = characteristic of opera
[2] **Restoration** (1995) is another film directed by Michael Hoffman. It is a historical drama set in 17th century England, which is based on the 1989 novel by Rose Tremain

---

c) Describe Roger Ebert's explanation about Shakespeare's ongoing popularity in your own words.
d) What "quick flashes of brilliance" can you find in the play?
e) Write your own film review of Michael Hoffman's version of *A Midsummer Night's Dream*. You can find support for writing a film review on p. 93.

Topic: A Midsummer Night's Dream

Dream and reality

1

a) Have you ever woken up from a dream or nightmare? Can you remember your dreams? What role do dreams or nightmares play for us?

b) Read the quotes about dreams and explain what notions of dreams they describe.

1 "A dream doesn't become reality through magic; it takes sweat, determination and hard work." – Colin Powell

2 "Make your life a dream, and a dream a reality." – Antoine de Saint-Exupéry

3 "All that we see or seem is but a dream within a dream." – Edgar Allan Poe

4 "I believe in everything until it's disproved. So I believe in fairies, the myths, dragons. It all exists, even if it's in your mind. Who's to say that dreams and nightmares aren't as real as the here and now?" – John Lennon

5 "Dreams are illustrations from the book your soul is writing about you." – Marsha Norman

c) Write an acrostic about your associations with dreams.

D

R

E

A

M

> **Info**
>
> **Acrostic**
>
> An acrostic is a poem in which particular letters, for example the first letters of each line, make a new word or phrase.

d) **Pair work** Compare your ideas with a partner.

Mediation

2 → **Workshop:** Mediation → **S19:** How to improve your mediation skills → **S8:** How to improve your text

You are a guest student at an English college and your class is working on a project about the role of dreams in literature. You have been asked to contribute an article and you have found an interview about dreams from the German magazine *GEO*. Read the interview and write an article for the project website in which you describe how dreams and nightmares work and how they can be interpreted or dealt with.

Traumdeutung: „Träume zu verstehen, ist nicht schwer"
von Johanna Romberg

Wie sind Träume zu verstehen? Kann man Albträume loswerden? Und was ist dran an Sigmund Freuds Traumdeutung? Über das und mehr sprach GEO-Redakteurin Johanna Romberg mit dem renommierten
5 Traumforscher Michael Schredl

GEO: Herr Professor Schredl, darf ich Ihnen einen Traum erzählen?
Michael Schredl: Gern.
Neulich nachts befand ich mich in Gesellschaft einer
10 *korpulenten amerikanischen Komikerin und von Sigmar Gabriel. Wir hatten ein Dreiecksverhältnis, das ich beendete, indem ich meinen Koffer packte. Beide waren sehr traurig, ich fühlte mich schuldig. Was sagt dieser Traum über mich?*
15 Wenn der Traum keine direkten Erfahrungen aufgreift …
Um Himmels willen. Ich bin seit 23 Jahren glücklich verheiratet.
… dann stellt er vermutlich ein Thema dar, das Sie gerade beschäftigt. Offenbar gibt es etwas in Ihrem Leben,

das Ihnen lange Zeit Spaß gemacht hat, beruflich oder privat. Davon wollen Sie jetzt aber weg. Und Sie sind sich bewusst, dass Ihre Entscheidung nicht positiv aufgenommen wird.

Das Muster mag stimmen. Aber warum wählt mein Traumbewusstsein ausgerechnet diese Komikerin und den Vizekanzler aus, um es darzustellen?

Die Personen haben keine besondere Bedeutung. Sie können sich das Traumbewusstsein wie einen Regisseur vorstellen, der ein Skript vor sich hat und dazu die passenden Bilder und Darsteller aussucht.

Passend erscheinen mir diese beiden nun gerade nicht ...

... weil Sie die Szene mit Ihrem wachen Verstand beurteilen. Im Traum arbeitet Ihr Bewusstsein aber anders. Es hat Zugriff auf Erinnerungen, die Ihnen im Wachzustand nicht zugänglich sind – weil jene Teile Ihres Gehirns, die Gedanken sortieren und logisch verknüpfen, weitgehend inaktiv sind. So führt Ihnen Ihr Traumbewusstsein, in dieser Szene, nicht nur eine aktuelle Situation vor Augen, es lässt darin auch Erinnerungen an andere, lange zurückliegende Abschiede wieder aufleben. Offenbar mit passenden Bildern – sonst hätte der Traum bei Ihnen nicht so starke Gefühle ausgelöst.

Was für „Skripte" werden im Traum inszeniert, und wie erkennt man sie?

Zu den häufigsten Handlungsmustern gehört etwa dieses: Man rennt in Panik vor Monstern davon, die einen verfolgen. Das Thema dahinter: Der Träumende scheut die Auseinandersetzung mit einem Problem, das als bedrohlich empfunden wird.

Ich packe im Traum ständig Koffer und werde damit nie fertig.

Ein klassisches Traumthema, hinter dem eine heutzutage gängige Erfahrung steht: Man hat zu viele Projekte zu erledigen und gerät darüber in Zeitdruck.

Die Erklärungen klingen einleuchtend. Aber auch irgendwie – zu einfach.

Sie sind einfach. Das Interpretieren von Träumen erfordert keine großen Dechiffrierkünste.

Wirklich nicht? Ich dachte immer, Träume seien voller verdeckter Botschaften, die man nur durch genaue Analyse entschlüsseln kann.

Das ist, vorsichtig gesagt, eine überholte Vorstellung.

Treppensteigen bedeutet Koitus, Höhlen und Gefäße stehen für weibliche Genitalien ...

Sie spielen auf die Theorie von Sigmund Freud an, die immer noch viele gängige Vorstellungen über Träume prägt. Ich finde diese Art der Interpretation problematisch; sie sagt oft mehr über den Interpreten aus als über den Träumenden selbst.

Und woher wissen Sie, dass Ihre Form der Traumdeutung richtig ist?

Es gibt keine „Deutung", die „stimmt". Ich würde diese Begriffe nicht verwenden. Für mich liefern Träume schlicht Anregungen, im Wachzustand über etwas nachzudenken. Zwar kommt man meist nicht „über Nacht" zu neuen Erkenntnissen. Aber wenn sich nach einiger Zeit das Gefühl einstellt, ich kann bestimmte Verhaltensmuster genauer erkennen, womöglich konstruktiv verändern – dann war die Traumarbeit erfolgreich.

Es gibt aber auch Träume, die man nach dem Aufwachen am liebsten gleich vergessen würde.

Gerade mit Albträumen sollte man sich unbedingt auseinandersetzen. Das ist oft die einzige Möglichkeit, sie loszuwerden.

Und wie funktioniert das konkret?

Man sollte die Traumhandlung zunächst aufschreiben oder aufzeichnen, mit allen Details. Dann kann man darangehen, den Traum umzuschreiben. Man erfindet, zum Beispiel, ein Fabelwesen, das die verfolgenden Monster besiegt. Die neue Wendung ruft man sich von nun an täglich ins Gedächtnis. In etwa 80 Prozent aller Fälle verschwinden die Albträume bereits nach zwei Wochen.

Was bringt es gesunden, unbelasteten Menschen, sich mit ihren Träumen zu beschäftigen?

Ich glaube, dass die Beschäftigung mit den eigenen Träumen jedem weiterhilft, unabhängig vom psychischen Befinden. Träume können lehren, die eigenen Stärken und Schwächen zu erkennen, und sie geben immer wieder kreative Anregungen.

Sie sprechen auch aus Erfahrung. In Ihrem Buch „Träume" ist zu lesen, dass Sie seit über 20 Jahren Ihre Traumerlebnisse protokollieren.

Und sie überraschen mich immer wieder. Neulich erst stürmte nachts eine Menschenmenge in mein Zimmer, um mich von der Arbeit abzulenken.

Und was haben Sie aus diesem Traum gelernt?

Es ging um das Thema Abgrenzung. Was ich daraus lerne – das ist noch die Frage. Träume liefern ja niemals fertige Lösungen. Sie sind immer nur eine Anregung zum Weiterdenken.

Topic: A Midsummer Night's Dream

DREAM AND REALITY IN *A MIDSUMMER NIGHT'S DREAM*

3
Read the following quotations from the play. Identify the speaker and the context in which they are said. Then analyse how dream is displayed in these extracts.

1. "Four days will quickly steep themselves in night;
Four nights will quickly dream away the time; [...]"
(Act I, Scene 1)

2. "When they next wake, all this derision
Shall seem a dream and fruitless vision,
And back to Athens shall the lovers wend
With league whose date till death shall never end.
Whiles I in this affair do thee employ
I'll to my queen and beg her Indian boy;
And then I will her charmed eye release
From monster's view, and all things shall be peace."
(Act III, Scene 2)

3. "And, gentle Puck, take this transformed scalp
From off the head of this Athenian swain,
That, he awaking when the other do,
May all to Athens back again repair,
And think no more of this night's accidents
But as the fierce vexation of a dream."
(Act IV, Scene 1)

4. "My Oberon, what visions have I seen!
Methought I was enamour'd of an ass."
(Act IV, Scene 1)

5. "Are you sure
That we are awake? It seems to me
That yet we sleep, we dream. [...]"
(Act IV, Scene 1)

6. "I have had a most rare vision. I have had a dream, past the wit of man to say what dream it was. Man is but an ass if he go about to expound this dream."
(Act IV, Scene 1)

7. "If we shadows have offended,
Think but this, and all is mended:
That you have but slumber'd here
While these visions did appear;
And this weak and idle theme,
No more yielding but a dream,
Gentles, do not reprehend;
If you pardon, we will mend."
(Act V, Scene 1)

4

a) Read an extract from Jerome Mandel's article "Dream and Imagination in Shakespeare" from *Shakespeare Quarterly* (1973). Explain how Jerome Mandel differentiates between two kinds of reality.

> It will be necessary to distinguish between two kinds of reality. One is the reality of Renaissance England in which burghers, apprentices, and aristocrats composed an audience watching a play. They lived in a world of experiential reality in which phenomena are verifiable. Within such a real world is a play-world, fabricated in the mind of the poet. To the audience, the play-world is not real in the sense that the world they live in is real. But from another point of view, the play-world is a reality in which the actors are not actors but real people – kings and nobles and clowns – who suffer passion, anguish, the human condition. They suffer as real people in a real world. But their reality differs from that of the audience in that theirs is an imaginative reality, a product of the playwright's mind.
>
> Jerome Mandel: "Dream and Imagination in Shakespeare." In: Shakespeare Quarterly, Vol. 24, No. 1 (Winter, 1973). Oxford: Oxford University Press, p. 61. Reprinted by permission of Oxford University Press on behalf of the Folger Shakespeare Library.

b) Revise the function of the play-within-the-play in Act V, Scene 1 (extract 21, p. 159ff. and info box on p. 164). Then examine how the play-within-the-play contributes to a "third reality".

A Midsummer Night's Dream — Topic 6

5
Explore what role one's imagination plays for the theme of dream and reality by examining Theseus's concept of it. Read the following extract and explain Theseus's line of argumentation.

Extract 23 (Act V, Scene 1)

Athens, the palace of THESEUS:
Enter THESEUS, HIPPOLYTA, PHILOSTRATE, *Lords and Attendants*
HIPPOLYTA. 'Tis strange, my Theseus, that these lovers speak of.
THESEUS. More strange than true. I never may believe
These antique fables, nor these fairy toys.
Lovers and madmen have such seething brains,
5 Such shaping fantasies, that apprehend
More than cool reason ever comprehends.
The lunatic, the lover, and the poet
Are of imagination all compact:
One sees more devils than vast hell can hold;
10 That is the madman. The lover, all as frantic,
Sees Helen's beauty in a brow of Egypt.
The poet's eye, in fine frenzy rolling,
Doth glance from heaven to earth, from earth to heaven;
And as imagination bodies forth
15 The forms of things unknown, the poet's pen
Turns them to shapes, and gives to airy nothing
A local habitation and a name.
Such tricks hath strong imagination
That if it would but apprehend some joy,
20 It comprehends some bringer of that joy;
Or in the night, imagining some fear,
How easy is a bush supposed a bear!
HIPPOLYTA. But all the story of the night told over,
And all their minds transfigur'd so together,
25 More witnesseth than fancy's images,
And grows to something of great constancy;
But howsoever, strange and admirable.

Annotations
l. 3 **toys** = *here:* silly tales
l. 4 **seething** = boiling, full of restless activity
l. 5 to **apprehend** = *here:* to think up, to imagine
l. 6 to **comprehend** = to understand
l. 7 **lunatic** = a person driven mad by the moon
l. 8 **compact** = *here:* composed
l. 10 **frantic** = in a state of extreme emotion
l. 11 **Helen** = Helen of Troy is a figure in classical mythology. She is said to have been the most beautiful woman in the world.
 in a brow of Egypt = in the face of a gypsy
l. 12 **frenzy** = *Rausch, Wahnsinn*
l. 14 **bodies forth** = creates
l. 16 **airy** = *luftig, leicht*
l. 17 **habitation** = a place to live
l. 20 to **comprehend** = *here:* to include
l. 24 **transfigur'd** = changed, usually in a positive and often spiritual way

6
a) What dreams do the characters have at the beginning of the play? Write thought bubbles for …
- Theseus
- Hermia
- Demetrius
- Oberon
- Egeus
- Lysander
- Helena
- Titania.

b) Pair work Have their dreams come true at the end of the play? Compare your answers with a partner.

7
Write an essay in which you elaborate on the function of dream and reality in *A Midsummer Night's Dream*.

Language support

a positive adventure | a nightmare | a mechanism to speed up time | (to) be linked to magical mishaps | (to) explain bizarre events | (to) be unable to understand magical happenings | (to) be seen as the result of sleeping | (to) impact or misrepresent reality | a sense of illusion | gauzy fragility | fantastical experience | (to) foreshadow events | (to) recap events | (to) intertwine dreams and reality | a way of framing one's own experiences | a dream can win over reason | …

Topic: A Midsummer Night's Dream

Love and marriage

1

a) Listen to the song "Love and Marriage" recorded by Frank Sinatra in 1955. Tick (✓) the correct answer. **Webcode** DSW-73684-12

1. What are love and marriage compared to?
   - ❏ a) brother and sister
   - ❏ b) horse and carriage
   - ❏ c) cat and dog

2. Can you love somebody without getting married according to the song?
   - ❏ a) You can't have one without the other.
   - ❏ b) You can have one without the other.
   - ❏ c) You can only have one of them.

3. How are love and marriage assessed in the song?
   - ❏ a) They are of no importance.
   - ❏ b) They used to be an institution.
   - ❏ c) They are an important institution.

4. What do the locals think about this union? They think it is …
   - ❏ a) essential.
   - ❏ b) compulsory.
   - ❏ c) significant.

5. What happens if you try to separate love and marriage?
   - ❏ a) You will fail.
   - ❏ b) You will be happy.
   - ❏ c) You will be disillusioned.

b) Outline the attitude towards love and marriage in the song in one or two sentences.

c) **Group work (4)** Placemat: Discuss this attitude in groups of four. (If you need more information, reread the info box on p. 166.)

2

a) Read the quotation below and explain it in your own words.

> "In England you marry the women you love. In India we love the women we marry. You fall out of love after marriage. We fall in love after marriage."
> – Mark Tully quoting the headman of a village near Delhi in *Ram Chander's Story*

b) **Group work** Research some background information on arranged marriages and prepare for a debate. Split the class into two groups. Group A collects arguments in favour of arranged marriages and group B collects arguments against arranged marriages.

c) Stage a debate.

LOVE AND MARRIAGE IN *A MIDSUMMER NIGHT'S DREAM*

3

What did the Elizabethans think about love and marriage?
Read the extracts from an article from the website of the British Library.

A Midsummer Night's Dream — Topic 6

Marriage and courtship

by Eric Rasmussen 15 March 2016

[...] In the early modern period, customs of courtship and marriage were undergoing significant shifts. Throughout the medieval period, money, class or alliance governed and regulated marriage. As Europe modernized, however, the Puritans and others began to champion the novel idea of marriages based on mutual inclination and love. Time and again Shakespeare's plays dramatise the conflict between the old order in which fathers chose husbands for their daughters and the new order in which daughters wished to choose their own mates based on affection. [...]

In Shakespeare's England, the process for getting married could be complex. A couple wishing to marry had first to obtain the blessing of the church, either by obtaining a licence to marry, or by having the 'banns' read – that is, announcing the couple's names and their intent to marry – on three successive Sundays from church pulpits in the home parishes of both parties. Couples who paid for a license and testified that there were no obstacles to their union still had to wait one month before they could be married. For some, the process was too slow.

Consequentially, a culture of clandestine marriage emerged. The 'Fleet marriage' was so named because the Fleet prison in London offered the venue; as a prison it claimed to be independent of church marriage strictures, and rapid – or secret – marriages could be carried out. Before the custom was outlawed in 1754, tens of thousands of 'Fleet marriages' were solemnized. [...]

a) Describe how the customs of courtship and marriage have developed.
b) Compare the customs with those displayed in *A Midsummer Night's Dream*.

4 → **S15**: How to describe pictures
a) Look at the painting by Edwin Landseer. Identify the different elements and describe the picture.
b) Analyse the portrayal of love in the painting.
c) How did Shakespeare deal with the theme in *A Midsummer Night's Dream*? Assess to what extent the picture mirrors the attitude towards love in the play.

Edwin Landseer: Scene from *A Midsummer Night's Dream*. Titania and Bottom (1848–51)

Topic — A Midsummer Night's Dream

5 **Pair work**

a) Read the assertions about love and marriage below and find evidence from the play to prove or disprove them.
1. Duty and law dominate love and desire.
2. Love is a source of amusement and playfulness.
3. Love is a feeling ruled not by reason but by fairy interventions.
4. Love seems to be a dream, some sort of madness.
5. Love reaches its culmination in marriage.
6. Marriage is a catalyst for conflicts.
7. Marriage is seen as a tool for healing wounds.
8. A wedding implies harmony.

b) Write further assertions and test your partner.

_____

_____

_____

_____

6

a) Briefly explain how love and marriage are presented in *Pyramus and Thisbe* (extract 21, p. 159ff.).
b) Compare the story of Pyramus and Thisbe with that of the four lovers.
c) Comment on the interruptions made by the audience during the performance. What do they reveal?

7 → **S9:** How to structure a text   → **S8:** How to improve your text

Based on your findings from the previous tasks, write an essay on one of these topics.
- Love and marriage in Shakespeare's time
- Why Titania had to obey
- *Pyramus and Thisbe* – a mirror to the newly-weds?
- Why all the couples had to get married
- The importance of a happy ending in *A Midsummer Night's Dream*

Language support

Introduction:
This essay will be about … | In this essay I shall discuss / look at …

Main part:
first of all | next | then | furthermore | besides | finally | for example | for instance | such as | similarly | likewise | on the one hand …, on the other hand … | however | in contrast | …

Conclusion:
to sum up | all in all | in conclusion | …

| A Midsummer Night's Dream | Topic 6 |

Gender roles

1

a) **Pair work** How do you explain the term "gender role"? Write a definition with your partner.
b) Look up the term on the Internet. Choose the definition you think is the most appropriate.
c) Compare your definition from a) with the one you have found on the Internet.

2

a) Look at the adjectives in the box. Decide which adjectives are typically attributed to women and which ones to men. Sort them into the grid below.
b) **Pair work** Compare your results with a partner.

> active | aggressive | analytical | blunt | competitive | cruel | dependent | dominant | easily influenced | emotional | gentle | graceful | home-oriented | independent | innocent | logical | obedient | self-confident | submissive | talkative | tough

Traditional gender stereotypes	
feminine	masculine

3

Read about the campaign *Look Beyond* by UN Women and UNFPA (United Nations Population Fund) on the organisation's website. **Webcode** DSW-73684-13

a) Answer the following questions.
   1. How has the COVID-19 pandemic affected the field of work?
   2. How are women affected in particular?
   3. What is the aim of the campaign?
   4. Why is the pandemic seen as an opportunity to change the situation for women?
   5. Why is unpaid care work important for communities?
   6. What results have surveys shown?
   7. What chores are usually attributed to women?
   8. How does the reshaping of gender roles relate to domestic violence?
   9. How does the campaign try to bring about the changes?
b) **Group work** Discuss the importance of such campaigns for gender equality.

4 → **Workshop:** Analysing a cartoon → **S17:** How to work with cartoons

Visit the UN Women website and look at some cartoons which are part of the book *Make way for women!* and were created by members of Cartooning for Peace, a non-profit international network of cartoonists.
Webcode DSW-73684-14
Group work Each of you picks one of the cartoons and prepares a short presentation about it.
- Introduce the cartoon. (Name the cartoonist and the topic.)
- Describe the cartoon. (Give a detailed account of its pictorial elements and its caption.)
- Analyse the cartoon. (Explain the function of its elements and its message.)
- Evaluate the cartoon. (Do you agree with the message?)

Topic: A Midsummer Night's Dream

5 Pair work

Partner A: Read the following extracts from an article from the website of the British Library. Describe the situation of women in Shakespeare's time. Then exchange the information with your partner.

Daughters in Shakespeare: dreams, duty and defiance

by Kim Ballard   15 March 2016

[...] When we consider that Shakespeare lived in an age when all actors were male and the subject matter of serious drama focused heavily on the exploits of men, it's hardly surprising that female characters are in a minority in his plays. And yet Shakespeare created many complex and engaging female roles for his young male actors to perform. Parent-child relationships feature heavily, and a significant number of these involve fathers and daughters. Interestingly, mothers are often absent from the drama, throwing the daughter/father relationship into sharp relief. A father of two daughters himself, Shakespeare's dramatic daughters make a formidable line-up of young women, most of them at a transitional stage between the protection of their childhood home and an adult life beyond it. The transition is rarely a smooth one: in both comedies and tragedies, tension rises as daughters go in search of love, adventure and independence. [...]

In Shakespeare's time, daughters of respectable families, like Juliet, could expect their fathers to have a significant involvement in choosing their future husband. This reflected the subordinate position of women in a patriarchal society, and particularly the traditional view that daughters were a commodity and could be used in marriage to forge useful alliances. Paternal involvement in husband selection provided fertile material for Shakespeare in many of his plays, and he makes considerable dramatic use of the resulting family clashes. [...]

The obedient way young women of the 16th century were meant to behave towards their parents was not only reflected in religious teaching but also well documented in publications known as 'conduct books'. [...]

Partner B: Read the following extracts from an article from the website of the British Library. Outline the practice of playing female roles. Then exchange the information with your partner.

Shakespeare and gender: the 'woman's part'

by Clare McManus   15 March 2016

[...] The stages of the earlier 17th-century commercial theatres were all-male preserves: women were part of the play-going audience and worked in the theatre buildings but they did not act on the commercial stages. So when *Hamlet* was first staged in 1600–01 and *Julius Caesar* in 1599, female roles were taken by a small cohort of highly trained boys. The small number of female roles in each play (usually no more than three or four roles that could be described as more than walk-on parts), have shaped and constrained opportunities for actresses on the modern stage. [...]

As we know, [...] women did not play Shakespearean roles. Instead, the practice of casting boy actors in female parts meant that the playful exploration of gender was written into these plays from the start. Elizabethan and Jacobean theatre used cosmetics and cross-dressing to exploit audiences' awareness that they were watching a boy playing a female character and to tease them with that knowledge. [...] Shakespeare's theatre layered gender roles to tantalise audiences, drawing on the virtuosic skill of the highly trained young men (aged between 12 and 21 years old) who played these complex female characters. Not that the boy-as-woman was universally accepted: those opposed to the theatre feared that cross-dressing would corrupt its audience and destroy the distinction between the sexes. Much of this fear and much of the energy of Shakespeare's cross-dressed dramas depends on desire. [...]

A Midsummer Night's Dream — Topic 6

GENDER ROLES IN *A MIDSUMMER NIGHT'S DREAM*

6

a) Read the following quotations from the play. Identify the speaker and the context in which they are said.

1. "Be it so she will not here, before your grace,
   Consent to marry with Demetrius,
   I beg the ancient privilege of Athens;
   As she is mine, I may dispose of her;
   Which shall be either to this gentleman
   Or to her death, [...]" *(Act I, Scene 1)*

2. "Your wrongs do set a scandal on my sex!
   We cannot fight for love, as men may do;
   We should be woo'd, and were not made to woo." *(Act II, Scene 1)*

3. "Tarry, rash wanton! Am not I thy lord?" *(Act II, Scene 1)*

4. "But, gentle friend, for love and courtesy
   Lie further off, in human modesty;
   Such separation as may well be said
   Becomes a virtuous bachelor and a maid,
   So far be distant, and good night, sweet friend;
   [...]" *(Act II, Scene 2)*

5. "Egeus, I will overbear your will; [...]" *(Act IV, Scene 1)*

b) Find adjectives to describe the characters. You can use adjectives from the box on p. 177.

c) Analyse how and to what extent the characters in the play fulfil the roles that are expected from them.

7

In class, discuss if Shakespeare can be considered a critic of gender inequality.

8 Group work

Each group member slips into the shoes of one of the characters from the play in their respective situation.

CHOOSE Write their soliloquy, in which you reflect upon the following questions:
- What is your situation like?
- What do you think about the other character(s) on stage?
- What is expected of you? How do you feel about the situation you are in? Why?
- What would you like to change?
- What are your hopes and dreams?

Then present your soliloquy to your group members. (You can find more information about soliloquies in the box on p. 127.)

OR

Have a discussion on gender roles and expectations.

Copyrights

TEXTQUELLEN

6	Quote by Martin Luther King Jr.: "Forgiveness is …" San Francisco: Goodreads, Inc. https://www.goodreads.com/quotes/57037-forgiveness-is-not-an-occasional-act-it-is-a-constant (19.04.2022)
6	Quote by Wil Zeus, *Sun Beyond the Clouds*: "Always forgive, but …" San Francisco: Goodreads, Inc. https://www.goodreads.com/quotes/247513-always-forgive-but-never-forget-else-you-will-be-a?page=4 (19.04.2022)
6	Quote by Gordon B. Hinckley: "The whole essence …" https://www.allgreatquotes.com/authors/gordon-b-hinckley/page/3/ (19.04.2022)
6	Quote by Deb Caletti: "I guess forgiveness …" San Francisco: Goodreads, Inc. https://www.goodreads.com/quotes/75628-i-guess-forgiveness-like-happiness-isn-t-a-final-destination-you (19.04.2022)
21 f.	Geoff Dyer: "Who's afraid of influence?" In: *The Guardian*, 22.09.2001. Copyright Guardian News & Media Ltd 2023. https://www.theguardian.com/books/2001/sep/22/fiction.ianmcewan (24.02.2022)
24 f.	"What is Britishness?"	"Identification with Britishness." In: *Citizenship and Belonging: What is Britishness? A research study*. London: Commission for Racial Equality, November 2005, S. 6–7. http://www.ethnos.co.uk/pdfs/9_what_is_britishness_CRE.pdf (03.05.2022)
25 f.	„Wie ein Schülerlied Großbritannien entzweit – ‚Untersteht euch, meinem Kind das Gehirn zu waschen!'" Jörg Schindler, DER SPIEGEL, 24.06.2021. https://www.spiegel.de/ausland/grossbritannien-wie-ein-patriotisches-schuelerlied-das-land-entzweit-a-0175d1c6-39a6-43a3-96a0-8f624da32b9a (24.02.2022)
28	Quote by Ivanka Trump, *The Trump Card*: "Perception is …" In: *Vanity Fair*, 24.04.2017. https://www.vanityfair.com/hollywood/2017/04/john-oliver-jared-kushner-ivanka-trump-last-week-tonight (02.03.2022)
30–35	Nafissa Thompson-Spires: "Heads of the Colored People: Four Fancy Sketches, Two Chalk Outlines, and No Apology." In: Nafissa Thompson-Spires: *Heads of the Colored People*. London: Vintage/Penguin Random House 2019, S. 1–14.
37 f.	Anonymous: "I was very interested in …", 26.03.2021	Danielle Hawthorne: "Nafissa Thompson-Spires is …", 26.03.2021	Phoenix Johnson: "Thompson-Spires has a special …", 25.03.2021 – Haley Reading (Group 1) Nafissa Thompson-Spires's "Heads of the Colored People" Comments. Hrsg.: Professor Howard Rambsy II, Edwardsville, Illinois, USA, 24.03.2021. https://www.culturalfront.org/2021/03/haley-reading-group-1-nafissa-thompson_24.html?m=1 (18.04.2022)
39–47	Camille Acker: "Mambo Sauce." In: Camille Acker: *Training School For Negro Girls*. New York: The Feminist Press 2018, S. 129–158.
52	"Ethnic identity." In: *APA (American Psychological Association) Dictionary of Psychology*. Washington, DC: American Psychological Association. https://dictionary.apa.org/ethnic-identity (20.04.2022)
52	Quote by Malcolm X, *The Autobiography of Malcolm X*: "I believe in recognizing …" San Francisco: Goodreads, Inc. https://www.goodreads.com/work/quotes/47400-the-autobiography-of-malcolm-x (02.03.2022)
63	Quote from the film *The Founder* (2016): "Persistence. … all day long." MovieQuotesandMore, Hrsg.: Parissa Janaraghi. https://www.moviequotesandmore.com/the-founder-best-quotes/ (09.05.2022)
63	Quotes from the film *The Founder* (2016): "McDonald's can be the new American church. … One word, persistence." MagicalQuote: https://www.magicalquote.com/moviequotes/mcdonalds-can-be-the-new-american-church/ (09.05.2022)
68 ff.	Marinela Potor: „Wie nachhaltig ist McDonald's Deutschland wirklich?" Berlin: BASIC thinking GmbH, 30.03.2021. https://www.basicthinking.de/blog/2021/03/30/mcdonalds-deutschland-klimacheck/ (02.05.2022)
71	"11 Facts LGBT Life In America." New York: Do Something, Inc. https://www.dosomething.org/us/facts/11-facts-lgbt-life-america (11.05.2022) (verändert)
78 f.	Amnesty International: "Discrimination." © 2022 Amnesty International. https://www.amnesty.org/en/what-we-do/discrimination/ (12.05.2022)
80	"Diversity Wheel." Adapted from: Loden, Marilyn & Rosener, Judy, "Workforce America! Managing Employee Diversity as a Vital Resource." McGraw-Hill Professional Publishing, 1990. (verändert)
88	"The 12 Steps of AA." Alcoholics Anonymous Great Britain and English Speaking Continental Europe. https://www.alcoholics-anonymous.org.uk/about-aa/the-12-steps-of-aa (13.05.2022)
88	Quote from the film *Boy Erased* (2018): "Your father's asked me … Any questions?" MovieQuotesandMore, Hrsg.: Parissa Janaraghi. https://www.moviequotesandmore.com/boy-erased-best-movie-quotes/ (13.05.2022)
89	Quotes from the film *Boy Erased* (2018): Sarah: "I would look at other girls … forgive me all these things."	Gary: "Dear Heavenly Father … path to righteousness." IN: BOY ERASED (2018) – FULL TRANSCRIPT. https://subslikescript.com/movie/Boy_Erased-7008872 (13.05.2022)
90	Quote from the film *Boy Erased* (2018): "I imagine I'm him sometimes. …" MovieQuotesandMore, Hrsg.: Parissa Janaraghi. https://www.moviequotesandmore.com/boy-erased-best-movie-quotes/ (13.05.2022)
95	Quote from the film *Boy Erased* (2018): "I wish none of this had ever happened. …" MovieQuotesandMore, Hrsg.: Parissa Janaraghi. https://www.moviequotesandmore.com/boy-erased-best-movie-quotes/ (16.05.2022)
95 f.	„Gesetz gegen „Homoheiler" – Ein Meilenstein für Deutschland." Markus Kowalski im Gespräch mit Stephan Karkowsky. Köln: Deutschlandfunk Kultur, Deutschlandradio, 07.05.2020. https://www.deutschlandfunkkultur.de/gesetz-gegen-homoheiler-ein-meilenstein-fuer-deutschland-100.html (16.05.2022)
97 f.	Salomé Kofler: „Was ist ein Ally?" München: Zeitjung.de, Z-LIVE GmbH, 11.08.2020. https://www.zeitjung.de/was-ist-ein-ally-gesellschaft-allyship-engagement-definitionen/ (16.05.2022)